CITIES BEYOND BORDERS

Cities Beyond Borders

Comparative and Transnational Approaches to Urban History

Edited by

NICOLAS KENNY
Simon Fraser University, Canada

REBECCA MADGIN
University of Glasgow, UK

Routledge
Taylor & Francis Group

LONDON AND NEW YORK

First published 2015 by Ashgate Publishing

Published 2016 by Routledge
2 Park Square, Milton Park, Abingdon, Oxon OX14 4RN
711 Third Avenue, New York, NY 10017, USA

First issued in paperback 2017

Routledge is an imprint of the Taylor & Francis Group, an informa business

British Library Cataloguing in Publication Data
A catalogue record for this book is available from the British Library

The Library of Congress has cataloged the printed edition as follows:
Cities beyond borders : comparative and transnational approaches to urban history /
edited by Nicolas Kenny and Rebecca Madgin.
    pages cm
Includes bibliographical references and index.
ISBN 978-1-4724-3479-1 (hardcover)
1. Cities and towns—History. I. Kenny, Nicolas, 1977– editor.
II. Madgin, Rebecca, editor.
HT111.C538 2015
307.7609—dc23

                                                                        2015017521

ISBN 13: 978-1-138-30712-4 (pbk)
ISBN 13: 978-1-4724-3479-1 (hbk)

Contents

REFLECTIONS

List of Figures

List of Maps

List of Contributors

Stefan Couperus is Assistant Professor of Politics and Society (European Languages and Cultures Department) at the University of Groningen. He has worked on the history of urban governance and municipal transnationalism in early twentieth-century Europe. Currently he is working on a project entitled 'Beyond New Jerusalem. The Governance of Planning in Rotterdam, Coventry and Le Havre: 1920–1960', which examines governance practices and community-building discourses in bombed cities.

Jeffry Diefendorf is Professor of History at the University of New Hampshire. His book, *In the Wake of War: The Reconstruction of German Cities after World War II* (Oxford University Press, 1993), and other publications examine different forms of postwar planning.

Shane Ewen is Senior Lecturer in Social and Cultural History at Leeds Beckett University. He is the co-editor of *Urban History* and the UK Representative on the International Committee for the European Association of Urban History. He has written extensively on issues related to urban governance, disasters and transnational urban history. His publications include *Fighting Fires: Creating the British Fire Service* (Palgrave, 2010) and, with Pierre-Yves Saunier, *Another Global City: Historical Explorations into the Transnational Municipal Moment* (Palgrave, 2008). He has also written *What is Urban History?*, forthcoming with Polity Press.

Dan Horner is Assistant Professor in the Department of Criminology at Ryerson University. He has published a number of articles on public life in mid-nineteenth-century Montreal.

Nicolas Kenny is a member of the History Department at Simon Fraser University. His research examines the bodily and emotional relationship to the urban environment in the nineteenth and twentieth centuries, focusing especially on Montreal and Brussels in a comparative and transnational context. He is the author of *The Feel of the City: Experiences of Urban Transformation* (University of Toronto Press, 2014).

Rebecca Madgin is Senior Lecturer in Urban Development and Management in the School of Social and Political Sciences at the University of Glasgow.

She currently researches the economic and emotional values of heritage in relation to urban development. Her work is located in an international context spanning the twentieth and twenty-first centuries, and she is the author of *Heritage, Culture and Conservation: Managing the Urban Renaissance* (VDM Verlag, 2009).

Carl H. Nightingale is Professor of Urban History and World History in the Department of Transnational Studies at the University at Buffalo, State University of New York. He is the author of *Segregation: A Global History Divided Cities* (University of Chicago Press, 2012) and numerous articles concerning the transnational dynamics of the politics of race and urban space.

Harold L. Platt is Professor of History Emeritus at Loyola University Chicago. He is the author of several books on the city, the environment, and technology, including *The Electric City: Energy and the Growth of the Chicago Area* (University of Chicago Press, 1991), and *Shock Cities: The Environmental Transformation and Reform of Manchester and Chicago* (University of Chicago Press, 1991). His most recent book is *Building the Urban Environment: Visions of the Organic City in the United States, Europe, and Latin America* (Temple University Press, 2015).

Marion Pluskota is a Postdoctoral Researcher on crime and gender at Leiden University, The Netherlands. Her current research focuses on criminality and gender interactions in nineteenth-century Europe. This project uses a comparative methodology to explain gender constructions in a criminal and in a court setting. Her other research interests include the history of prostitution and colonial crime history.

Janet Polasky is Presidential Professor of History at the University of New Hampshire. Her most recent publications include: *Routes to the City, Roots in the Country* (Cornell University Press, 2010) and *Revolutions without Borders: The Call to Liberty in the Atlantic World* (Yale University Press 2015).

Nikhil Rao is Associate Professor of History at Wellesley College, where he teaches South Asian and urban history. His book, *House, But No Garden. Apartment Living in Bombay's Suburbs, 1898–1964*, was published by the University of Minnesota Press in 2013. He is currently working on a history of cooperative housing.

Richard Rodger is Professor of Economic and Social History at Edinburgh University. He has published widely on the history of British towns and cities, and on the evolution of urban history as a field of study. For many years he was

Editor of *Urban History*, General Editor of Ashgate's Historical Urban Studies series, and Director of the Centre for Urban History. He was elected to the Academy of Social Sciences in 2004, and currently is directing a historical GIS project on Edinburgh.

Jordan Stanger-Ross is Associate Professor of History at the University of Victoria, British Columbia. He is the author of *Staying Italian: Urban Change and Ethnic Life in Postwar Toronto and Philadelphia* (University of Chicago Press, 2009) and currently the Project Director of *Landscapes of Injustice* (www. landscapesofinjustice.com).

Janet Ward is Professor of History and Faculty Director of the Humanities Forum at the University of Oklahoma. She is the author most recently of *Post-Wall Berlin: Borders, Space and Identity* (Palgrave Macmillan, 2011) and co-editor of two volumes, *Transnationalism and the German City* (with fellow *Cities Beyond Borders* contributor Jeffry M. Diefendorf, Palgrave Macmillan, 2014) and *Walls, Borders, Boundaries: Spatial and Cultural Practices in Europe* (Berghahn, 2012). Her two current book projects are 'Sites of Holocaust Memory' and 'Blitz Cities: Nazi Urban Planning for War and Terror'.

Preface

What is to be gained by studying two or more cities in historical perspective? What new insights does a comparative or transnational approach offer? And why, for that matter, should one particular set of cities be privileged over another combination? These are vexing questions for the historian seeking to understand wider urban processes by juxtaposing, blending, comparing and contrasting the experience of multiple places, spaces and sites. They will no doubt be familiar to anyone who has attempted such an endeavour, and who may even on occasion have felt a twinge of resentment at the seemingly heavier burden of justification placed on multisite studies than on those based on just one city. Having each spent years working on comparative and transnational urban history projects, encountering these questions and accounting for our rationale at every stage, we began this project unable to shake these preoccupations, but equally eager to get to the bottom of them.

In a scholarly era that more than ever encourages international collaborations while embracing transnational and global 'turns', we knew intuitively that working across and beyond borders could only broaden our horizons, help us understand the dynamics of urban life in unsuspected ways and raise new research questions about what it has historically meant to live in cities (not to mention amplify the pleasures of research in exciting locations). However, comparative and transnational approaches have traditionally had their sceptics, and doubts have often been raised as to the heuristic benefits, feasibility or apparent idiosyncrasies of such topics. Wanting to pursue a reflection on the epistemological potential, theoretical grounding and methodological challenges of comparative and transnational urban history, we were convinced that a project like this one, bringing together emerging and established historians who each had expertise with these approaches, would undoubtedly be of interest to many others grappling with similar questions. With a volume like this in mind, we thus began the conversation formally in the context of a three-hour round table at the European Association of Urban History conference held in Prague in the summer of 2012, followed two months later by a subsequent panel at the Urban History Association conference in New York City. Drawing on feedback the contributors had prepared for one another at these sessions, and encouraged by the spirited responses shared by audience members, the authors embarked on the challenging task of reflecting critically on the comparative and transnational approaches underlying their work.

Cities Beyond Borders, then, is the product of these stimulating conversations and debates around the question of how and why we can better understand the nature of urban life when we broaden our interpretative lens to include more than one city. The chapters all reflect on the advantages, as well as some of the downsides, of comparative and transnational historical approaches, illustrating with examples set in a diversity of urban settings around the world. We are grateful first and foremost to the 12 contributors who answered our call, participated wholeheartedly at every stage and gave generously of their insights and efforts. Nearly all the authors gathered in these pages took part in one or both of the conference sessions, and we thank those who accepted to join us along the way. In the ensuing two years, the authors have continued the discussion, reflected on these exchanges, and laboriously refined and revised their chapters. Their dedication and good-natured patience with the inevitable delays a project like this entails has made it a pleasure and a privilege to assemble this collection of original and enticing approaches to urban history. Our thanks to Simon Gunn for his input at the project's earliest stages, and to Carl Nightingale for suggesting that after Prague we 'take the show on the road' to New York. At Ashgate Publishing, Emily Yates greeted this project with enthusiasm and Sadie Copley-May has offered invaluable support in the various steps toward publication, while anonymous readers offered welcome suggestions for improving the individual chapters as well as the book's overarching arguments. We would also like to express our gratitude to Michèle Dagenais, Prashant Kidambi and Richard Rodger for supporting this project and graciously accepting to comment on previous iterations of the introductory chapter, as well as to Jordan Stanger-Ross for his thoughts on the book's promise and purpose. Very special thanks go to Pierre-Yves Saunier who cheerfully commented on an earlier draft of the entire manuscript, and whose sharp discernment and extensive expertise helped us define the scope and structure of the present volume. Without the critical but entirely constructive feedback of these friends and colleagues, the final result would not look the same.

Shaped through years of research, conferences and discussions that have taken us over countless borders and across continents, this book is itself a product of the transnational exchanges that define urban history, and we hope it will be read as a testament to the vibrancy, uniqueness and collegiality of this very rich area of study. Closer to home, the ideas in the book have also been developed through conversations with our colleagues and students in our respective universities, and this lively research and teaching culture evident in Glasgow and Vancouver has been a constant source of stimulation. It may be that in the end this book raises more questions than the ones it set out to answer. If nothing else, we wish for it to encourage other scholars to consider the sense of place, social dynamics and political processes that have shaped city life the world over from these different angles, and hope that they will find their travels as rewarding as we have.

INTRODUCTION

Chapter 1

'Every Time I Describe a City': Urban History as Comparative and Transnational Practice

Nicolas Kenny and Rebecca Madgin

'Sire, now I have told you about all the cities I know'.
'There is still one of which you never speak'.
Marco Polo bowed his head.
'Venice', the Khan said.
Marco smiled. 'What else do you believe I have been talking about?'
The emperor did not turn a hair. 'And yet I have never heard you mention that name'.
And Polo said: 'Every time I describe a city I am saying something about Venice'.[1]

These lines from Italo Calvino's *Invisible Cities* beautifully illustrate the complexity of understanding what makes a city. The author uses Marco Polo's urban travelogue to trick both the main protagonist – the emperor Kublai Khan – and the reader into believing that the renowned explorer is talking about 55 different cities. Only well into the story is the verisimilitude shattered by Polo's revelation that 'Every time I describe a city I am saying something about Venice'. The series of conversations around which the novel is structured leave the reader with a sense that cities are at once the same and different, unique and universal. For Calvino's characters, Venice is as much a jewel among cities as it is every-city. Indeed, our knowledge of and relationship to a given city inherently depends on our appreciation of other cities and, by extension, of the countless relationships that unfold between them. For the urban historian, disentangling these connections implies careful attention to a further layer of relationality, namely the dialogue between the concepts, methods and sources through which the relationships between people and place, and between cities themselves, can be brought to light. Drawing on a body of research that is global in scope, the purpose of this book is to reflect on the methodological and heuristic implications of studying cities in relation to one another, principally through comparative and transnational approaches. Understanding the particularities of urban life on the

---

[1] Italo Calvino, *Invisible Cities*, trans. William Weaver (New York: Harcourt Brace, 1974), 86.

ground, the way people inhabit, imagine and arrange their urban environments, we argue, requires an urban history that approaches individual cities not as fixed entities, but as nodes of relationships between people, space, and the research methods used to examine them.

The original chapters collected in this volume draw on research projects covering primarily Europe and the Americas, stretching also to Asia and Africa, from the mid-eighteenth century to the present. They each ask how some of the fundamental questions of urban history, such as the way issues like governance, planning, segregation, injustice and criminality play out in cities and find new answers when individual case studies are confronted against others in comparative and transnational terms. Before introducing the chapters, we lay the groundwork for the volume by examining the dynamics of comparative and transnational history, how these approaches are related, how they have shaped urban historiography and the potential they offer for recasting the way we conceive of the relationship between cities and their inhabitants. We start from the premise that cities are complex entities, a myriad of contested places, shifting spaces and elusive ideas. Large or small, recent or established, central or peripheral to economic and political power, it may be tempting to define cities in terms of their uniqueness rather than according to shared features. Yet it is just this diversity that makes cities so compelling to residents and researchers alike, and that, perhaps paradoxically, offers up certain commonalities. For all that differentiates a booming metropolis from a quiet provincial town, a port city from a resource hub, a futuristic technopole from an ancient capital, it is their constant flux, their energy, the flows of people shaping and reshaping them according to often conflicting objectives that allows us to use the single word 'city' in designating these units of social organization.

To understand what makes the city, then, involves not just accounting for its various manifestations, but more probingly, requires us to think of cities as plural, in relation to one another, both comparatively and transnationally. Cities are the products of numerous colliding processes, whereby the material and environmental characteristics of these spaces meet the organizational imperatives of urban actors whose decisions are shaped by their knowledge of more than one city. For the historian, grasping the nature of these processes, and the urban outcomes they have produced, implies crossing both conceptual and geopolitical borders. We cannot consider the story of one city without comparing it, even implicitly, to other cities, either within or outside the same national boundaries. Nor can we hope to know what cities are more generally unless we account for the exchange of information and ideas among them, and ground our understanding of processes and practices from within and across other urban centres. What is defined as a city in England, for example, may not be defined as such in India, and what was considered a world city in the nineteenth century may not necessarily be seen as a global city in the twenty-first century, further confirming the extent to which the very act of designating a geographical and social entity as a city is impossible without some form of comparison, whether in space or though time.[2] *Cities Beyond Borders* offers a reflection on the nature of these comparisons and flows, and argues that to make sense of how cities functioned in places like England or India, among many others, requires both setting specific examples against one another and accounting for the economic, migratory and colonial entanglements that have historically connected, and thus unremittingly reshaped, cities around the world. Moving fluidly between comparative and transnational methods, as well as across regional and national lines, the chapters gathered in this volume demonstrate the necessity of this broader view in assessing not just the fundamentals of urban life, the way cities are occupied and organised on a daily basis, but also the urban mindscape, the way cities are imagined and represented.

As his fictional conversation with the Khan continues, Polo reveals his deep attachment to Venice, and his fear of 'losing' this connection merely by 'speaking of other cities', suggesting that through his travels, his own sense of self evolves as a function of his urban emplacement. Touching on a diversity of specific urban settings and problems around the world, the contributors to this volume take as the starting point of their respective investigations the fundamental connections between city dwellers, the urban environments they inhabit and the wider regional, national and global contexts in which cities are imbricated. These everyday interactions with and actions upon the city are at the heart of what literary scholar Andreas Huyssen refers to as the 'urban imaginary', that is to say the 'cognitive and somatic image which we carry within us of the places where we live, work and play'. But if our understanding of the city is intimately bound to the personal, interior and affective relationships to the spaces and places that frame our daily lives, a growing body of urban scholarship shows that the urban experience also surpasses the immediacy of daily life. It is equally defined by contact and exchange with other urban centres near and far, and as Huyssen notes, urban imaginaries are themselves 'sites of encounters with other cities', mediated through travel, migration and the circulation of images, goods and

---

[2] See Clark's 'Introduction', in Peter Clark, ed., *Cities in World History* (Oxford: Oxford University Press, 2013) for an explanation of the difficulty of definition. Clark also calls for a less 'catholic definitional matrix' which recognizes the 'multi-functionality of urban communities over time'. See also John V. Beckett, *City Status in the British Isles, 1830–2002* (Aldershot: Ashgate, 2005); Lewis Mumford, *The City in History: Its Origins, its Transformations, and its Prospects* (New York: Harcourt, Brace and World, 1961) for differing conceptions of how to define a city. The definition of a city also varies according to linguistic and cultural context. For a nuanced discussion, see Christian Topalov et al., *L'aventure des mots de la ville à travers le temps, les langues, les sociétés* (Paris: Robert Laffont, 2010).

ideas.[3] The challenge, then, is to bridge these scales, to explore and unpack urban dynamics in ways that account simultaneously for the immediate and the distant, for the everyday contact with the built environment and the social tensions that animate it, as well as for the much wider regional, national and international flows in which it is immersed. We seek, as urban analyst Michael Peter Smith suggests, to jettison conceptions of local and global as binaries, concentrating instead on 'the complexity of transnational connections, the dynamics of cross-border networks, and the shifting spatial scales at which agency takes place.'[4]

With this objective in mind, the chapters gathered here are underpinned by a basic question: how is our understanding of what it has historically meant to live in a city enhanced by a widened lens that encompasses multiple urban settings? If the question has long intrigued researchers, it is worth appraising the distance travelled to reflect on the added value of comparative and transnational approaches. To the extent that cities are the products as much of local imaginaries as of transnational flows, the portrait of their development, transformation and socio-cultural significance appears more fully when we question not just their similarities and differences, but also the impact of movement through and among different places. Cities, noted sociologist Charles Tilly, 'offer privileged sites for study of the interaction between large social processes and routines of local life.'[5] If segregation, prostitution laws or housing policies differed according to whether they were enacted in Hong Kong, Nantes or Bombay, what emerges from the entanglement of these stories is an opportunity to bridge this gap between a specific setting and developments on a broader scale. As historical geographer Richard Dennis has noted, 'the point of overlaying examples from different cities' is not to explain 'some form of economic or political determinism' caused by 'local variation', but rather to uncover the 'broadly similar responses' to the challenges posed by the cohabitation of ever-growing numbers of people in dense urban settings.[6]

Several decades ago, analysts seeking to jolt scholars out of the 'myopia of parochialism' afflicting the 'great majority of urban research' encouraged 'more extensive comparative work premised on a broader range of theoretical viewpoints.'[7] They were hardly the first to make this suggestion, but if, in our

[3] Andreas Huyssen, ed., *Other Cities, Other Worlds* (New York: Palgrave Macmillan, 2008), 3, 5.

[4] Michael Peter Smith, *Transnational Urbanism: Locating Globalization* (Malden: Blackwell Publishers, 2001), 174.

[5] Charles Tilly, 'What Good Is Urban History?', *Journal of Urban History* 22 (1996): 704.

[6] Richard Dennis, *Cities in Modernity: Representations and Productions of Metropolitan Space, 1840–1930* (Cambridge: Cambridge University Press, 2008), 25.

[7] John Walton and Louis H. Masotti, eds, *The City in Comparative Perspective: Cross-National Research and New Directions in Theory* (New York: Sage, 1976), 2–3.

own hyper-globalized times, such entreaties might strike us as artefacts of another historiographical era, the challenge they pose to urban scholarship remain salient. Comparison implies analysing two or more objects side by side in order to demonstrate how the similarities and differences that appear provide a more nuanced portrait of historical phenomena than when they are observed in isolation.[8] By examining the garment industry in Paris and New York for example, historian Nancy Green showed how from different localized experiences a more multidimensional appreciation of the 'spatial, ethnic and temporal' patterns of urban labour and migration can be attained.[9] Many of the contributors to the present volume have, in their earlier work, skilfully compared various phenomena, from reform movements, to industrial expansion, to modes of ethnic community formation, to reveal not only how they have transformed cities on both sides of the Atlantic, but also how the complexity of these issues arises from their distinctively urban condition.[10]

Comparison homes in on specificities, while at the same time questioning what is in fact unique about a particular city's experiences and development. Some critics, however, see comparison as overly static, boxing complex phenomena into narrow categories, presuming the units and societies under study to be closed off from one another, and failing to account for the interactions and movement across regions and over borders through which these phenomena take shape. Instead, they argue, it is precisely the dynamics of contact and exchange between societies, among individual, group, corporate or state actors, that explain the development of phenomena on the ground. For Sanjeev Khagram and Peggy Levitt, this transnational perspective implies

---

[8] Scholars have long been intrigued by the methodological possibilities, and limitations, of comparison for historical research. See for example Marc Bloch, 'Pour une histoire comparée des sociétés européennes', *Revue de synthèse historique* 46 (1928): 15–50; Deborah Cohen and Maura O'Connor, eds, *Comparison and History: Europe in Cross-National Perspective* (London: Routledge, 2004); George M. Fredrickson, 'From Exceptionalism to Variability: Recent Developments in Cross-National Comparative History', *Journal of American History* 82 (1995): 587–604; Raymond Grew, 'The Case for Comparing Histories', *American Historical Review* 85 (1980): 763–8; Jürgen Kocka, 'Comparison and Beyond', *History and Theory* 42 (2003): 39–44; Khaldoun Samman, 'The Limits of the Classical Comparative Method', *Review (Fernand Braudel Center)* 24 (2001): 533–73; Michael Werner and Bénédicte Zimmermann, 'Penser l'histoire croisée: entre empirie et réflexivité', *Annales Histoire, Sciences Sociales* 58 (2003): 7–36.

[9] Nancy L. Green, *Ready-to-Wear and Ready-to-Work: A Century of Industry and Immigrants in Paris and New York* (Durham: Duke University Press, 1997), 9.

[10] Harold L. Platt, *Shock Cities: The Environmental Transformation and Reform of Manchester and Chicago* (Chicago: University of Chicago Press, 2005); Janet Polasky, *Reforming Urban Labor: Routes to the City, Roots in the Country* (Ithaca: Cornell University Press, 2010); Jordan Stanger-Ross, *Urban Change and Ethnic Life in Postwar Toronto and Philadelphia* (Chicago: University of Chicago Press, 2009).

adopting 'an optic or gaze that begins with a world without borders, empirically examines the boundaries and borders that emerge at particular historical moments, and explores their relationship to unbounded arenas and processes.'[11] In this sense, the 'national' in 'transnational' should pose little discomfort to urban historians. For if transnational history was to some extent conceived as a way to liberate the discipline from the strictures of a single national framework as a privileged unit of analysis, it does not by necessity take the nation, constructed as it may be, as its sole object of inquiry. Instead, the point is to problematize the very borders that migrants, travellers, investors or colonial agents, whose actions have built, destroyed and reconfigured cities around the world, first had to cross. On the other side of these lines, they found urban settings that were equally produced by the cultural, economic and legislative frameworks imposed by national units, as they were transformed by the porosity of these boundaries. Situating cities at the heart of the analysis while at the same time accounting for the way they are shaped, bound and transformed by larger political systems allows for the writing of 'a history with nations that is not a history of nations.'[12] While much work remains to be done in this vein,[13] many of the contributors to this book have previously focussed on transnational linkages, tracing the flow of intellectual capital that have resulted in outcomes ranging from the reconfiguration of municipal governance in Europe, to post-war urban planning in Germany, to suburbanization in South Asia, to patterns of racial segregation in cities around the world.[14]

In sum, comparison problematizes specific units of analysis, locating the fundamentals of urban life directly on the landscape of cities, while

---

[11]   Sanjeev Khagram and Peggy Levitt, eds, *The Transnational Studies Reader: Intersections and Innovations* (New York: Routledge, 2008), 5. For a thoughtful discussion on the impact of transnational approaches to historical research, see also Christopher A. Bayly et al., 'AHR Conversation: On Transnational History', *American Historical Review* 111 (2006): 1440–64.

[12]   Pierre-Yves Saunier, *Transnational History* (Houndmills, Basingstoke, Hampshire: Palgrave Macmillan, 2013), 8.

[13]   Recently, a group of leading American urban historians participating in the 2014 Urban History Association conference issued a call for the field to further 'transnationalise' itself. Andrew K. Sandoval-Strausz and Nancy Haekyung Kwak, et al., 'Why Transnationalize Urban History?'. For further information, see http://uha.udayton.edu/2014Conf/UHA%20Program%20FINAL%20Web.pdf, 22. See also Stefan Krätke, et al., *Transnationalism and Urbanism* (New York and Oxon: Routledge, 2012).

[14]   Jeffry M. Diefendorf and Janet Ward, eds, *Transnationalism and the German City* (New York: Palgrave Macmillan, 2014); Carl H. Nightingale, *Segregation: A Global History of Divided Cities* (Chicago: University of Chicago Press, 2012); Nikhil Rao, *House, but No Garden: Apartment Living in Bombay's Suburbs, 1898–1964* (Minneapolis: University of Minnesota Press, 2013); Pierre-Yves Saunier and Shane Ewen, eds, *Another Global City: Historical Explorations into the Transnational Municipal Moment, 1850–2000* (New York: Palgrave Macmillan, 2008).

transnationalism locates them in between, opening our eyes to the connections between cities. In a comprehensive theoretical and methodological overview of transnational history, Pierre-Yves Saunier suggests that long-standing debates between proponents of one or the other have subsided in favour of 'attempts to combine the two approaches'. Working with both offers the possibility to juxtapose 'different questions', and while Saunier concedes that transnational historians require a comparative sensibility if only to 'understand what happens to the ties and flows they follow through different polities and communities', he ultimately sees comparison as 'a topic of study more than a tool for the study of the topics'.[15] Khagram and Levitt establish a more explicit hierarchy between the two approaches, stating that comparison 'necessarily comes up short', in the face of transnationalism, which they privilege for the fuller portrait they suggest results from its mobility.[16]

Recognizing that comparison and transnationalism pursue somewhat different objectives, however, one of the key aims of this volume, in this spirit of movement and interaction through, between and beyond borders, is to overcome the epistemological boundaries and hierarchies that have tended to set the two approaches apart, and instead to examine cities 'as units of comparison and, at the same time, as components of a larger whole'.[17] For one, it is important to avoid thinking of comparison as static, as it too implies movement, if only on the part of researchers required to adopt transnational postures in moving between, and immersing themselves within, different cultural, linguistic, archival and historiographical contexts. From this perspective all urban research is intrinsically comparative. Even in choosing to conduct an urban biography, the comparative merits of the specific city under study need to be considered and justified against other possibilities. Nor can a focus on a single city ignore migratory flows or economic exchanges that necessarily place a given city in the orbit of many others. Most importantly, though, the specific, empirical topics that preoccupy urban historians stand to be enriched as much by attending to the similar ways in which they are played out in different contexts, as by interrogating the relationship between these contexts, and the methods used to analyse them. As geographer Kevin Ward suggests, an approach that is at once 'relational' and 'comparative' allows us to escape the notion that cities can somehow be seen as 'bounded and closed', and to focus instead on the 'overlapping and mutually constitutive aspects of comparative and transnational urbanisms'.[18]

[15]   Saunier, *Transnational History*, 5.
[16]   Khagram and Levitt, *The Transnational Studies Reader*, 1.
[17]   Kocka, 'Comparison and Beyond', 44.
[18]   Kevin Ward, 'Towards a Comparative (Re)Turn in Urban Studies? Some Reflections', *Urban Geography* 29 (2008): 408.

Our purpose here is not to rank, or even simply to combine, these approaches, but rather to tune into the answers that emerge from a line of questioning that places comparison and transnationalism themselves in relationship to one another. A fuller picture of the urban imaginary, of the connections urban dwellers make with the cities they live in and move through, emerges when both of these vectors are accounted for, when elements of fixity in the city, its embeddedness in the history, geography, culture and materiality that forges its individuality, are viewed in tandem with the flows of people, goods and ideas that descend upon it. A new 'experimental phase'[19] in urban research need not expand the linguistic canon with yet another term to a busy lexicon of 'comparative', 'transnational', 'translocal' or even 'cosmopolitan'. Instead, through a careful and varied reflection on methodologies and the interrelationships of the comparative and the transnational, we can extend our understanding of how the fundamentals of urban life operate in cities through time and across space.

The chapters that follow reveal the extent to which comparison and transnationalism are intertwined. Authors adopting an ostensibly comparative method do not avoid reflecting on the linkages between the cities they study, while those who focus more directly on the movement of people and ideas from one city to another invariably pause to reflect on the similar and different ways in which the dynamics at stake operated in various locales. Indeed, many of the chapters cannot be defined as one or the other, so seamlessly do their authors integrate the two, so much is their very research process informed by a comparative and transnational take on urban environments and on the way in which historical actors themselves made choices based as much on their movement between cities as on the similarities and differences they observed along the way. Urban place making happens as a function not of the city's rootedness or of its fluidity, but of both. And like Calvino's Marco Polo, the contributors here grapple with urban processes as much by interrogating the movement between cities as by comparing one city to another.

Assessing these dynamics has long been the preserve of historians and social scientists seeking to understand the urban variable, that is to say how particular historical episodes and processes are shaped by their specifically urban condition. This line of questioning has often been informed by two distinct approaches, labelled as 'descriptive' or 'interactional',[20] set up as a series of spatial and temporal dichotomies between the urban biography and the comparative

[19] Jennifer Robinson, 'Cities in a World of Cities: The Comparative Gesture', *International Journal of Urban and Regional Research* 35.1 (2013): 2.

[20] Richard Rodger, *European Urban History* (Leicester: Leicester University Press, 1993), 1.

method,[21] the historian versus the social scientist[22] and taking the city either as a 'site' or as a 'process'.[23] Common across each of these teleologies is the belief in the capacity of the urban variable to illuminate socio-economic, cultural and political characteristics which are actively shaped by their interaction with the city. Indeed, H.J. Dyos, a pioneer of urban history in Britain argued that:

> the authentic measure of urban history is the degree to which it is concerned directly and generically with cities themselves and not with the historical events and tendencies that have been purely incidental to them [...] it is the study of the characteristically symbiotic relationships of their (cities') different characteristics, of the ways in which their components fitted together or impinged on other things that distinguishes urban historians from those who may be said merely to be passing through their territory.[24]

In essence, the city is not a stage-set upon which events are acted out, but instead the urban variable actively shapes and conditions human behaviour and it is in this relationship between space and society that urban historians locate their research. This pursuit of the urban variable manifested itself in the UK, North America and Australia,[25] firstly, through the urban biography: the single-site study which aimed to produce a micro *histoire totale*. According to urban historians Richard Rodger and Roey Sweet, this biographical focus emerged from a number of wider considerations, including antiquarian approaches to understanding cities often adopted by pre-modern historians faced with the constraints imposed by the limited methods and sources at their disposal.[26] Despite the conviction, expressed in the mid-1970s, that 'the day of the individually posed idiosyncratic study of a town that has no particular analytical purpose ... is now on the wane',[27] the urban biography has stayed relevant because it is seen as 'providing the empirical bedrock for the systematic analyses of the

---

21   Clark, *Cities in World History*.

22   Richard Rodger and Roey Sweet, 'The Changing Nature of Urban History', *History in Focus* (2008).

23   See Theodore Hershberg, 'The Future of Urban History', in Derek Fraser and Anthony Sutcliffe, eds, *The Pursuit of Urban History* (London: E. Arnold, 1983), 428–48.

24   H.J. Dyos, 'Editorial', *The Urban History Yearbook*, 1974, 5.

25   See Richard C. Wade, *The Urban Frontier: Pioneer Life in Early Pittsburgh, Cincinnati, Lexington, Louisville, and St. Louis* (Chicago: University of Chicago Press, 1964) for more on the North American context, Lionel Frost and Seamus O'Hanlon, 'Urban History and the Future of Australian Cities', *Australian Economic History Review* 49 (2009): 1–18 for more on the Australian context and Rodger and Sweet, 'The Changing Nature of Urban History' for the UK context.

26   'The Changing Nature of Urban History'.

27   H.J. Dyos, 'Editorial', 3.

processes at work within towns and cities'.[28] Indeed, the approach has gained renewed vigour to the extent that urban historian Peter Clark, introducing the 2013 *Oxford Handbook of Cities in World History*, challenged readers to think about how this 'upsurge of specialist literature' can be directed 'into a new comparative analysis of cities'.[29]

Geographer Jennifer Robinson echoes this desire to develop 'alternative approaches to comparative research' but from her position in the broader urban studies field.[30] As with urban history, urban studies has fluctuated between the 'individualizing' tendencies of micro research on one city and comparative research focussing on multiple sites. However, notes Robinson, urban studies scholars have, until recently, been 'relatively reluctant to pursue the potential for international comparative research'.[31] Nevertheless, the *International Journal for Urban and Regional Research* (IJURR) published in 2014 a special online issue which provided a series of reflections on the state of comparative urbanism since the journal's inception in the 1970s.[32] The dominance of 'metrocentricity'; the dangers of Euro- and/or Anglo-American-centrism; questions concerning how to 'decentre' comparative urbanism and how to build a more 'global urban studies' sit alongside more methodological issues concerning how to achieve more 'innovative and experimental' comparisons, particularly those 'which consider variations amongst cities within and across regions, including comparisons which challenge or bypass Northern or Western reference points',[33] These questions are as relevant for urban history as they are for urban studies, and demonstrate that while the collision of the comparative agendas of urban history and urban studies is partly the product of different traditions of scholarship, it is also the result of the demands placed on researchers by contemporary urban issues.[34] The questions that lie at the heart of Robinson's editorial in the IJURR develop from the shifting concepts of what constitutes a world city as the process of globalization forces the lens on the interplay of international and local urban ideals and processes. Just as urban history developed in close relationship with the urban crisis of many western cities during the 1960s, this refreshed consideration of comparative urbanism is located within ever-shifting urban

[28] Rodger, *European Urban History*, 2.
[29] Clark, *Cities in World History*, 3.
[30] Robinson, 'Cities in a World of Cities', 1.
[31] Robinson, 'Cities in a World of Cities', 1.
[32] Virtual Issue on Comparative Urbanism, *International Journal of Urban and Regional Research* (published online, April 2014).
[33] Jennifer Robinson, 'Introduction to Virtual Issue on Comparative Urbanism', *International Journal of Urban and Regional Research*.
[34] For more on the Urban Studies literature on comparative/transnational urbanism, see both the Virtual Issue of IJURR, 2014 and the Special Issue 'Comparative Urbanism', *Urban Geography* 33 (2012): 765–915.

relations in the context of postcolonialism, economic power and the unravelling complexities of globalization.[35]

This book is partly a desire to meet these academic challenges, but it also seeks to explore how comparative urban histories can engage with the recent critique of grand processes, universalist narratives and the privileging of dominant vocabularies and views.[36] The danger of comparative urban history lies in the risk of falling into a seemingly out-dated 'one for all, all for one model [...] that overlooks the local context and aims to find universal solutions to global social, economic and environment urban problems'.[37] In the postmodern, postcolonial intellectual world we inhabit, where the certainties once attributed to empirical data have been replaced with questions about the language and assumptions that construct such information, it no longer seems relevant to simply understand similarities and differences between cities and to use these as a lens to understand urban development. Rather, the urban vocabularies and grammars within cities, between cities and at the intersection of physical and virtual communication need to be examined. Only by understanding the innate framings, cultural traditions, fluidities and complexities that subliminally and often implicitly underpin these processes can comparative and transnational urban history start to meaningfully examine how the experience of urbanism varies both within and between regions, nations and continents.

At the heart of this comparative and transnational approach lies the imperative to examine relationships not just across cities, but also across materials and methods. Saunier's suggestion that a transnational historian 'may invent new sources as well as revisit or rearrange existing ones' highlights the possibilities for a more dynamic urban history, one that explores the flows and relationships between cities as much by seeking them out in unfamiliar locations as by posing uncustomary questions of more familiar materials.[38] One accusation often levelled at comparative urban histories is the apparently arbitrary nature of case study selection, or the tendency to formulate 'major' and 'minor' case studies which seem predicated as much on the availability and symmetry of sources, as on their heuristic promise. Such critiques tend to miss the key point that the intellectual reward of comparison lies not in finding a supposedly ideal match –

---

[35] The relationship between contemporary urban issues and the development of the field of urban history is covered in Gary Davies, 'The Rise of Urban History in Britain, c. 1960–1978' (PhD diss., University of Leicester, 2014).

[36] Robinson, 'Cities in a World of Cities'; Kevin Ward, 'Towards a Relational Comparative Approach to the Study of Cities', *Progress in Human Geography* 34 (2010): 471–87. Charlotte Lemanski, 'Hybrid Gentrification in South Africa: Theorising across Southern and Northern Cities', *Urban Studies* 51 (2014): 2943–60.

[37] Rebecca Madgin, *Heritage, Culture and Conservation: Managing the Urban Renaissance* (Saarbrucken: VDM Verlag, 2009), 27.

[38] Saunier, *Transnational History*, 134.

an impossible task to be sure – but in the original questions and unsuspected answers these pairings can yield. Much urban history research has sought to pair or categorize cities on the basis of the complementarity of existing source material.[39] However, we suggest that these categorizations could be disrupted by a creative use of sources, an increasing inclination to fuse different sources and the adoption of original methods emerging from recent interdisciplinary scholarship. To fully explore the urban imaginary we need to avoid a reductive typology of cities that labels them, boxes them into narrow categories and shies away from juxtaposing very different cities in historical perspective. The future of urban history, we contend, may be shaped by a comparative urbanism that willingly forgoes neat categorizations in favour of producing 'relational comparisons that use different cities to pose questions of one another'.[40]

Rather than searching in vain for exact replicas of source material in various settings, the approach we advance is premised on the acceptance that urban problems and processes are subject to cultural nuances which shape the formulation and implementation of ideas and policies. Comparative and transnational approaches can reveal how similar types of sources tell us about the dynamics of different places, but by the same token, they need not be abandoned if available materials do not correspond. Oral histories, for example, may not exist with the same richness in two different cities, but ethnography or diaries may work just as well for interrogating the research question. A rich literary tradition in one city can bring the researcher to search for unexpected imaginative insights in another city's periodicals or ephemera.[41] Juxtaposing seemingly unlikely materials offers precisely the unexpected, perhaps surprising, questions and insights that cannot arise from more conventional pairings.[42]

Stemming from this re-examination of method, the very terminology used to explain urban processes has also been called into question, notably amid concerns that the existing linguistic canon unduly privileges, and universalizes, terms associated with Western contexts. Geographer Charlotte Lemanski offers a telling example in questioning the applicability of the term 'gentrification' and its connotations in the South African context. Gentrification, Lemanski argues, is a 'northern' concept not readily transportable to the Global South. Calling for a reflective engagement with the terms that scholars use to describe and understand urban processes, Lemanski points to the importance of examining

[39] For port cities, market towns and small towns see the chapters in Peter Clark, *The Cambridge Urban History of Britain*, Volume II 1540–1840 (Cambridge: Cambridge University Press, 2000).
[40] Ward, 'Towards a Relational Comparative Approach', 480.
[41] Nicolas Kenny, *The Feel of the City: Experiences of Urban Transformation* (Toronto: University of Toronto Press, 2014).
[42] Marcel Detienne, *Comparing the Incomparable*, trans. Janet Lloyd (Stanford: Stanford University Press, 2008).

the way these take shape in their own right in diverse settings (rather than merely by transplanting concepts developed elsewhere), and hence the need to broaden the comparative scope of urban analysis beyond familiar western confines.[43] A creative use of source material requires us to be more critical of language that may block, inhibit or alter our ability to understand the ways urban problems and processes play out within different contexts. Here the methodological aspect of urban research assumes increased importance. Returning to the tension between biographies and interactional studies, the sources and methods available for research profoundly condition not just the type of study that can be undertaken but the extent to which those urban vocabularies, frameworks, fluidities and traditions can be accessed and used to inform comparison. If we are to answer Clark and other critics, and move beyond similarities and differences in order to deepen our understandings of how cities functioned, then our first line of enquiry has to be a re-examination of the sources, methods and vocabularies that shape the ways we conduct comparative and transnational urban history. In light of the increasingly transnational outlook of historical practice in general, interrogating the ways in which comparative and transnational research extends the methodological and conceptual frameworks of urban history in particular is thus a timely endeavour.

In the chapters that make up this volume, scholars deeply immersed in comparative and transnational methods discuss the widened perspective these bring to fundamental components of urban history. In scholarly research, the full implications of a particular argument or method often do not come to light during the writing process, but after the work has appeared in print and been shared with its readership. Many of the chapters have a contemplative quality to them, their authors taking stock of their recent work and reflecting on what they have learned about the process of comparative and transnational methodologies through their research on multiple urban sites. The chapters, as a result, blend theory with the historian's practice, illustrating the advantages, and challenges, of dwelling upon and navigating between multiple cities in uncovering the complexities of urban problems and characteristics, ranging from segregation, to migration, to prostitution, to planning and reform. They are grounded in the relatively recent past, beginning in the mid-eighteenth century and showing how these issues resonate in the urban world we inhabit today. Movement between cities has, to be sure, constituted a defining element of urban societies since their inception, but this book concentrates on a time during which cities

---

[43] Lemanski, 'Hybrid Gentrification in South Africa: Theorising across Southern and Northern Cities'. Similarly, historian Alan Mayne has described the constructed nature of the word 'slum', and in a Global South context the words 'favela' and 'slum' are not synonyms. See Alan Mayne, *The Imagined Slum: Newspaper Representation in Three Cities, 1870–1914* (Leicester: Leicester University Press, 1993).

reached their apogee as modes of organising human society.[44] This was a period in which travel and communications between cities were not only facilitated by new technologies, but in which this movement itself became a primary driving force in urban development and thus in different forms of organization.[45]

In many ways, urban life in the last two-and-a-half centuries appears as a matrix of local and global relations mediated by an increasingly diverse set of actors, and forged through contact, dialogue and conflict across borders. The relationship between cities and their inhabitants has, in the modern period, been characterized by ever-more urgent questions of how to structure, plan and govern these distinct forms of human habitat. The authors question our understanding of how cities were redeveloped at crucial turning points in their histories, moments defined by larger transnational patterns such as industrialization, war and colonialism, and highlight discrepancies between expressed ideals of governance and planning, and the way they took form on the ground. If urban elites have sought to consolidate their influence and hegemony through actions designed to impose material and moral order on cities, as these chapters show, these actions have been contested and resisted by workers, migrants, prostitutes and other marginalized local populations seeking to carve out their own space and spheres of influence on the urban landscape. This book address the ways in which comparative and transnational perspectives reveal urban planning and governance to be the product of perpetual collisions between highly local factors and experiences on one hand, and increasingly international movement on the other.

The authors of *Cities Beyond Borders* thus share a common objective of unpacking the relationships between people, places and methods that animate comparative and transnational urban history. While Part I emphasizes methodological concerns and Part II delves more specifically into historical narrative, each of the chapters dwells on the rich interplay between practice

---

[44] To be sure, this volume's focus on the recent past does not imply that movement between cities was an exclusively modern phenomena. For more on earlier periods, see for example Peter M.M.G. Akkermans and Glenn M. Schwartz, *The Archaeology of Syria: From Complex Hunter-Gatherers to Early Urban Societies, c.16,000–300 BC* (Cambridge: Cambridge University Press, 2003), Michael C. Howard, *Transnationalism in Ancient and Medieval Societies: The Role of Cross-Border Trade and Travel* (Jefferson, NC: McFarland, 2012), Patrick O'Flanagan, *Port Cities of Atlantic Iberia, c. 1500–1900* (Aldershot: Ashgate, 2008). For other comparative studies see the *Historical Urban Studies* general series edited by Jean-Luc Pinol and Richard Rodger and published by Ashgate, in particular Jaroslav Miller, *Urban Societies in East-Central Europe, 1500–1700* (Aldershot: Ashgate, 2008).

[45] Daniel T. Rodgers, *Atlantic Crossings: Social Politics in a Progressive Age* (Cambridge, MA: Harvard University Press, 1998); Pierre-Yves Saunier, 'Transatlantic Connections and Circulations in the 20th Century: The Urban Variable', *Informationen zur modernen Stadgeschichte* 1 (2007).

and content. A closing section reflects on the lessons this relational approach teaches us about cities and urban historical research today. Addressing both the interpretive possibilities these approaches offer and the risks they entail, Part I begins with Carl Nightingale sailing the seven 'Cs'[46] of transnational urban historical practice in search of what historian Thomas Bender 'hauntingly' refers to as the 'explanatory payoff' of transnationalism. Mulling over his experience of writing about urban racial segregation on a global scale, Nightingale reminds us that the primary challenge of doing transnational history resides in avoiding the risk of producing what amounts to a collection of individual stories on a given topic, or worse, that we 'pigeonhole' urban problems according to our own assumptions rather than explain how they derive from 'the large-scale historical experiences' of cities themselves. Understanding how a widespread phenomenon like racial segregation emerged in the cities and at the historical junctures it did, he urges, requires following various incarnations of this reality around the globe. Achieving this requires careful attention to the 'dialectical interplay' between commonalities and contrasts within different cities and between the connections and contingencies that both link them together and highlight their uniqueness. Despite the difficulties inherent in such large-scale research, he concludes, this opens up possibilities for an urban history premised on a wide geographic *scope* within which multiple cities are placed into *dia*logue, prompting Nightingale to suggest that the intellectual reward for such work lies in the adoption of what he somewhat provocatively calls a 'disacopic' perspective.

Dan Horner pursues this reflection on movement, in this case by discussing the benefits of comparison and transnationalism for understanding how imperial and migratory connections underpinned urban governance. Interested in the way people and ideas traversed the Atlantic, and in what happened to them on either side, Horner explains why the port cities of Montreal and Liverpool work to explore the connections between mid-nineteenth-century migratory waves, particularly from Ireland, and the spread of liberal conceptions of urban governance. Urban elites took cues from one another, particularly through the press, as they contributed to building a 'transnational liberal public sphere' premised on 'reason, restraint and decorum'. But it is by wielding the tools of comparison, exploring the similarities and differences between Montreal and Liverpool, that Horner is able to show how the liberal project was 'established, resisted and, ultimately, negotiated' according to specific circumstances in these two 'laboratories'. Comparison, argues Horner, shows how a transnational phenomenon like liberalism operated in distinct sites, revealing how the ideology both shaped, and was shaped by, developments in the specific places

---

[46] Nightingale discusses seven elements of transnational urban history, all of which begin with the letter C: case studies, chronology, causality, commonalities, contrasts, connections and contingencies.

in which it alighted. Moreover, by focussing on the city, on the mobility and circulation that animated it and on the tension between governing elites and the marginalized subjects of liberal reform, Horner also shows the importance of considering political developments outside of the national framework from which they are typically studied.

Questions of space, place and identity are at the heart of Jordan Stanger-Ross's methodological reflection on the use of digital methods in researching the settlement patterns of Italian communities in post-war Toronto and Philadelphia. As in the two preceding chapters, Stanger-Ross is interested in unpacking the ramifications on the ground of transnational flows, and his chapter discusses the unsuspected findings that can arise from analysing highly localized data, in this case the residential address listed in marriage records. Stanger-Ross points to the rich interpretive possibilities of GIS and digital historical mapping in bringing to life the complex 'choreographies' of migrant communities as they settled into new urban environments. Discarding the perception that quantitative data limits scholars to analysing maps and censuses, Stanger-Ross points to the qualitative stories of social practice that hide beneath these figures, discussing the way individual performances of ethnic and gender identities shine through the plotting of their movement through urban space. Only when such information is analysed in a comparative framework do the full possibilities of such methods become evident, he emphasizes. By examining the way 'geographies of intimacy' take shape differently in two cities, Stanger-Ross shows the importance of local circumstances and spatial relations in the production of 'everyday urban life', demonstrating how the concepts of ethnicity and gender wielded by social historians are themselves shaped by the urban localities in which they are rooted.

Also attentive to the interplay between local and transnational scales, Jeffry Diefendorf discusses the insights that both a broad global sweep and point-to-point comparison bring to the history of post-Second World War planning and reconstruction in Eastern Europe, the Soviet Union, Japan, France and Great Britain, showing how the specific variables at work in these different contexts collide with transnational influences. Fusing these perspectives, he notes, allows both for a broader understanding of the forces driving reconstruction and for a freedom from the methodological constraints posed as much by the nation-state as by 'intensely local, self-limiting perspectives'. But Diefendorf also notes that while transnational models were applied broadly in urban planning before, during and after the war, initiatives by national governments, municipal politics and the desires of local populations meant that planning ideas circulating around the globe were often refashioned or resisted in the localities upon which they descended. Diefendorf thus closes Part I with a word of caution, reminding us that while a broader perspective opens new horizons, there is always a danger in getting 'carried away' with transnationalism at the risk of overlooking significant developments that do occur at the local and national levels.

In Part II the dialogue between cities and the conceptual apparatus of historians centres on specific areas of urban historical research – from reform and housing to planning and governance – to reveal the unsuspected shapes these take when viewed through the prism of comparison and transnationalism. Marion Pluskota addresses the question of prostitution in Bristol and Nantes between 1750 and 1830 with the larger goal of explaining the way comparison brings out the local specificities of concerns that crossed borders. This was a period, she notes, in which the systematic collection of statistical information at an urban level was in its infancy, raising the need for historians to forgo the search for equivalent data sets and instead think comparatively with qualitative sources that tell us about the nature of the elites involved in the regulation of prostitution, and the specific contexts in which they functioned. Pluskota explains that comparing the two cities displays the extent to which local traditions, social structures and legislative frameworks produced important differences in what were outwardly similar processes. Comparison on a highly localised scale, she further posits, brings to our attention municipal cultures that, despite sharing certain values and norms, acted on issues of governance in ways that not only illustrate national differences, but that also bring out the particularities of 'provincial cities' with respect to dominant metropoles like London or Paris. Comparative methods, Pluskota argues, are essential for grasping how the 'interplay' between local and external factors moulded shifting attitudes toward prostitution, and its regulation, during the period.

Janet Polasky, in her chapter, considers urban reformers in nineteenth-century London and Brussels, observing these cities in tandem to reveal previously unrecognised patterns in their reconfiguration during the Industrial Revolution. Polasky embraces the interconnectedness of comparison and transnationalism, as much in her own method as in her analysis of urban reformers who themselves both compared the two cities and moved between them in their search for solutions to the overcrowding wrought by the need for concentrated labour forces. For the author, boundaries between British and Belgian historiographical traditions have proved more impermeable than the geopolitical boundaries reformers' frequently crossed as they observed one another's differing attempts to achieve similar goals. Noting that comparison on an urban scale affords the opportunity for more in-depth, archival analysis than is possible at the level of the 'unwieldy nation state', Polasky observes that while urban reform was 'shaped by global mentalities and movements and buffeted by national politics', it nonetheless 'unfolded pragmatically at a municipal level'. Beyond the specific lessons about the reformist endeavours that are learned by comparing the two cities, Polasky's multi-pronged approach allows her to reconsider larger historiographical conventions about housing policies and the roles of the state and of private enterprise in these respective contexts. Ultimately, the reorganisation of both London and Brussels around the avenues and monuments international tourists appreciate today originates in divergent, though mutually shaped efforts to exclude workers from the historic centres of these cities.

Nikhil Rao also investigates the flow of urban planning ideas through cross-border circuits, asking how such an approach can help 'disengage' the transnational aspects of Indian urban history from the colonial framework in which it tends to be discussed. As he points out, Indian historiography has long been preoccupied with questions of colonial rule and the emergence of the nation and of nationalism, an outlook which has had a 'distorting' effect on our understanding of Indian cities. Examining the transnational dimensions of the integration of Salsette Island into Bombay during the early twentieth century allows Rao to move beyond the traditional focus on the 'England-India colonial axis' and to show that even within this relationship, interactions at the urban level were not necessarily all 'colonial as such'. The development of Salsette Island is especially illustrative of the circuitous routes along which urban planning emerged during the period. Ideas borrowed from Germany modified the application of British principles in Bombay, and these in turn made their way back to London where they inspired new outlooks among English planning experts. Rather than seeing urban planning as merely another instance of colonial imposition, Rao also shows how debates about urban development on the ground were themselves important factors in the development of Indian nationalism itself.

Stefan Couperus and Shane Ewen take the conversation about early twentieth-century transnational planning in a new direction by concentrating specifically on the people who made these networks function. While the organizations bringing together municipal administrators and experts have attracted growing historical attention, Couperus and Ewen point out that the individual personalities driving these institutions forward are most often overlooked at the expense of the institutions they embodied. And yet the decisions, priorities and concrete actions that resulted from these bodies, and through which urban change was effected, were coloured by the values, identity and temperament of the specific individuals at the helm. Appreciating how transnational networks of urban governance actually functioned thus requires knowing and understanding the 'human stories' that shaped them. Focussing on two successive presidents of the Union Internationale des Villes/International Union of Local Authorities (UIV), Floor Wibaut and George Montagu Harris, Couperus and Ewen propose a 'decentring' of the 'macro-institutional' politics of the UIV in favour of 'thick descriptions' that speak to the personal backgrounds, politics and agency of the two men. It is this human dimension, they show, that makes the 'link between the local and the international spheres', revealing how urban planning and governance was constituted by the overlapping of various scales, ranging from the personal to the transnational.

The relationship between urban planning and politics had a much more sinister appearance in Second-World-War Germany, as the following chapter demonstrates. Janet Ward examines the transnational underpinnings of the Nazi Party's plans to reshape the cities of Central and Eastern Europe according to an ideology of racial purity. Adopting an explicitly spatial perspective on the Third Reich, Ward shows how the application of Final Solution objectives to urban planning were envisaged as a transnationally exportable 'urban re-formation' and corresponding 'racial de-formation'. National Socialist planners imagined the cities of the region as future sites of 'genocidal colonisation', serving to extend and reinforce a *domus* conceived in relation to 'the German blood and soil'. This vision was itself informed by knowledge acquired elsewhere, as Ward demonstrates through the example of the 'grotesquely transnational intersection' at play when Treblinka concentration camp guards drew on their experiences with the destruction of corpses in the clean-up of Dresden after the allied bombings of the city. While we often think of cross-border knowledge acquisition as a sign of openness and extended horizons, Ward too reminds us to stay critical: the work of Nazi planners dispels persistent 'assumptions that transnationalism somehow carries its own progressive politics within itself'.

We conclude the volume with two chapters that reflect on the insights comparative and transnational approaches bring to our understanding of both the contemporary world and the practice of urban history today. Harold Platt offers further evidence of the inequalities that underlie transnational urbanism by examining new forms of urban segregation generated by global flows of capital in the post-1973 energy crisis world. Ebenezer Howard's garden city ideal of a century ago, he posits, has morphed into a proliferation of exclusive gated communities embodying the interplay of global market forces, national policies and local regulation that have resulted in the privatisation of public space. Tracing these realities through São Paulo, Los Angeles and San Salvador, Platt discusses how notions of First and Third worlds collide and are inverted, producing in these cities 'Fourth World' zones of racial and class-based marginalization. At stake is the very connection between urban dwellers and their surroundings, producing unresolved tensions between the gated communities of the wealthy and the ghettoes and prisons to which the poor are confined, between globalised space and the quest for place-based identities.

Finally, against the 'examples of man's inhumanity to man' that have always underlain urban development, Richard Rodger nonetheless contemplates the intellectual potential that comes with thinking beyond individual cities. Without overlooking the sense of place and deep local knowledge offered by specific urban case studies, he argues, an approach rooted in comparison and transnationalism attunes us to the way cities function as part of larger social, economic or cultural systems, operating at scales that are not just national, but regional or global as well. The theoretical and methodological innovations of contemporary historiography, from cultural studies to the digital humanities, offer new ways to consider the 'everyday experiences of everyday people' in these urban systems, across the longue durée and into the twenty-first-century world, where the transnational movement of people, technology and culture has radically transformed the realities of city life.

* * *

Blending comparative and transnational approaches, as we suggest here, implies abandoning neat comparable boxes or tidy transnational linkages, and instead reflecting on urban knowledge as the dynamic product of thick local experiences rooted in an asymmetrical global context. Whilst this volume engages with a number of cities located across the globe, our purpose is to interrogate existing methodologies and practices as urban historians rather than to address the global history field more broadly. As such, recognizing that contemporary scholarship across the humanities and social sciences has taken a decidedly global turn, the perspective offered here suggests possible remedies to globalization studies that are often criticized for making universalistic generalizations at the expense of attention to local variations,[47] paying insufficient heed to historical context[48] and for ignoring social and cultural processes in favour of coldly economic developments.[49] As social units distinct from the nation, cities, notes sociologist Saskia Sassen, are not only intrinsically embedded in the mechanics of globalization, but are also the sites on which identities and communities are themselves reconfigured by global processes.[50] The call for urban studies research to 'trace the multiplicity of connections which exist amongst cities around the world', to 'bring many different cities into closer conceptual proximity' and to 'address the demand that insights from cities beyond the West be launched as starting points for new theoretical conversations' in the twenty-first century can be extended to urban historians.[51] Future research into urban development need not focus on these contexts solely in the twenty-first century, as detailed and innovative archival research can inform a greater awareness of the interplay

---

[47]   Khagram and Levitt, *The Transnational Studies Reader*, 3–4.

[48]   Saunier and Ewen, *Another Global City*; Michael Peter Smith, 'Transnational Urbanism Revisited', *Journal of Ethnic and Migration Studies* 31.2 (2005).

[49]   Xiangming Chen and Ahmed Kanna, eds, *Rethinking Global Urbanism: Comparative Insights from Secondary Cities* (New York: Routledge, 2012); Huyssen, *Other Cities, Other Worlds*.

[50]   Saskia Saasen, *Globalization and its Discontents: Essays on the New Mobility of People and Money* (New York: New Press, 1998).

[51]   Robinson, 'Introduction'.

of international, national, regional and local factors and above all the lived experience of urbanism across space and through time. Joining critics who see the local, in particular the urban, and the global not as binaries or hierarchies but as mutually constitutive domains of human action and identity, this book emphasizes the centrality of urban space and place to processes occurring on an international scale.[52]

Putting cities side by side and examining the flows and linkages between them allows us to examine how the picture of urban organizations and experiences on the ground comes into sharper focus only when the lens is sufficiently wide to account for the global scope of local place making. For both the Marco Polos who travel the world and the Kublai Khans who stay put, urban imaginaries are rooted in the bridging of these scales. The pursuit of the urban variable has long been the preserve of scholars uncovering the relationships between people and space, between economy and society, the natural and the human-made and the mental and physical urban landscape. Common across biographic and interactional approaches is a desire to set the internal dynamics of urban spaces against the externalities that govern both stasis and change. At the heart of the urban historian's approach is thus a capacity to think relationally – within spaces and hierarchies, between people and places and across temporal and spatial borders. Pursuing the relational aspect of urban history in a comparative and transnational perspective, as the chapters in this volume show, broadens the examination of the fundamental relationships that guide how we have historically organized and lived in our cities.

---

[52]   Smith, *Transnational Urbanism: Locating Globalization*.

PART I

Chapter 2

The Seven Cs: Reflections on Writing a Global History of Urban Segregation

Carl H. Nightingale

Books like this one, packed with diverse and stimulating chapters, make it indisputable: urban history has embraced its 'transnational turn'. Celebrations are certainly in order and so are the ongoing critical conversations that are essential to any innovative academic departure. Moreover, as transnational urban history transforms from a theoretical call to a real and burgeoning practice, we also need to continuously reflect back on how it is we *do* this kind of history. In that spirit I offer these thoughts on my experience writing a book called *Segregation: a Global History of Divided Cities*.[1] These are retrospective musings, and they describe the techniques I used to research the book and develop its argument far more systematically than they ever appeared to me while I was actually writing the book. The overall drift is this: when we embrace the 'transnational' we must not conceive of it so much a radical departure, but the beginnings of potent dialectical interchanges between many newer and more traditional forms of thought and practice about urban history. There are seven elements to the practice that I used in the book, and it happens that all seven can be introduced using words beginning with the letter C: case studies, chronology, causality, commonalities, contrasts, connections and contingencies. In actual practice, I did not 'sail' upon these seven Cs so smoothly, and their confluence as a set of practices actually came to me largely by means of another important activity beginning with C: casting about in the dark! That last C is perhaps just as important – for I now realize that not always knowing the direction I was sailing or where I was casting my lines actually allowed fruitful dialectical dynamics to develop between the seven other Cs.

That dialectical dynamic – that 'tavern of the seven Cs', we might call it – is worth preserving. It is in that interchange that we can discover the true potential of the transnational turn in urban history – the realization that approaches often deemed opposed to each other – not only the 'transnational' and 'traditional' or the macro and the micro, but also comparative history and global history – in

---

[1] Carl H. Nightingale, *Segregation: A Global History of Divided Cities* (Chicago: University of Chicago Press, 2012).

fact offer potent benefits to each other. Moreover, this dialectical urban history, while certainly set in motion by the transnational turn, may also ultimately transcend the strict sense of 'transnational' itself and become something even more valuable.

Case Studies

What we know about the history of urban segregation – and specifically what we know about urban residential segregation by race, the central focus of my book – mostly came into being because of case studies of individual cities. For the prospect of writing a larger-scale history of urban segregation, local case studies have some weaknesses, but they must also be treated as essential assets. Case studies alone, obviously, only allow historians to speculate about larger historical patterns – that is, after all, largely why we have called so loudly for more transnational urban histories. But over the past 100 years or so the collectivity of urban historians has written so many case studies that we have created in effect a massive secondary archive – filled with rich analytical insight as well as basic information. Without it, let us be clear, it would be inconceivable to write larger-scale stories. This indispensability, in fact, creates a lovely paradox: urban historians' efforts to go global must start with a deep plunge into the rich and pulsing sea of local studies.

There are several risks to this plunge. One is the overwhelming amount of information – how to keep track of it all? Another is the risk that instead of a transnational history, we surface from our dive with a product that looks suspiciously like another collection of chapters that only recapitulate the case studies on which each is based. Another potential outcome, also in my mind falling short of a transnational history, would be a kind of typological study, one that subjects a specific urban topic, such as urban segregation, to a system of pigeonholes that derives from a historian's own *a priori* categorical imperatives rather than from within the large-scale historical experiences of those cities themselves.

My own plunge into the secondary archive was, as I have suggested, less organized and less efficient than it should have been. What ultimately gave it structure, I now realize in retrospect, is that I focussed on finding and cataloguing evidence that helped me solve problems relating to the other 'C' questions: What chronological sequence can we build between these cases? How is this case similar or different from other places? Is there evidence of connection in this case, or are there contingencies operating in these cases that might have limited or deflected connections in some way or another?

Meanwhile, the weaknesses and assets of case studies for transnational history themselves operated in a productive dialectical fashion as I went about my work. The secondary archive as a generality did not provide full answers for all the larger-scale urban historical questions I faced. Accordingly, my only solution in many instances was to embark on my own case studies. That, in turn, brought up another productive question: which cities should I chose as cases? (Obviously, I could not conduct primary research on every segregated city in world history.) Once again, it was only by navigating the secondary archive with the particular focus provided by the other 'Cs' that I was able to identify likely candidates, in my case cities where significant changes occurred in the larger-scale chronological narrative of segregation or cities that operated as significant nodes of the larger-scale connections that helped to direct the broader flow of segregationist practice.

The result was the basic methodological structure of the book, what I sometimes call the 'synthetic reading with post-holes': a broad narrative constructed through a synthetic reading of the published literature, punctuated by in-depth, and in some cases, chapter-length original research studies on five individual cities that were crucial to the larger chronological, causal, comparative, connective and contingent patterns of my developing transnational story. These five cities were Madras, Calcutta, London, Chicago and Johannesburg. As the narrative came into further focus, I found it necessary to delve into less-exhaustive primary work on a few incidents that occurred in other cities as well, in the 'cantonments' of British India, Hong Kong, Paris, Algiers and Baltimore. All of these case studies also allowed me to bring the richness of human-scale urban experience into a narrative that often had swept across much larger scales.[2]

The last and perhaps most important strength of case studies' local perspective, ironically, turned out to be a rather abstract and sweeping insight – one that derives not so much from the geographical scope of the inquiry but from the disciplinary style urban historians bring to questions such as the nature of segregation and the ways it operates historically. As useful as sociologists' approaches are to this subject, their focus on the quantification of 'dissimilarity' or on modelling such dynamics as 'invasion and succession' did not provide the empirically verifiable connective tissue I needed for a larger-scale narratives based around the other Cs. Where urban historians excel, it is in recreating the messiness of the politics of urban space – the unceasing and uncertain contests over dividing lines, the jagged stories in which people mobilize other people, ideas, money, practices and institutional power to make those boundaries stick despite near-constant resistance. To write the worldwide spread of segregation, I would have to trace the spread of the constitutive elements of this politics, hopefully as evocatively as urban historians have rendered them in individual

---

[2]   These primary case studies can be found in Nightingale, *Segregation*, Chapters 2, 3, 8, 9, 10 and 11. Material from the less-extensive studies can be found in Chapters 4, 5, and 7.

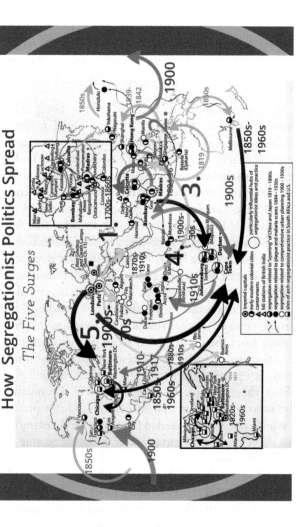

Figure 2.1   The five surges of racial segregation in the modern era. This map shows the global geography of the spread of racial segregationist politics and practices, starting in South Asia (1), then travelling to East Asia and the Pacific (2), then becoming a worldwide phenomenon because of turn-of-the-twentieth-century public health panics that fuelled 'segregation mania' (3), and also because of the city-splitting imagination of globe-trotting professional urban planners (4) and finally culminating in the European-inspired 'archsegregationist' politics of the United States and South Africa (5)

Source: Carl Nightingale, 'Urban Segregation: A 'Diascopic' World Atlas', a forthcoming on-line reference tool.

cities, and in so doing also measure the extent that segregationists were able to adapt and recreate these elements in many, extremely diverse, local places.[3]

Chronology

When did segregation begin? Where did it appear next? When did it spread and peak? What happened after that? These problems were among the most important and fundamental I could solve as someone engaged in larger-scale urban history. Chronology would allow me to create a story-line, after all, and most clearly distinguish my history from a collection of essays or a typological study.

As for the book as a whole, my search for chronological answers started in the oceans of the secondary archive. To establish, for example, that Madras was the first place where officials used the terms White Town and Black Town to designate separate zones of a colonial city, I had to read dozens of works on early modern colonial cities stretching from Mexico City to Moçambique to Macao, where possible confirming important points in the original sources.[4] From there, the chronological imperative provided a crucial organizing principle for the vast amounts of information from the secondary archive. The timeline I developed of incidents of segregationist practice and politics began to reveal striking patterns not only across time but also across hemispheric, continental and ocean-sized swaths of space. Race itself may have been originally an Atlantic phenomenon, but urban segregation by colour and race began in the Indian Ocean and spread far eastward and then jumped the Pacific long before it swung towards the West.

Five overlapping periods – or 'surges of segregation' as I ultimately called them – emerged, determined both by their geographical extent and some of the central themes of segregationist politics and practice involved in each. First, a series of segregationist practices – which represented modified versions of those that occurred in the colonial cities of Madras, Calcutta and Bombay – spread across the Indian subcontinent in tune with the British conquest.[5] Then, new innovations of these practices spread eastward in step with the West's forced 'opening' of China and the subsequent migration of Chinese people across the Pacific. This second surge helped explain, for example, why campaigns for segregation ordinances in the USA first arose in San Francisco in the 1870s, and only came to the country's east coast and heartland after 1910.[6] It also clarified the climax of my story, the third and largest surge, dating from 1894 to 1920,

---

3   Nightingale, *Segregation*, 9–10.
4   Nightingale, *Segregation*, Chapter 2.
5   Nightingale, *Segregation*, Chapter 4.
6   Nightingale, *Segregation*, Chapter 5.

that I call 'segregation mania'. The mania began with the outbreak of plague in Hong Kong and the first official uses of 'segregation' to describe practices of dividing urban space for public health reasons there and in Bombay. From Asia, this form of segregationism spread, once again, across the Pacific (occasioning a second segregation ordinance in San Francisco in 1900, for example), and at the same time also westward across much of the rest of Asia, Africa and ultimately to the eastern shores of the Americas. The conceptual scope of public health-related segregation measures widened as well, to cover diseases like malaria in West Africa and tuberculosis in Baltimore.[7]

Amidst this mania for segregation, a fourth parallel surge crested as well. It was tied to the expansion of the urban planning movement, and particularly to the work of planners influenced by French traditions of monumental urbanism. They endorsed segregation in far loftier terms, as a means to distinguish the dynamic West from the stagnant if noble East. Their work is best exemplified by particularly ambitious plans of urban racial division as those at Rabat, Morocco and at the new capital of British India at New Delhi.[8] Those examples marked the outer chronological limits of segregationist colonial urbanism, for specifically racialized plans for divided cities in the colonies largely disappeared once nationalist movements dissolved the structures of formal European empires during the mid-twentieth century. In only two societies did race segregation expand during this period: South Africa and the United States. The persistence of these two systems in the face of attacks from powerful anti-segregationist movements earned them the title 'archsegregation'. Though South African segregation, and later apartheid, relied more heavily on explicitly racist state legislation than urban segregation in the United States, the two systems were deeply connected. City-splitters in both countries depended on importing people, ideas, money and a vast array of organizational forms, techniques, practices and legal instruments that urban authorities, reformers and real estate practitioners had developed in Britain and other European countries. As such, the simultaneous development of the two enormously complex and resilient engines of segregation in South Africa and the US represented a fifth transnational surge in segregationist practice.[9]

Causality

The words of Thomas Bender, delivered as part of a keynote lecture at my university in 2004, haunted this project throughout. Transnational history,

---

[7] Nightingale, *Segregation*, Chapter 6.
[8] Nightingale, *Segregation*, Chapter 7.
[9] Nightingale, *Segregation*, Chapters 8–11.

he warned, will only prove itself if there is 'explanatory payoff'. In my case the most obvious payoff would come from being able to explain the plot line of my story. Why did segregation appear in the particular cities and regions it did, in the particular chronological order it did and to the changing extent that it did? 'History is a contextualizing discipline', Bender had declared as part of the la Pietra Report, the manifesto for a transnational history of the United States. My bigger narrative would pay causal dividends only if it could illuminate the politics of segregation in any one city by placing that politics within the broader currents that in turn determined the geographical vectors and the timing of my five surges.[10]

How could I explain these surges then? Here is where I began to rely on the dialectical interplay of the four remaining Cs – commonalities and contrasts on the one hand, and connections and contingencies on the other.

Commonalities and Contrasts

Comparative history has a long and illustrious pedigree, and the work of comparativists has provided much of the scaffolding upon which any hopes for larger-scale histories have been built. In the past, urban historians have not played a large role in the business of comparative history, and the recent expansion of work that compares and contrasts two or more cities is a refreshing trend, as the more comparatively oriented articles in this book richly attest.[11]

Comparative analysis of cities across time was critical to establish both my choice of case studies and to clarify the integrity of my analysis of the five surges of segregation. Without a clear sense of how localities resembled each other and differed, I would not be able to determine when and where innovations in segregationist practice occurred. Comparisons also gave rise by themselves to

[10]   Thomas Bender, 'Keynote Address' at Conference on the Atlantic in Global Perspective, University at Buffalo, State University of New York, Buffalo, NY, 2004. See also Jorge Cañizares-Esguerra and Erik Seeman, eds, *The Atlantic in Global Perspective, 1500–2000* (Upper Saddle River, NJ: Pearson Prentice Hall, 2007). Organization of American Historians (OAH), 'The La Pietra Report: A Report to the Profession' (2000) at http://www.oah.org/about/reports/reports-statements/the-lapietra-report-a-report-to-the-profession/.

[11]   For some comparative approaches to urban history see the following chapters in this volume: Jordan Stanger-Ross and Janet Polasky. Also see book-length studies such as Jerome I. Hodos, *Second Cities: Globalization and Local Politics in Manchester and Philadelphia* (Philadelphia: Temple University Press, 2011); Jordan Stanger Ross, *Staying Italian: Urban Change and Ethnic Life in Postwar Toronto and Philadelphia* (Chicago: University of Chicago Press, 2009); Lisa Keller, *Triumph of Order: Democracy and Public Space in New York and London* (New York: Columbia University Press, 2009).

what I thought were important insights, such as the fact that the segregationists' policies of the British and French empires differed internally far more than they did from each other. There were plenty of similarities between the two as well, and neither deserves to be called intrinsically more segregationist than the other, even if the British were responsible for building a larger number of segregated colonial towns. Such insights also fit into a much broader one, that global history is not fully global unless it happens in a multitude of local places.[12]

That point also highlights a weakness of comparative history when practiced in isolation from an analysis of connections and disconnections. Overall, the act of comparing and contrasting did focus my attention more on the particular than the general, and on contrasts more than on any larger story that could encompass both or all the cities involved in my comparisons. Prophets of the broader transnational turn in history have accused practitioners of national comparisons for exactly that: their choice of objects to compare tends to reinforce the boundaries around nations and thus to justify the nation as the principle 'container' of our historical narratives.[13]

In addition, any act of comparison and contrast between cities raised the vexed 'apples and oranges' question: what exactly determines that segregationist politics in any two or more cities is, in fact, truly comparable? To the extent that comparativists have answered this question, they have done so by establishing inherently questionable *a priori* standards from outside the historical experience of the compared societies, not from within that experience. In this respect, their work often shares an epistemological attribute with typological approaches.[14]

The biggest limitation I sensed from relying solely on comparison and contrast, though, had to do with the causal imperative. While comparing attributes of segregated cities gave me an enormously richer descriptive portrait of the politics that lay behind the dividing lines, I could not explain how those

---

[12]   Nightingale, *Segregation*, 195–8.

[13]   The quotation about the nation as a 'container' of our histories is from the OAH's 'La Pietra Report'. On comparative history's focus on contrasts, see Daniel T. Rodgers, *Atlantic Crossings: Social Politics in a Progressive Age* (Cambridge, MA: Belknap Press of Harvard University Press, 1998), 4–5.

[14]   For one of the greatest comparative historians, George M. Fredrickson, 'comparison works best when the two cases being considered show a demonstrably high degree of similarity'. But by what standard do we 'demonstrate' a 'high degree of similarity?' In *White Supremacy*, he rejects the possibility of direct comparison of Jim Crow and South African segregation because the 'differences [between the two systems] ... are too great', once again raising the question: how great *is* too great? George M. Fredrickson, *The Comparative Imagination: On the History of Racism, Nationalism, and Social Movements* (Berkeley: University of California Press, 1997), 4; and George M. Fredrickson, *White Supremacy: A Comparative Study in American and South African History* (Oxford: Oxford University Press, 1981), 250.

attributes came into being solely by using comparative methods. In fact, by engaging in comparisons, I only multiplied the number of explanatory questions I faced. Not only did those comparisons fail to explain my big chronological story, but they also forced me to explain why the cities within each of my five surges – which I based on broad commonalities – nonetheless also varied so widely. Questions like this could only be answered if I moved beyond comparative history into what we have traditionally called transnational or global approaches,[15] and specifically if I placed comparisons in dialogue with connections on the one hand, and contrasts in dialogue with contingencies on the other.

Commonalities and Connections

Of course, my own comparative work for *Segregation* did not proceed as blindly as I have just portrayed it – I suspect that no comparative work ever really does. In my case, the main goal of comparing and contrasting cities was always to make an initial test to establish whether or not any one city's segregationist politics could be connected in some way to that of others. Establishing the existence of those connections was crucial, because I wanted to assess whether those connections, in their turn, could serve as an important part of the explanation for the broader spread of racial segregationist politics, as well as for the particular forms it took within each of the five surges. One of several virtuous dialectical interchanges between comparative and global history began to emerge for me: commonalities between cities would provide empirical hints that connections were present, and connections, if they were indeed demonstrably present by other empirical tests, would help me to reaping some 'explanatory payoff', namely by explaining patterns of commonality. Note that I was aware of the dangers of setting up a circular argument here. Commonalities could *hint* at, but *only* hint at, the presence of connections: the existence of these connections would have to be independently researched as well. And in turn, the actual impact of connections on commonalities had to be proven by evidence other than the commonality itself. That said, if connections did exist, I could reap the benefits of another type

---

[15]   For examples of this approach see the following chapters in this volume by Stefan Couperus and Shane Ewen, Nikhil Rao and Harold Platt. Also see: Rodgers, *Atlantic Crossings*; Gwendolyn Wright, *The Politics of Design in French Colonial Urbanism* (Chicago: University of Chicago Press, 1991); Paul Rabinow, *French Modern: Norms and Forms of the Social Environment* (Cambridge, MA: MIT Press, 1989); Pierre Yves Saunier and Shane Ewen, eds, *Another Global City: Historical Explorations into the Transnational Municipal Moment, 1850–2000* (New York: Palgrave Macmillan, 2008); Christopher Klemek, *The Transatlantic Collapse of Urban Renewal: Postwar Urbanism from New York to Berlin* (Chicago: University of Chicago Press, 2011).

of virtuous analytical payoff. Those connections could act as a truly historical standard of comparability – if two things were connected historically, either directly or through some third source of connective influence, their historical experiences of that mutual connection can be compared.

By these guidelines, it quickly became clear that segregation did not just appear randomly in different places and different times: it spread, and deliberate action was involved in making it spread. The most important commonality I found in modern-era segregationist politics was the presence of three institutions. All three could project power and influence over long distances, including within the local politics of many cities. These three institutions include governments (imperial ones being the most important, but national and local ones played critical roles); international networks of academics and urban reformers; and the loosely related group of institutions that combined to form a global urban real estate industry. In the sources, these institutions left behind a surfeit of evidence that they acted as agents of connection, and as such they became central to the book's main explanatory argument. It was they who were most responsible for spreading the people, ideas, money, practices and power needed to divide hundreds of cities in a vast variety of settings over the long course of the modern era. Though these institutions did not always work together everywhere – and indeed sometimes contributed to the messiness of local politics by opposing each other – it was also clear that the five surges of segregation coincided with surges in the influence of at least one and usually more than one of these three institutions.[16]

It also became clear that certain cities – and certain webs of inter-city connections – were especially important to the development of segregationist practice. For example, it was in Calcutta – and in Calcutta's deepening connection to London – that the three modern institutions first developed practices and rationales for segregation that would be exported and adapted elsewhere. Calcutta also influenced other cities negatively: the city's relatively attenuated colour line was often seen as something to avoid in other places.[17]

Elaborating the role of each of these three connective institutions required another crucial step in the enterprise of large-scale urban history: I also needed to move beyond the secondary archive of urban historiography – including both its rich case studies and the handful of transnational histories that do exist – -and connect what we know about cities to historiographies of the three institutions themselves: the history of empire; the growing literature on transnational reform movements, medical history and the intellectual history of race; and making some initial explorations into the transnational history of urban land markets, which has yet to spawn much of a transnational historiography at all.

---

[16]   This argument is first articulated in Nightingale, *Segregation*, 5–8.

[17]   Nightingale, *Segregation*, chapter 3.

Taking my cue from recent transnational histories of urban planning and social policy, I also made a few forays into biography. There, it was possible to see how individual segregationists themselves carried practices from one place to another, whether as representatives of governments, as experts or reformers or as land market agents. In this way, for example, I could show why Ronald Ross, who discovered how mosquitoes transmitted malaria, was so astounded when he found no separate zone for whites upon his arrival in Sierra Leone: he had been born in the segregated Himalayan hill station of Almora and lived most of his life in various other white compounds and bungalow districts across British India. These experiences influenced his endorsement of the Sierra Leone Governor's decision to build separate districts for whites and blacks in the colonial capital of Freetown. There was also the case of William Simpson, a public health expert whose career took him from Calcutta in the 1890s to various medical research centres in Britain, to Hong Kong, to West Africa, and then to East Africa by 1910, in a sense making him a personification of the connections that made up the period of segregation mania.[18]

My analysis of commonalities and connections, finally, helped me establish the contexts I needed for an adequate transnational analysis of urban segregation in the United States and South Africa. The archsegregationist practices adopted in both countries were similar in their complexity and sheer durability – they were the only forms of race-segregation that outlived the anti-colonial movements of the mid-twentieth century. I also discovered that both countries' segregationist politics revolved around a shared network of connections across the Atlantic: both countries based their racist segregation systems upon a long list of imported practices, legal precedents, legislation, institutional forms, as well as people and money that largely originated as non-racial phenomena in Europe, primarily in Britain. The list includes public health justifications for segregation, restrictive covenants in title deeds and the jurisprudence that clarified the terms under

---

[18]   These stories can be followed in Nightingale, *Segregation*, 164–5, 168–77, 181. Other transnational biographies can be found on 242–4 (Lionel Curtis); 277–8 (William K. Tucker); and 322, 326–7 (Richard T. Ely). See also Couperus and Ewen in this volume, and Shane Ewen and Michael Hebbert, 'European Cities in a Networked World during the Long 20th Century', *Environment and Planning C: Government and Policy*, 25.3 (2007): 327–40; Stefan Couperus, 'Backstage Politics. Municipal Directors and Technocratic Ambitions in Amsterdam, 1916–1930', in Stefan Couperus, Christianne Smit and Dirk Jan Wolffram, eds, *In Control of the City: Local Elites and the Dynamics of Urban Politics, 1800–1960* (Leuven, Paris and Dudley, MA: Peeters, 2007), 175–90; Shane Ewen, 'Transnational Municipalism in a Europe of Second Cities: Rebuilding Birmingham with Municipal Networks', in Saunier and Ewen, eds, *Another Global City*, 101–18; Stefan Couperus, 'In Between "Vague Theory" and "Sound Practical Lines": Transnational Municipalism in Interwar Europe', in Daniel Laqua, ed., *Internationalism Reconfigured: Transnational Ideas and Movements Between the World Wars* (London: I.B. Taurus, 2011), 65–87.

which they operated, slum clearance legislation, zoning laws, public housing policies and state-backed mortgage support programs for first-time home buyers. In addition, the same land development companies sometimes operated in both places, guaranteeing the flow of British capital, surveyors, lawyers, land agents and suburban planning models needed for the creation of segregated districts. Neighbourhood protective associations based on British ratepayer associations also operated in both countries. In the context of multiracial white supremacist settler societies, all of these tools provided a means to transform local housing markets into segregationist institutions that operated under the racialized economic logic of what W.E.B. DuBois called the 'bearded lie' – that black people living in white neighbourhoods brought down local property values.[19]

Contrasts and Contingencies

As significant as these results were for the book's central argument, the dialectic of commonalities and connections did not accomplish everything. I still had to explain the sheer diversity of segregationist 'dramas' within my broader stories of segregation's surges.

Why was it that contrasts persisted despite connection? The best transnational historians have dealt with this question by acknowledging that connections are not completely determinative: people in one nation or locality may import something – say a promising policy model – through large-scale connective networks, but they usually have to adapt whatever it is they import to suit local circumstances. Sometimes therefore they invent radically new forms of practice, and in so doing influence other places in ways that the original creators or importers of the policy did not envision. Sometimes, only some segments of a multi-faceted set of practices or ideas make it through; some pieces have to be discarded. Processes sometimes called 'friction', 'filtering', or 'adaptation' are at work and must be explained to account for what is essentially a process of transnational differentiation operating through connections.[20]

I think the term 'contingency' best encapsulates the many possible causal forces responsible for these forms of differentiation. I argue, for example, that local contingencies operating in Hong Kong explain its unique 1904 segregation

[19] These connections are discussed in Nightingale, *Segregation*, 229–36, 275–84, 307–17, 341–50, 358–73.

[20] A classic example of this kind of analysis is Daniel T. Rodgers' treatment of the various kinds of welfare-state policies that American reformers imported to the United States from the 1870s to the 1940s in his monumental *Atlantic Crossings*. Also See Marilyn Lake and Henry Reynolds, *Drawing the Global Colour Line: White Men's Countries and the International Challenge of Racial Inequality* (Cambridge, UK: Cambridge University Press, 2008).

ordinance. The colony's location on a mountainous island, combined with the fact that British authorities acquired the large New Territories in 1898–99 meant that a deal could be struck with local Chinese residents for legislation allowing Britons exclusive residence on the geographically distinctive Victoria Peak in exchange for quiet assurances that Chinese real estate speculators who had stymied segregation for most of the previous 60 years would have access to new opportunities on the Chinese mainland. These contingencies led to a striking exception to a wider rule: in virtually all other colonial cities that contained wealthy elites of colour, those elites were a source of formidable opposition to neighbourhood racial segregation of any form – and separation by law was largely unthinkable.

Furthermore, contingencies, just like connections, can operate on a variety of geographical scopes, in this case both larger and smaller than that of the urban territory itself. This was especially evident to me when I sought to explain how segregationist policies in the US and South Africa diverged so sharply despite the fact that both societies imported so many of the same practices from Europe. The main difference was that South African urban segregation, later consolidated as apartheid, was brazenly and publically a state-run, fully legislated affair, whereas in the United States segregationists needed to forswear the tool of racial legislation, and when they did use the state in other ways, they had to keep their initiatives as far from the political limelight as they could. Numerous contingencies explain this difference, the most important being the national contexts of each country's black-white politics, which had very different pasts. In South Africa, whites' power over blacks was based on a history of conquest and land dispossession, and a right-of-conquest legal system that severely undermined blacks' civil, voting and property rights (not to mention those of mixed-race 'coloureds' and Indians). In the US, the matrix of black-white racial politics was the regional conflict over slavery and emancipation, which gave political parties in the victorious North an overwhelming incentive to enfranchise black men and enact some protections of their civil and property rights after the Civil War. Though Southern leaders subsequently erased many of these rights, blacks, especially those living in the North, nonetheless retained far more political clout than any group of people of colour in South Africa. As one result, the fledgling National Association for the Advancement of Colored People was able to marshal property rights claims against the residential segregation ordinances that American cities across the South and Midwest passed in the wake of an infamous precedent set in Baltimore in 1910. By contrast, in South Africa local 'natives locations' ordinances, which had roots in the British conquest of the Eastern Cape, enjoyed full constitutional sanction, and acted as precedents that encouraged white settlers to look to the law and the state to remedy the what they saw as the weaknesses of a segregation system that otherwise relied heavily on restrictive covenants.[21]

South Africa's rural reserve system, and the pass laws that were rooted in it, were also possible in the national constitutional climate established by conquest – and were equally impossible to enact against blacks in the US. In South Africa, these policies also came into being because of other contingencies that were larger than nations in scope, transnational connections that cut across the policy importations mentioned above that connected both countries to Europe. These contingencies consisted of a traffic in ideas about native reserves systems and anti-'Asiatic' immigration restriction laws that connected South Africa's 'native policy' architects with other parts of the British empire, notably Australia and Canada, and also to some extent to the anti-Native and anti-Asian policies of the US. Indeed, it is possible to say that US native reservation systems and Asian immigration restriction influenced the black-white politics of South Africa more than that of the US itself. The weak resistance to such policies in South Africa represents another empire-sized contingency, since any liberal protests in London and from the rising nationalist movements of India against the reserve system and the pass laws were undermined by Liberals' countervailing insistence on stronger home rule for what emerged as the constitutionally white supremacist Union of South Africa in 1910.[22]

Important contingencies could also operate on far smaller scopes as well: the metropolitan region, the industrial district, the municipal territory, the neighbourhood and street and even the more intimate spaces of the domestic realm. The fact that the South African mining economy, unlike the US industrial economy, relied on a majority black workforce, meant that urban slumlords in Johannesburg were less likely to cater to white poor people's calls for separate accommodations than those in American cities like Chicago, where European immigrants were in the vast majority. As a result, blockbusting was a more effective strategy in the slum belts, and soon the middle-class neighbourhoods, of Chicago than it was in Johannesburg. Black-white segregation was, partly as a result, far more effective in Chicago than in Johannesburg until the mid-1930s. The reliance by Witwatersrand mining companies and other entities such as the municipality of Johannesburg on a seasonal migrant labour system also meant that segregated worker compounds were more common in South Africa than in the US. The fact that the domestic labour force for most of the first two decades of Johannesburg's history was largely made up of black men meant that whites there focussed more intently on the black peril than in northern US cities

---

[21] This argument can be followed in greater depth in Nightingale, *Segregation*, 229–36, and 295–304.

[22] Nightingale, *Segregation*, 229–36, 295–304.

like Chicago. However, because of the durability of South African legislated precedents, these fears were channelled into ultimately more durable agitation for expanded residential segregation ordinances, in addition to petty Jim-Crow-like laws regulating blacks' use of sidewalks, tea rooms and public trams, or attempts at the regulation of black latrines and servants' quarters in suburban households. In Chicago the Great Migration, combined with the NAACP's court victory against segregation ordinances led to a massive week-long street riot and a five-year rash of house bombings, both of which were largely absent in cities like Johannesburg.[23]

After the First World War, South African authorities and lawmakers expanded legislation for urban segregation, first in the Natives (Urban Areas) Act of 1923 and its subsequent revisions, then in the Slums Act of 1935 and then in the various efforts to curb Indian and coloured residence that culminated in the apartheid-era Group Areas Act of 1950. These laws envisioned 'permanent' racial zones in South African cities, whose boundaries were supposed to remain inviolate even as cities grew. In the US, by contrast, the system relied more heavily on the racially discriminatory implementation of ostensibly non-racial legislation, such as zoning ordinances forbidding apartment buildings in all-white suburban municipalities, home mortgage supports for suburban homebuyers, public housing legislation and slum-clearance and urban renewal legislation. The American system also depended heavily on the power of such institutions as the National Association of Real Estate Boards which made racial steering a professional obligation for its members. The combination of these tools created rigid colour lines, but never permanent ones: as blacks moved into cities, they spilled over into white neighbourhoods. The great burden of the US system of mortgage supports was to enable whites to flee these 'transitional' neighbourhoods for racially exclusive zones largely in suburban areas.[24]

From the Transnational to the 'Diascopic'

As this example and others from the book suggest, my explanations for commonalities and contrasts in segregationist politics – for both the spread of segregation and its diversification – thus relied on connections and contingencies operating on a wide range of geographical scales. Our most common word for this type of history is 'transnational', a word that reflects its recent origin in the effort to pry our histories out from what Bender called 'the container of the nation' and to guarantee that the profession abjure any tacit or active support for ideologies of national exceptionalism. Nations may be unique, Daniel T. Rodgers

23 Nightingale, *Segregation*, 261–84, 307–17.
24 Nightingale, *Segregation*, 327–31, 371.

has argued, but none are 'exceptions' to some arbitrarily defined 'rules of history'. The *trans*national connections that bind them are evidence of that reality.[25]

To the extent that urban historians, with our traditional focus on phenomena that operate on a much smaller scopes than nations, have nevertheless contributed to nationalist myths, we would do well to heed this advice and embrace the 'transnational' with fervour. However, to the extent that understanding 'the urban' means understanding a global phenomenon that manifests itself in relatively smaller, localized or regionalized places, but that in turn varies according to both connective and contingent forces operating on levels that span the geographic spectrum from the most intimate through the domestic, from the street and neighbourhood-level to the municipal, metropolitan, provincial, colonial, national, regional, continental, imperial, oceanic, hemispheric and global (or at least quasi-global), we need to begin our conversations at a more precise point.

The 'dialectic of the seven Cs' I have offered here does not only describe the need to recognize the advantages of the mutual interactions of our best historical practices. It also operates within a complex geographical dialectic. Since words like 'glocal' and 'deterritorialized' do not identify the multidimensionality of this spatial dialectic any better than the term 'transnational', I will go out on a limb and offer another word – 'diascopic'. Though I am ordinarily not much of a fan of neologisms, I hope just the mention of this one might jolt us into adopting a new and I think productive starting point for future conversations about larger-scale urban history. To imagine cities diascopically is to keep the geographic *scope* of our inquiry open, as something we need to establish empirically. While urban historians surely benefit from analyses that explicitly bring the 'nation' into question, nations are by no means the only geographic unit we need to interrogate. The word 'diascopic' also reminds us, that our goal is not to '*trans*cend' any one particular scope of historical influence active in urban space, but rather it is to analyse the forces of many sizes that play out in cities in *dia*logue or *dia*lectically with others. To dive into larger-scale histories of cities – and to do that in ways that appreciate the same level of messiness, richness and liveliness that urban historians have celebrated in local case studies – we need to start with as deep and flexible an appreciation as we can muster for the both the historical and the geographical confluences that our cities are made of. Such an inquiry is now possible, thanks largely to the transnational turn in our field. But that inquiry also allows us to transcend the transnational itself, and in so doing further widen our methodological and geographical imaginations.

---

[25] Daniel T. Rodgers, 'Exceptionalism', in Anthony Molho and Gordon S. Wood, eds, *Imagined Histories: American Historians Interpret the Past* (Princeton: Princeton University Press, 1998), 21–40.

Chapter 3

Port Cities in Crisis: Considering Urban Governance, Modernity and Migration in Mid-Nineteenth-Century Montreal and Liverpool in a Transnational Context

Dan Horner

During the summer of 1847 the project of creating an orderly, prosperous and modern city faced an imposing threat that was global in reach. Hundreds of thousands of Irish migrants were fleeing the social and economic upheaval unfolding in their homeland, and most were taking up residence in port cities across the North Atlantic World.[1] Montreal and Liverpool, two outposts of the British Empire that shared numerous similarities and differences, were amongst the cities most deeply affected by the arrival of tens of thousands of highly mobile men, women and children.[2] To contemporary observers, the pace and the unpredictability of these events was staggering, and threw widely accepted assumptions about urban governance and public order into doubt. The crises that accompanied this rapid urban growth posed an enormous threat to the vision of public order shared by a broad cross-section of the urban elite. Many of these migrants arrived in their adopted communities in a state of near destitution, and some contracted diseases on their long and insalubrious journeys. Ill and destitute migrants became a common sight on the urban street, and their need for assistance quickly drained the coffers of both public and private charities. The ensuing events fuelled longstanding conflicts that simmered just beneath the

---

[1] There is an extensive literature on the Irish Famine and the wave of migration that accompanied. A few that I find particularly illuminating are Christine Kinealy, *The Great Irish Famine: Impact, Ideology and Rebellion* (London: Palgrave Macmillan, 2002); Kerby Miller, *Emigrants and Exiles: Ireland and the Irish Exodus to North America* (Oxford: Oxford University Press, 1998); Stuart John McLean, *The Event and its Terrors: Ireland, Famine, Modernity* (Redwood City, CA: Stanford University Press, 2003).

[2] I have written about the impact of the famine migration crisis of 1847 and the ensuing typhus epidemic in Dan Horner, "'If the evil now growing around us be not staid': Montreal and Liverpool Confront the Irish Famine Migration as a Transnational Crisis in Urban Governance'. *Histoire sociale/Social History* 46 (2013): 349–66.

surface of public life in the nineteenth-century North Atlantic World – between Protestants and Catholics, elites and the popular classes and between different levels of government.[3] A social and political crisis that had originated in the pastoral countryside of Ireland had become a global crisis in urban governance.

This chapter examines some of the factors that led me to pursue a comparative analysis of crises in urban governance in mid-nineteenth-century Montreal and Liverpool. As an historian of urban governance and public order in the nineteenth-century city, the importance of the global context for the policies implemented in Montreal, the city that I began my academic career studying, became increasingly clear as my research progressed. Montrealers from across the linguistic and sectarian divides kept abreast of how urban elites in other cities were negotiating the challenges that came with mass migration, epidemic disease, environmental deterioration and popular violence. The accelerating speed at which people and texts could travel great distances was creating a public sphere of urban elites engaged in discussions on questions around governance. That Montreal and Liverpool shared a common trajectory during the Irish Famine migration is certainly worth noting. Adopting a comparative perspective, however, provides an opportunity to move this observation one step further. Urban governance in both Montreal and Liverpool was shaped by the liberal values and practices that had taken hold in the first half of the nineteenth century. Comparing how civic leaders in these two cities responded to this shared experience of crisis provides an opening to begin charting the complicated and messy implementation of liberal public policy during this period. Liberal urban governance did not come with a set of rigid policy solutions to urban crises. Instead, civic leaders attempted to implement responses to events like epidemics and riots that adhered to their political values while placating as broad a cross-section of the public as possible. This was a contentious and complicated process that led to significantly different results from city to city. Adopting a comparative approach to writing urban history is thus an attempt to think about the multiple and even contradictory ways that liberal approaches to urban governance were proposed, debated, implemented and resisted in the nineteenth-century North Atlantic World.

By examining Liverpool and Montreal from a comparative perspective, I am conceptualizing them as complicated laboratories of liberal urban governance. Urban elites in both cities were ceded new powers from the national and colonial authorities during this period. Existing power structures and tensions

---

[3] For an overview of sectarian and political conflict in mid-nineteenth-century British North America, much of which was centred in Montreal, see Jacques Monet, *The Last Cannon Shot: A Study in French-Canadian Nationalism, 1837–1850* (Toronto: University of Toronto Press, 1969). For Liverpool, see Philip Waller, *Democracy and Sectarianism: A Political and Social History of Liverpool, 1868–1939* (Liverpool: Liverpool University Press, 1981).

in both jurisdictions, however, continued to play a definitive part in shaping how urban elites wielded power in both cities. Access to positions of political and cultural authority in both Montreal and Liverpool remained a contentious issue, with claims of legitimate authority being asserted by still powerful vestiges of a feudal elite, a young and dynamic urban capitalist bourgeoisie and, especially when it came to social questions around public health and education, the clergy. In Montreal, an increasingly assertive French Catholic elite overlaid additional layers of sectarian and linguistic tension into this mix. Attempts to negotiate these local dynamics left both cities with unique local public cultures, institutional structures and political practices. Examining how these local political structures responded to moments of crisis is an opportunity to trace how liberal practices of urban governance were shaped by both local specificities and ideas that were circulating on a global scale. It provides us with an opportunity to reflect upon the adaptability and the flexibility of liberal governance during this period.

Take, for example, the debates over quarantine that gripped Montreal and Liverpool during the typhus outbreak of 1847. As Irish migrants arrived in both cities in numbers without precedent at the height of the famine crisis, local residents in Montreal and Liverpool demanded that their local governments take whatever measures necessary to protect them from the spread of epidemic disease.[4] Local officials on both sides of the Atlantic hesitated to act, insisting that managing the emerging crisis was the responsibility of the imperial authorities, who could have summoned the powers necessary to curb the flow of migrants fleeing Ireland. Public outrage over the weak official response to the epidemic led to mounting public anger in both cities, but only officials in Montreal remained steadfast in their refusal to impose harsher quarantine restrictions on Irish migrants. In response to popular agitation, officials in Liverpool drew up hasty plans to begin deporting Irish migrants claiming relief in the city back to their native country.[5] News of the plan reached Montreal quickly, where several newspapers responded with editorials demanding why the authorities in their city could not have reacted in such decisive terms.[6] This is an example of how local authorities in two cities negotiated the gap between their political principles and the demands of an assertive public sphere during a moment of crisis. It also demonstrates how, through the local press, urban elites kept a close eye on how their counterparts across the North Atlantic World were dealing with similar challenges to public order in their cities.

Furthermore, a comparative approach to writing urban history destabilizes my understanding of historical events which, like generations of fellow

---

[4] Horner, 'If the evil now growing around us be not staid'.

[5] *Liverpool Mercury*, 22 June, 29 June and 2 July 1847.

[6] See, for example, *The Pilot*, 13 July 1847.

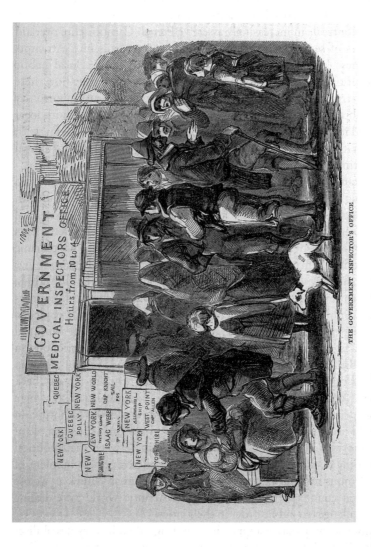

Figure 3.1   The government inspector's office. The arrival of thousands of Irish migrants each week at the height of the Irish Famine crisis turned the harbour fronts of port cities like Montreal and Liverpool into contentious, crowded and bustling spaces that raised concerns about the limits of state authority

Source: McCord Museum, M993X.5.1529.1.

historians, was forged through a national perspective. When reflecting on the issues with which this project is concerned, the necessity of thinking critically about national spaces and borders quickly became apparent. The comparative perspective allows me an opportunity to more effectively grapple with the global nature of these crises. This was, first and foremost, a set of circumstances and processes rooted in mobility and circulation.[7] Writing about two cities keeps both the reader and the writer focused on the way that the impact of these crises was not contained in a single city or national territory, but rather spread or convulsed across the North Atlantic World – with a handful of port cities experiencing them in their greatest intensity.[8]

Secondly, comparing two cities where civic elites shared a similar ideological approach to the challenge of urban governance is a way of exploring the flexibility and the fragility of the liberal project. In both cases, the sorts of liberal policy approaches to these crises raised public ire that brought the political legitimacy of the elite into doubt. The measures that the authorities took in response to these crises shaped the contours of the liberal project. Local circumstances, histories, power structures and problems informed the priorities of public officials in both cities in conjunction with transnational currents of political thought. Liberal governance, in other words, was not a monolith – its power lay in the way that it gave civic elites flexibility when it came to addressing the concerns of the broader community.[9] Comparing two cities and how this liberal project of governance was carried out over several decades allows me a chance to reflect on the complex interaction between the global and the local during this period.

Writing comparative urban history provides an opportunity to examine the impact that global transformations had on local communities outside of the conventional framework of national history. My generation of Canadian and Quebec historians has been profoundly influenced by the turn towards writing global history. Be it in the form of transnational or translocal history, or through studies of the various manifestations of the colonial project. Important

---

[7]   My understanding of circulation and mobility during this period has been shaped by David Harvey, *Paris: Capital of Modernity* (New York: Routledge, 2003); Marshall Berman, *All that is Solid Melts into Air* (London: Verso, 1983).

[8]   For more on the famine migration as a global crisis, see James Matthew Gallman, *Receiving Erin's Children: Philadelphia, Liverpool, and the Irish Famine Migration, 1845–1855* (Chapel Hill, NC: University of North Carolina, 2000); Margaret Mulrooney, ed., *Fleeing the Famine: North America and the Irish Refugees, 1845–1851* (Westport: Greenwood, 2005).

[9]   My efforts to think through liberal governance are indebted to Antonio Gramsci. See Quintin Hoare, ed., *Antonio Gramsci: Selections from Political Writings (1921–1926)* (Charlottesville: University of Virginia Press, 1978); For a survey of urban governance, see Robert J. Morris and Richard H. Trainor, eds, *Urban Governance: Britain and Beyond since 1750* (London: Ashgate, 2000).

historiographical interventions, like those of Adele Perry[10] and Sean Mills[11] – to name just two – pushed us to think more seriously about Canada and Quebec's role in social movements and transformations that were unfolding on a global scale. For several preceding generations of Canadian historians, the national perspective had been taken for granted as the starting point for historical inquiry. In both Canada and Quebec, historians deeply engaged in nationalist political projects loomed heavily over the historiography by the closing decades of the twentieth century. Placing Canada and Quebec in a global context addressed crucial questions about the workings of the colonial project,[12] about the impact of imported political traditions and practices had on North American society,[13] and about the relationship between colonizing peoples, indigenous populations and the environment.[14] What proved particularly appealing about this approach was that it could more accurately portray the experiences of the men and women who resided in the territory that would become Quebec and Canada, whose lives and social networks commonly poured across borders and oceans. Taking this global or transnational approach, therefore, more accurately captures the complexities of an historical moment when the most pressing challenges were not contained within national borders.

There is an underlying awkwardness to writing comparative history. Those of us who adopt this approach are forced to extend a great deal of energy in justifying the decision to compare multiple cities that can be as distinct as they are similar. Attempting to grapple even with two cities requires mastering multiple bodies of archival evidence and mastering a historiography that, because of different national or regional contexts, or because of different national or regional approaches to the historian's craft, can often make the task of drawing

[10] Adele Perry, *On the Edge of Empire: Gender, Race and the Making of British Columbia, 1849–1871* (Toronto: University of Toronto Press, 2001); Adele Perry, 'Nation, Empire and the Writing of History in Canada in English', in *Contesting Clio's Craft: New Directions and Debates in Canadian History*, eds Michael Dawson and Christopher Dummitt (Vancouver: University of British Columbia Press, 2008), 123–40.

[11] Sean Mills, *The Empire Within: Postcolonial Thought and Political Activism in Sixties Montreal* (Montreal: McGill-Queen's University Press, 2010); Sean Mills, 'Quebec, Haiti and the Deportation Crisis of 1974'. *Canadian Historical Review* 94 (2013): 405–35.

[12] See, for example, David McCrady, *Living With Strangers: The Nineteenth-Century Sioux and the Canadian-American Borderlands* (Toronto: University of Toronto Press, 2009).

[13] Michel Ducharme, *Le concept de liberté au Canada à l'époque des Révolutions atlantiques (1776–1838)* (Montreal: McGill-Queen's University Press, 2009).

[14] For example, Richard White, *The Middle Ground: Indians, Empires and Republics in the Great Lakes Region, 1650–1815* (Cambridge: Cambridge University Press, 1991); John, J. Bukowczyk et al., eds, *Permeable Border: The Great Lakes Basin as a Transnational Region, 1650–1900* (Pittsburgh: University of Pittsburgh Press, 2012).

comparisons especially challenging. Adding a comparative element loads another layer of analysis onto a project, forcing the historian to contemplate not only an event or phenomenon, but also the obvious and subtle differences between their impact in multiple settings.

This would be a very different project if it focused on a single city. Doing so would not be without its benefits, primarily in the way that it would concentrate the attention of both the writer and the reader on the way that the global transformations of the mid-nineteenth century impacted a contained geographic, social and political space. The comparative and translocal approach taken with this particular study, however, is an attempt to rethink the various mental maps adopted by people from across the social spectrum during this period. Public officials in British North America did not conceptualize the crises unfolding around them in the middle decades of the nineteenth century as a Canadian problem, but rather as a structural problem in the British Empire.[15] Power, in all of its social, cultural and political manifestations, was rooted not only in local relationships and structures, but in practices and networks that stretched across the globe.

There is no greater illustration of this than in the blossoming public sphere of these decades. Newspapers from across the globe demonstrate that local elites were engaged not only in the political conflicts being waged in their own communities, but also in cities around the world.[16] The revolutions in technology, transportation and consumption that occurred during this period paved the way for the emergence of a dynamic, though exclusive, public sphere that was rooted in the press.[17] Newspapers became a means for the reading public in places like Montreal and Liverpool to share ideas and engage in debates about the issues that preoccupied them which, during this period, tended to be discussions of public order and urban governance. Newspapers on both sides of the Atlantic Ocean reflected the view that cities were defined by a series of social problems that needed to be tackled through ambitious yet restrained projects of reform. These publications, produced and read on a daily basis, provided a space for urban elites to think through and subsequently problematize their changing surroundings. In many ways, these papers shrunk the distances between cities. A Protestant reader flipping through the pages of the *Gazette*

---

[15]   For an overview of British imperialism's impact on Canada, see Phillip Buckner and R. Douglas Francis, eds, *Canada and the British World: Culture, Migration and Identity* (Vancouver: University of British Columbia Press, 2006).

[16]   Simon Potter's *Newspapers and Empire in Ireland and Britain: Reporting the British Empire c. 1857–1921* (London: Four Courts, 2004) examines how debates circulated across the British World in the nineteenth and twentieth centuries.

[17]   See Geoff Eley, 'Nations, Publics, and Political Cultures: Placing Habermas in the Nineteenth Century', in Craig Calhoun, ed., *Habermas and the Public Sphere* (Cambridge: MIT University Press, 1992), 289–339.

would have encountered reports on outbreaks of sectarian violence occurring on the streets of Liverpool, and thus would have conceptualized the tensions that simmered on the streets of Montreal as part of a broader confrontation occurring across the globe. Similarly, an advocate of democratic reform reading the *Liverpool Mercury* would have stumbled across reports of similar political debates that were flourishing in different ways across the world. While the transnational approach to the study of the past has blossomed in recent years, there is still much work to be done to flesh out these sorts of analytical shifts. Thinking through the circulation of people and ideas in the mid-nineteenth-century North Atlantic World is an attempt to contribute to this growing body of literature.[18] Newspapers provide historians of this period with a vital source for tracing how ideas circulated.

The comparative approach has proven to be particularly illuminating when it comes to understanding the social, political and cultural impact of the sorts of public crises that frame my project. It lifts analyses of events like riots, epidemics and environmental disasters out of the realm of microhistory, thus bringing a unique perspective on the formation and reconstitution of national or transnational communities. Mary Ryan's *Civic Wars* examines the transformation of public life in three bustling nineteenth-century cities: New York, San Francisco and New Orleans.[19] As these three 'garishly diversified ... urban mongrels'[20] grew exponentially through the middle decades of the nineteenth century, public life began to splinter due to racial conflict and economic polarization. Although these three cities were very different with regards to demographic composition and economic structure, Ryan's comparative approach demonstrates a shared trajectory in American public life during this period, thus making a deeply nuanced contribution to our understanding of nineteenth century American democracy by placing these contentious urban spaces at the forefront of her study of political culture.

Comparative urban histories have also demonstrated how cities approached the challenges they shared with regards to urban governance, and how the construction of and debates around social problems fostered translocal and transnational networks of discussion. Lisa Keller's work on public order issues in the nineteenth century metropolis, *Triumph of Order*, shows how civic elites in the North Atlantic World's two great metropolises balanced competing demands

---

[18]   A number of books have shaped the way that I think about these patterns of circulation, including Catherine Hall, *Civilising Subjects: Metropole and Colony in the English Imagination, 1830–1867* (Chicago: University of Chicago Press, 2002); Perry, *On the Edge of Empire*, and the chapters in Philippa Levine, ed., *Gender and Empire* (Oxford: Oxford University Press, 2007).

[19]   Mary Ryan, *Civic Wars: Democracy and Public Life in the American City in the Nineteenth Century* (Berkeley: University of California Press, 1997).

[20]   Ryan, *Civic Wars*, 11.

for order and freedom.[21] Keller argues that how public officials and engaged intellectuals in New York and London approached this balance is crucial to understanding how they became the two leading centres of global capitalism over the course of the long nineteenth century. While located on opposite sides of the Atlantic, the cities shared a trajectory over the course of the nineteenth and twentieth centuries, serving as hubs of migration for those in search of fleeting opportunities for upward social mobility.[22] The continuous and rapid influx of migrants into the city during this period was a persistent threat to public order on a number of different fronts. Keller demonstrates that creating the social stability that capitalism's expansion required necessitated stringent regulation and vigorous policing, but officials in both cities realized that leaning too far in that direction would stifle the innovative ethos that flourished in both cities.[23] The ensuing attempts to strike a balance between order and freedom, Keller argues, highlights the interaction between transnational ideas and local circumstances in the shaping of urban public policy.

The contributions to this volume provide further demonstrations of the ways that comparative urban history can shed new light on historical processes by highlighting this interaction between transnational discussions and practices and local particularities. This was expressed in policy responses to emerging social problems like prostitution,[24] in approaches to urban governance[25] and in the culture formation of communities.[26] My project on urban crises and governance in mid-nineteenth-century Montreal and Liverpool attempts to make a similar contribution to this broader reflection on the shared trajectories and divergent paths followed by cities in this 200-year period marked by relentless urbanization across the globe.

The comparative perspective addresses another shortcoming of writing about a single city or nation, which is that these approaches have a tendency of presenting cities as far more stable and static than they were. My decision to adopt a comparative approach for this project on liberal urban governance was that it would help capture the essential role that mobility and circulation played in shaping politics, culture and society in the mid-nineteenth-century North Atlantic World. This was true on a number of different levels. The increased mobility of people and commodities was an essential component of the expansion of capitalist practices during this period. For the poor, decisions about mobility loomed over everyone during this period. With the North Atlantic World being

---

[21] Lisa Keller, *Triumph of Order: Democracy and Public Space in New York and London* (New York: Columbia University Press, 2013).

[22] Keller, *Triumph of Order*, xi.

[23] Keller, *Triumph of Order*, xiii.

[24] See Marion Pluskota in this volume.

[25] See Stefan Couperus and Shane Ewen and Janet Polasky in this volume.

[26] See Jordan Stanger-Ross in this volume.

restructured according to the ethos of liberal capitalism, migration became the leading strategy of those who struggled to make ends meet on a daily basis. Even those who chose not to migrate no doubt had to grapple with that decision, and likely had to navigate the consequences of other family members who chose to pursue a brighter future in a distant city.[27] As people, ideas and commodities circulated with increasing speed and volume around the North Atlantic World during this period, so did ideas and practices of resistance. While adhering to a liberal perspective on matters relating to urban governance, public officials and other commentators shared different perspectives on how to deal with events and behaviours that shook their confidence in the overarching project of the urban elite during this period – which was to create cities that were orderly, genteel, and where people, capital and commodities could circulate efficiently.[28] When civic elites addressed issues around migration, public health and public order, they were either consciously or unconsciously addressing the challenges that came in a world where people were moving around in larger numbers and in seemingly unpredictable ways.

The Irish Famine migration of 1847 was not an isolated incident. Both Montreal and Liverpool were growing rapidly during this period as a result of global patterns of urbanization. The speed at which this transformation was occurring made this a disorderly process. During the second half of the 1840s the population of each city was growing by thousands each year, to say nothing of the thousands more who passed through the city in the midst of extended migrations. For an assertive and engaged urban elite, the sequence of crises that marked their cities during this period – epidemics, riots, fires and a host of other problems rooted in poverty and dislocation – highlighted just how ambitious their project of creating an orderly, genteel and prosperous city was.[29]

How did I come to choose Montreal and Liverpool as the case studies for this project? Thanks to the doctoral work I had done on crowds and public life in mid-nineteenth-century Montreal, that city was a natural choice, seeing that I had already familiarized myself with the relevant historiography and

---

[27] Firsthand accounts of the Irish Famine migration, though rare, are illuminating here. See James Mangan, ed., *Robert Whyte's 1847 Famine Ship Diary: The Journey of an Irish Coffin Ship* (Dublin: Mercier Press, 1994); Shelley Barber, ed. *The Prendergrast Letters: Correspondence from Famine-era Ireland, 1840–1850* (Amherst: University of Massachusetts Press, 2006).

[28] Harvey, *Paris*, Chapter Four.

[29] For a case studies of the elite project of creating orderly public space, see Peter Baldwin, *Domesticating the Street: The Reform of Public Space in Hartford, 1850–1930* (Columbus: Ohio State University Press, 1989) and James Winter, *London's Teeming Streets, 1830–1914* (London: Routledge, 1993).

archival resources.[30] While holding a post-doctoral fellowship at the Centre for Urban History at the University of Leicester, I became immersed in debates and discussions around British urban history. It became apparent to me that Montreal and Liverpool shared a similar experience of the global upheavals of the mid-nineteenth century. Both were, first and foremost, commercial cities with bustling ports that both socially and culturally oriented them outwards in the direction of the North Atlantic World. When the economic transformations of the era began to produce a sharp increase in the scale of the circulation of both people and commodities across this region, Montreal and Liverpool, like a handful of other cities, were deeply affected.

As long-standing regional hubs of commerce and migration, Montreal and Liverpool were both profoundly implicated in the project of European imperialism. Liverpool had become a commercial powerhouse in the eighteenth century, serving as the primary port for British trade with Africa and the Caribbean. Much of the astounding wealth that was generated by the Liverpool mercantile elite was directly tied to the slave trade.[31] The city's bustling port was soon dotted with monuments to the astounding wealth that slavery created for a tiny white elite. On a more quotidian level, the city became an important site of cultural exchange, as Africans rubbed shoulders with migrants from closer afield flocking to the city in search of wealth and employment.[32]

Montreal, meanwhile, had been a centre of colonial administration in North America since the seventeenth century when, like much of the continent, it was under French jurisdiction. The settlement was on the geographic and political frontlines of the process of shifting sovereignty over the territory from aboriginal to European hands, a process that was marked by increasingly sporadic outbreaks of spectacular violence.[33] Just as the slave trade shaped Liverpool's orientation to the Atlantic World, the fur trade shaped Montreal's relationship to Britain, Europe and the North American continent.[34] As the city's economic reach continued to expand under British rule in the eighteenth century, Montreal,

---

[30]   Dan Horner, 'Taking to the Streets: Crowds, Politics and Identity in Mid-Nineteenth-Century Montreal' (PhD diss., York University, 2010).

[31]   The chapters in David Richardson, Suzanne Schwartz and Anthony Tibbles, eds, *Liverpool and Transatlantic Slavery* (Liverpool: Liverpool University Press, 2007) provide a helpful overview of Liverpool's role in the trade of African slaves.

[32]   John Belchem has contemplated the nature of pluralism on Liverpool's history in *Merseypride: Essays in Liverpool Exceptionalism* (Liverpool: Liverpool University Press, 2000).

[33]   See, for example, Gilles Havard, *The Great Peace of Montreal of 1701*, trans. Phyllis Aronoff and Howard Scott (Montreal: McGill-Queen's University Press, 2001).

[34]   For more on Montreal's role in the fur trade, see Carolyn Podruchny, 'Unfair Masters and Rascally Servants? Labour Relations between Bourgeois, Clerks and Voyageurs in the Montreal Fur Trade, 1780–1821'. *Labour / Le Travail* 43 (1999): 43–70.

like Liverpool, was increasingly defined by the cosmopolitan exchanges that occurred on its streets, where English public officials, French professionals and Scottish and American merchants encountered rural *Canadien* farmers and aboriginal traders on a regular basis.

The atmosphere of crisis that took hold under these conditions manifested itself in sectarian conflict. Montreal and Liverpool had both been cosmopolitan cities for nearly as long as they had existed, but the famine migration out of Ireland resulted in the massive growth of their Catholic communities, thereby destabilizing social relations in the city for much of what remained of the nineteenth century. In both cities, the contours of public life were increasingly negotiated through the framework of sectarian conflict.[35] Breaches of public order, whether they came in the form of popular violence, epidemic disease or in more routine manifestations of popular unrest were blamed on the other. In the contentious atmosphere that this created, competing factions of the urban elite framed their assertions of legitimate authority around the cultural and political project of public order. This became one of the leading venues in which difference was defined and discussed. In the contentious environment this created, assertions about public order carried considerable political weight.[36]

A dynamic popular culture emerged in these settings, as people engaged in activities that nurtured communities on the basis of familial, kinship, sectarian and national connections. There was a dark side to this cultural activity: in cities like Montreal and Liverpool, the demographic upheaval nurtured already-simmering social conflicts between rich and poor and, perhaps most prominently, between Protestant and Catholic.[37] The cosmopolitan exchanges that were quickly being woven into the fabric of social relations in these cities frequently teetered on the precipice of alcohol-fuelled interpersonal and collective violence. While their demographic compositions were not identical, public debate in both cities bore a close resemblance to each other. The sources available to historians reflecting on public life in the two cities, like newspapers

---

[35] Frank Neal, *Sectarian Violence: The Liverpool Experience, 1819–1914* (Manchester: Manchester University Press, 1988); Dan Horner, 'Shame upon you as men!': Contesting Authority in the Aftermath of Montreal's Gavazzi Riot'. *Histoire sociale/Social History* 44 (2011): 29–52.

[36] The chapters in Judith Rowbotham and Kim Stevenson, eds, *Criminal Conversations: Victorian Crimes, Social Panic and Moral Outrage* (Columbus: Ohio State University Press, 2005) shed light on multiple facets of this phenomenon. For the impact of this on political rhetoric, see Cecilia Morgan, *Public Men and Virtuous Women: The Gendered Languages of Religion and Politics in Upper Canada, 1791–1850* (Toronto: University of Toronto Press, 1996).

[37] For more on popular violence in the two cities, see Neal, *Sectarian Violence*; Horner, 'Shame upon you as men!'

and government records, were consumed by similar discussions of sectarian conflict, public health and urban governance.

The turbulence being experienced in the bustling port cities of the North Atlantic during the middle decades of the nineteenth century were marked by a profound crisis in the project of British imperial governance. Public life across the British Empire was wrapped up in deeply polarized debates around the democratic reform of political institutions and colonial sovereignty.[38] This conflict did not occur in a vacuum, but was debated in rapidly growing urban centres against the backdrop of accelerating economic polarization. The dynamic and occasionally unruly culture of the urban popular classes was seen by many as a threat to orderly and liberal deliberative democracy. It was in port cities like Montreal and Liverpool where the expansion and acceleration of the capitalist project was most visible – not only in the monuments built by the wealth that the project generated for the few, like suburban mansions, grand public buildings and massive infrastructure projects – but also in the growing visibility of urban poverty – the men and women begging on street corners, lined up to receive public assistance, and the hastily constructed working-class suburbs appearing on the urban periphery.[39] The moments of crisis that my project unpacks provide altogether rare opportunities to think through the ways that people who did not leave a historical record behind experienced the era's global transformations – through dislocation, mobility and material deprivation.

These urban centres of the North Atlantic World presented a difficult knot of contradictions to economic and cultural elites. On the one hand, the expansion of global trade and the process of industrialization made them both a producer of and a magnet for untold prosperity. On the other hand, many of that prosperity's essential ingredients, such as the continuous expansion of the working-class labour market through mass migration and the environmental degradation that came with industrialization, created cities where daily life was cumbersome and

---

[38] For more on discussions of democratic reform during this period, see James Vernon, *Politics and the People: A Study in English Political Culture, c. 1815–1837* (Cambridge: Cambridge University Press, 1993); Patrick Joyce, *Democratic Subjects: The Self and the Social in Nineteenth-Century England* (Cambridge: Cambridge University Press, 1994); Catherine Hall, Keith McClelland and Jane Rendall, eds, *Defining the Victorian Nation: Class, Race, Gender and the British Reform Act of 1867* (Cambridge: Cambridge University Press, 2005); Allan Greer, *The Patriots and the People: The Rebellion of 1837 in Rural Lower Canada* (Toronto: University of Toronto Press, 1993).

[39] See, for example, Richard Dennis, *English Industrial Cities of the Nineteenth Century: A Social Geography* (Cambridge: Cambridge University Press, 1986); Carolyn Steedman, *An Everyday Life of the English Working Class: Work, Self and Sociability in the Early Nineteenth Century* (Cambridge: Cambridge University Press, 2013). For the British North American context, see Bryan Palmer, *The Working Class Experience: Rethinking the History of Canadian Labour* (Toronto: McClelland and Stewart, 1992), Chapter One.

dangerous. Under these conditions, a disparate group of urban elites came to view the city as an object of reform.[40] The reforms that they proposed came in all shapes and sizes. There were calls for the establishment of public schools to get children – particularly boys – off the streets and prepare them for a moral and productive adulthood.[41] Support grew for the expansion and professionalization of police forces,[42] for investment in sanitary improvements[43] and the creation of public parks.[44] Some reformers focused their attention on questions of personal conduct, most notably by calling for heavy restrictions to be placed on the sale and consumption of alcohol.[45] For some of these elites, engaging in this sort of social and political activism flowed out of strong religious convictions. The chaotic bustle of the nineteenth-century city struck others as irrational and anti-modern, a troublesome reality that demanded a scientific response. Many likely felt the tug of both of these sentiments. While the aspirations and goals of these reform efforts might have been diffuse – and even, on occasion, contradictory – it is possible to trace an emerging elite consensus through it: that progress was inextricably tied to the fostering of a more genteel urban culture and landscape, where a growing emphasis on things like privacy and physical restraint could be carefully nurtured.[46]

---

[40] See Mary Poovey, *Making a Social Body: British Cultural Formation, 1830–1864* (Chicago: University of Chicago Press, 1995); Jean-Marie Fecteau, *La liberté du pauvre: crime et pauvreté au XIXe siècle québécois* (Outremont: VLB, 2004).

[41] Bruce Curtis, *Ruling by Schooling Quebec: Conquest to Liberal Governmentality – A Historical Sociology* (Toronto: University of Toronto Press, 2012); Michael Sanderson, *Education, Economic Change and Society in England, 1780–1870* (Cambridge: Cambridge University Press, 1995).

[42] Allan Greer, 'The Birth of the Police in Canada', in Allan Greer and Ian Radforth, eds, *Colonial Leviathan: State Formation in Mid-Nineteenth-Century Canada* (Toronto: University of Toronto Press, 1992), 17–42; David Taylor, *The New Police in Nineteenth-Century England: Crime, Conflict and Control* (Manchester: Manchester University Press, 1997).

[43] Christopher Hamlin, *Public Health and Social Justice in the Age of Chadwick* (Cambridge: Cambridge University Press, 1998); Thomas Osborne, 'Security and Vitality: Drains, Liberalism and Power in the Nineteenth Century', in Andrew Barry, Thomas Osborne, Nikolas Rose, eds, *Foucault and Political Reason: Liberalism, Neo-Liberalism and Rationalities of Government* (Chicago: University of Chicago Press, 1996), 99–121.

[44] For a case study of the cultural politics behind urban parks, see Roy Rosenzweig and Elizabeth Blackmar, *The Park and the People: A History of Central Park* (Ithaca: Cornell University Press, 1992).

[45] See Jan Noel, *Canada Dry: Temperance Crusades before Confederation* (Toronto: University of Toronto Press, 1992).

[46] For more on this cultural shift, see John Tosh, *A Man's Place: Masculinity and the Middle-Class Home in Victorian England* (New Haven: Yale University Press, 1999).

The cultural importance placed on reason, restraint and decorum was increasingly evident in every facet of public life during these years. It was the foundation of the era's liberal politics, which sought to create an orderly society where private initiative was encouraged and private property secure, all the while treading as lightly as possible on personal liberties. This political ideology found its most vocal advocates in the urban elite, especially amongst those whose wealth was owed to their engagement in industry and commerce. Liberalism flowed out of enlightenment ideas and the revolutions of the eighteenth century, and its influence changed the way that power and authority were wielded on both a local and a global scale.[47] Nowhere was its impact more keenly felt than in the relationship between people and the state, which was altered radically during this period. These ideas were circulating at a moment, however, when the actions and behaviours of the urban poor were increasingly being cast as a social problem and a target of reform. By the beginning of the final third of the nineteenth century, encountering different manifestations of state authority became a far more common part of the urban experience, whether it be through attending a school, meeting a police officer on his daily beat, having a census taker knock at the door or being confined to a workhouse or quarantine station.[48] Taking a comparative approach to the writing of urban history provides us an opportunity to consider how this political vision was shaped by both local circumstances and ideas that were clearly circulating through both the press and networks of imperial authority. Government correspondence and the press provide countless examples of public officials and elites in cities like Liverpool and Montreal keeping a close eye on how their counterparts across the North Atlantic World were dealing with crises of urban governance.

The crises addressed in this study were the principal impediment to the orderly and liberal vision of reform-oriented urban elites. The project of creating an orderly city was multi-faceted, complex and, on occasion, contradictory. As per the tenets of liberal governance, political elites expressed confidence that institutional innovations and reforms would be up to the task of fostering an orderly city without resorting to authoritarian measures.[49] This approach to governance shaped the sharp increase in public and private investment in

---

[47] Ian McKay, 'Canada as a Long Liberal Revolution: On Writing the History of Actually Existing Canadian Liberalisms, 1840s–1940s', in Michel Ducharme and Jean-François Constant, eds, *Liberalism and Hegemony: Debating the Canadian Liberal Revolution* (Toronto: University of Toronto Press, 2009), 347–452; Patrick Joyce, *Liberalism and the Modern City* (London and New York: Verso, 2003); Morris and Trainor, *Urban Governance*.

[48] Eric Evans, *The Forging of the Modern State: Early Industrial Britain, 1783–1870* (Harlow: Longman Group, 1983); Allan Greer and Ian Radforth, eds, *Colonial Leviathan: State Formation in Mid-Nineteenth-Century Canada* (Toronto: University of Toronto Press, 1992).

[49] Joyce, *The Rule of Freedom*, 5.

policing, prisons, workhouses, schools, asylums and quarantine stations during this period. The disorder of the urban street in the midst of the unrelenting cycle of crises that gripped cities like Montreal and Liverpool in the middle decades of the nineteenth century was a major impetus for the rethinking of these sorts of institutional responses. In the midst of these crises, however, is where we can see the contours of this liberal project being established, resisted and, ultimately, negotiated. The broader community exerted an important influence here, demanding radical measures and interventions from public officials whose first reaction was to let existing regulations and institutions work through the challenges posed by the crisis at hand. Furthermore, the agitation caused by these crises challenged one of the central tenets of the period's liberal political culture – that legitimate authority was rooted in the ability to demonstrate a very elitist and masculine form of independence, rationality and restraint.[50] In the midst of these public crises that threatened the lives and well-being of the broader public, these assertions of elite composure on the part of civic elites became deeply contested and politicized. This project, therefore, is my attempt to contribute to the literature on politics and urban governance in the mid-nineteenth century in a way that maps some of the spaces between theory and practice by looking at how public officials reacted when unfolding events were raising fundamental questions about their worldview.

Despite sharing the political and cultural reluctance towards interventionism that defined mid-nineteenth-century liberalism, sustained public pressure and popular agitation during these moments of crisis pushed local officials towards taking a more activist approach on a number of occasions in both Montreal and Liverpool. Cities or, to be more specific, the social, cultural and physical aspects of the urban landscape, became something of a laboratory where liberal approaches of governance could be put into practice.[51] To push this metaphor further, the sorts of urban crises that are the focal points of my project were the experiments, when hypotheses around liberal governance were put under the microscope, producing results that highlighted their shortcomings and complexities. Local civic elites, wielding newfound powers granted to them by superior levels of government in only recent memory,[52] used these moments

---

50   The recent literature on public life and popular politics is illuminating here, see Jeffrey McNairn, *The Capacity to Judge: Public Opinion and Deliberative Democracy in Upper Canada, 1791–1854* (Toronto: University of Toronto Press, 2000); Craig Calhoun, *The Roots of Radicalism: Tradition, the Public Sphere and Early Nineteenth-Century Social Movements* (Chicago: University of Chicago Press, 2012).

51   Joyce, *The Rule of Freedom.*

52   A municipal government had been established in Montreal in 1832, but suspended during the violent conflicts over democratic reform in 1837 and 1838, and reinstated in 1841. The 1835 Municipal Corporations Act had established an elected civic government in Liverpool, replacing a pre-existing body of self-appointed elites. For more on the impact

to test the boundaries of their authority. In many instances, particularly when their cities were in the midst of being struck by outbreaks of epidemic disease, a consensus emerged amongst them that their powers were by no means sufficient to deal with the challenges at hand.[53] It was in cities that the agenda and the legitimacy of the expansion of the state's authority in the second half of the nineteenth century and the first decades of the twentieth century was thought through by a broad cross-section of elites.[54]

There is a danger that historians face when writing on topics like urban governance to place too much emphasis on the men – and, of course, in this period we are speaking exclusively of men – who wielded the authority necessary to govern. For historians of the mid-nineteenth century, the voices of these elites, and the attitudes and assumptions that shaped their perspectives, have an almost exclusive grip on the historical record. When marginalized groups, including women, children, ethnic and racial minorities and the poor are discussed on the pages of mid-nineteenth-century newspapers, it is not as liberal individuals but as the target of reforms.[55] In order to truly grapple with questions around urban governance, however, it is crucial to think through the motivations and experiences of the people who came to be the subject of liberal reform. As the overarching principle of urban governance during this period, public order was not an assortment of edicts handed down from above. It can be more effectively conceptualized as a discussion, albeit one where imbalances of power played a key role. These moments of crisis are a valuable resource to historians because they draw our attention to the project of liberal governance at moments when resistance towards it was most visible. For example, during the outbreaks of cholera that struck Montreal and Liverpool in 1849, the efforts on the part of the authorities to enforce sanitary regulations with greater vigour brought acts of resistance into the spotlight. Newspapers were forced to engage with the question of why some people would look negatively upon the interventionist

---

of these municipal bodies, see Ramsay Muir and Edith May Platt, *A History of Municipal Government in Liverpool* (Liverpool: University of Liverpool Press, 1907), Part One and Michèle Dagenais, 'The Municipal Territory: A Product of the Liberal Order?' in Michel Ducharme and Jean-François Constant, eds, *Liberalism and Hegemony: Debating the Canadian Liberal Revolution* (Toronto: University of Toronto Press, 2009), 201–20.

[53] See Dan Horner, '"The Public Has the Right to be Protected from A Deadly Scourge": Debating Quarantine, Migration and Liberal Governance during the 1847 Typhus Outbreak in Montreal'. *Journal of the Canadian Historical Association / Revue de la Société historique de Canada* 23 (2012), 65–100; Gallman, *Receiving Erin's Children*, Chapters 1–2.

[54] These reform movements often brought together uneasy alliances of elites with different interests, like prosperous merchants, the clergy, professionals and people with aristocratic backgrounds whose wealth stemmed from property ownership, not to mention elites from different ethnic communities.

[55] See Poovey, *Making a Social Body*; Fecteau, *La liberté du pauvre*.

tactics of local authorities. The power of the liberal project, it has been argued, was that its scope was so expansive and pervasive that, over the course of a few decades, it came to be seen as natural and inevitable.[56] These crises were occasions when its methods and assumptions had to be vigorously asserted and defended in the face of sustained resistance. The comparative approach is yet another way to destabilize our perspective on urban governance by revealing how liberal attitudes towards governance proved to be malleable in the face of local complexities.

The urban crises of the mid-nineteenth century and the solutions crafted in response to them – including the expansion of public schooling and policing and the deeper commitment to enforcing stricter sanitary regulations – transformed the way that authority worked in urban settings. Its impact can still be felt in contemporary cities which, in the case of much of the North Atlantic World, are more genteel and orderly than even the most optimistic nineteenth-century reformer could ever have imagined. On a global scale, however, these same tensions and crises continue to pose a daunting challenge. Cities like Cairo, Lima, Mumbai and Shenzhen face a similar set of challenges that mid-nineteenth-century Montreal and Liverpool did. With all that has changed in the two centuries that have elapsed since this time, the capitalist practices of the twenty-first century continue to rely on the mobility of labourers to densely populated centres of industry and commerce, which quickly become blighted with conflict and environmental decay.[57] The threats of popular violence, epidemic disease and a slate of other challenges that tend to accompany the rapid growth of cities continue to vex public officials nearly 200 years later. By thinking through how the authorities grappled with these destabilizing processes, works of comparative history can help us better understand the complex impact that global transformations have on local communities.

---

[56]   Ian McKay, 'The Liberal Order Framework: A Prospectus for a Reconnaissance of Canadian History', *Canadian Historical Review* 81 (2000): 617–45; Joyce, *The Rule of Freedom*, 5.

[57]   For a discussion of twenty-first century global cities and their historical, political and economic contexts, see Mike Davis, *Planet of Slums* (London: Verso, 2006).

Chapter 4
Choreographies of Urban Life: Mapping the Social History of Cities

Jordan Stanger-Ross

This chapter proposes a new approach to the comparative history of urban social life. Following the recent turn by many historians to GIS (Geographic Information Systems), which facilitate the systematic integration of spatial analysis into the telling of the past, I argue that comparative urban social history stands especially to benefit from, and to contribute to, digital historical mapping. I offer no technical guide or demonstration – which abound already in better form than I could provide – but rather reflections on an orientation, or approach, that emerged in my own research and that I hope might inform others.[1] This approach aims to answer questions about the movement of people within urban space. As GIS historian Ian Gregory observes, 'almost everything that interests a historian ... moves from one place to another'.[2] Yet historians have largely neglected to analyse the constant movement of people within urban environments. Comparative analysis that mobilizes new mapping tools could pose novel questions, enrich our answers to old ones and convey urban social history in exciting new ways.

My interest in the 'choreography' of urban life (a term I borrow from Torsten Hagerstrand) emerged in the study of Italian immigrants and their children

Thank you to Nicolas Kenny and Rebecca Madgin for this initiative, which began with their organizing two excellent conference panels at the European Urban History Association and the American Urban History Association. Thank you also to Jacqueline Clare for her assistance with Maps 4.1 and 4.2 in this chapter. Finally, my deepest gratitude to the late Michael Katz, who inspired and supervised this work in its original form.

[1] In this respect, my aims are similar to those of Colin Gordon, who also retrospectively reflected on his experience with historical GIS after the completion of a book project. See: 'Lost in Space, or Confessions of an Accidental Geographer', Journal of Humanities & Arts Computing: A Journal of Digital Humanities 5 (2011): 1–22.

[2] Ian N. Gregory, "'A Map Is Just a Bad Graph": Why Spatial Statistics Are Important in Historical GIS', in *Placing History: How Maps, Spatial Data, and GIS Are Changing Historical Scholarship*, eds Anne Kelly Knowles and Amy Hillier, 1st ed. (Redlands, CA: ESRI Press, 2008), 127.

in North America.³ Historians of migration narrate movement: immigrant North America is the story of people transplanted across enormous distances. Historians of immigration have also been concerned with spatial dynamics on a smaller scale, seeking to understand the experiences of people within the local environments in which they settled. As such, scholars of immigrants in North America have often also been important historians of cities. Case studies of nineteenth- and twentieth-century American newcomers demonstrate that ethnic communities and identities emerge from an interaction between immigrant traditions and skills and the demands made, opportunities offered and limitations imposed in their (often urban) places of settlement. In the early 1990s, after a generation of this kind of scholarship, Kathleen Neils Conzen and colleagues reflected: 'That time and space conditioned the process of ethnicization is a truism, but the particular ways in which they operated and with what results are the stuff of history'.⁴

Within this larger scholarly setting, historians of Italian immigrants have been especially attuned to the city, as Italian immigrants have been understood as particularly influenced by the sites of settlement that they shared. The living rooms, pavements, corner stores, union halls and church pews of North American cities, historians have argued, served as sites for the transformation of regional to national identities and the emergence of a shared (although varied on gender and class lines) ethnicization as 'Italian'. Italians were shaped by 'the city' and also left an imprint upon it; 'Little Italies' made Italians perhaps the most conspicuously urban immigrant group in twentieth-century North America.⁵

My book, *Staying Italian*, joined the existing scholarship in its attention to urban settings, using GIS to trace the daily movement that animated the urban

---

³ See Torsten Hagerstrand, 'What about People in Regional Science?' *Regional Science Association Papers* 24 (1970): 7–21; Allan Pred, 'The Choreography of Existence: Comments on Hagerstrand's Time-Geography and its Usefulness', *Economic Geography* 53 (1977): 207–21; Anthony Giddens, 'Time, Space and Regionalization', in *The Constitution of Society: Outline of the Theory of Structuration* (Berkeley: University of California Press, 1984), chap. 3; and Derek Gregory, *Geographic Imaginations* (Cambridge, MA: Blackwell, 1994), chap. 2.

⁴ Kathleen Neils, Conzen, David A. Gerber, Ewa, Morawska, George E. Pozzetta and Rudolph J. Vecoli, 'The Invention of Ethnicity: A Perspective from the USA', *Journal of American Ethnic History* 12 (1992): 3–41.

In this chapter I use 'ethnicization' in much the same fashion as Conzen and her colleagues, viewing it as 'a process of construction or invention which incorporates, adapts, and amplifies pre-existing communal solidarities, cultural attributes, and historical memories'.

⁵ For a fuller explanation of the positioning of my work within this wider scholarship, see: Jordan Stanger-Ross, *Staying Italian: Urban Change and Ethnic Life in Post-war Toronto and Philadelphia* (Chicago: The University of Chicago Press, 2009).

ethnic community.[6] By the end of my project, I was convinced that a somewhat idiosyncratic comparative approach – one that mobilized *quantitative* social historical data to compare the *qualitative* features of community in two locales – had allowed me to trace new linkages between the history of ethnicity and the history of the city. Using data that revealed the geography of community life – the spatial dynamics of ethnicity as a communal practice – I was able to demonstrate that the experience of Italian ethnicity varied significantly in connection with its local surroundings. I aimed to illuminate 'the particular ways in which [space] operated' in the process of ethnicization. In doing so, I was able to detail how, precisely, place mattered. This orientation positioned the city at the centre of the story.

Ostensibly, GIS is a quantitative method, but it may have particular appeal to historians for its power to answer qualitative questions. Although I was counting and measuring (and testing statistical significance), my analysis centred on *how* ethnicity was practiced, rather than *how much*. I deliberately selected two sites – Toronto's Little Italy and Italian South Philadelphia – within which Italian ethnicity continued to have salience as a social organizational force throughout the twentieth century. My concern was not, as it had been for many previous historians, to measure assimilation, or, conversely, the 'amount' of Italian ethnicity that persisted in each neighbourhood, but rather to gauge how ethnicity worked, how it mattered in two very different urban historical settings. The ability of GIS to answer this kind of question in a systematic fashion – to offer quantitative evidence in support of qualitative analysis of city life – gives it particular promise in the field of urban social history.

Toronto and Philadelphia charted opposite paths during the second half of the twentieth century, setting dramatically different stages for Italian communal association. Toronto stood among the winners in the post-war restructuring of urban North America; Philadelphia, at least until the 1980s, stood among the losers. These divergences were felt locally within neighbourhoods. In Toronto's Little Italy, awash with newcomers, the real value of housing more than quadrupled between the 1940s and the 1980s. In stagnant South Philadelphia, the population of the historic Italian neighbourhood plummeted over the same period and housing prices scarcely increased until modest gains in 1980s. How did Italian immigrants and their children respond to these changes? How did urban change reverberate in the practices of communal life? Comparative quantitative analysis of the character of ethnic association – of how Italians did community – offered new answers to these questions. More than had been previously demonstrated, ethnicization bore the imprint of *varied* urban change. As my study cities, Toronto and Philadelphia, diverged from one another in the twentieth century, so too did processes of communal association in each place.

---

6   Stanger-Ross, *Staying Italian*.

In the remainder of this chapter, I briefly revisit the evidence with which I began the research for my book. Having first detailed this approach, I'll then reflect more broadly on the prospect of these methods for a broader comparative inquiry into urban social history.

Measuring Qualities

I stumbled by hunch into the method that lies at the core of *Staying Italian*. The book compares experience in central Italian parishes in Toronto and Philadelphia, and I began my research with Catholic marriage registers. Following the lead of previous scholars, and especially of John Zucchi, whose fine book on Toronto's Little Italy before the Second World War influenced my approach, I hoped to find in the registers evidence of the extent of ethnic endogamy in each city as well as of the role of Italian regional and hometown networks in marriage choices in Toronto, where (unlike in Philadelphia) new immigrants continued to arrive en masse in the post-Second World War era.[7] However, when I began to work with the registers, I discovered that they included another category of evidence altogether, which I had not anticipated. In addition to listing each spouse's place of baptism (which historians had used to analyse endogamy), the registers provided other information that could be used to illuminate the *movement of people through urban space*. Priests recording marital unions in the heavy, bound volumes stored at their rectories wrote down the stated addresses of each spouse at their time of marriage. Taken together with the address of the church itself, where the sacrament was performed, and sites of baptism, the registers provided five separate addresses for each marriage. The registers constituted a rich trove of spatial information about the intimate connections among Italians in each city.

Previous historians had used two of the addresses contained in the registers – those indicating the site of baptism and the site of marriage – to convey important social history. A girl baptized in 1949 in Catanzaro, a seaside city in the instep of Italy's boot, had traversed worlds by the time of her Toronto marriage in 1970. But my attention was also drawn to the hundreds of men and women in Philadelphia who had been baptized at the very sites of their marriages; this steadfastness in place told a history as well. Pairing sites of baptism with sites of marriage, historians can tell stories of movement over long periods of time. In my case studies the registers revealed one neighbourhood awash with newcomers, well accustomed to movement across long distances, and another in which almost all young people pronouncing vows in the local church had been born and bred in the neighbourhood.

---

[7]   John Zucchi, *Italians in Toronto: Development of a National Identity* (Montreal: McGill-Queens University Press, 1981).

At least as intriguing, and less well used by previous historians, were the residential addresses of the brides and grooms at the time of their marriages. Initially, I was surprised to find this information in the registers at all, especially in the last two decades of the twentieth century. Even as rates of co-habitation before marriage increased, brides and grooms in the Italian parishes continued to report separate addresses. When I aired my puzzlement to an office assistant at one of the rectories where I was conducting research, she rebuked me – 'they better not be living together before they marry!' – providing a clear enough indication of the reasons for women and men in the parish to report separate homes. This posed a question of interpretation. If brides and grooms were not always truthful about where they lived, then what did the addresses in the registers reveal? I proceeded on the assumption that the addresses they provided were almost certainly not fabricated whole cloth. In some instances the couples continued to live separately, or at least to maintain separate addresses, and in others the addresses were most likely representative of where they had lived: either a past address, or, perhaps, the address of their parents.[8] And on this basis, a new area of analysis emerged.

Marriage, though not an everyday choice, grows from a much wider array of activities, social surroundings and local practices. Young people come together in church and associational halls, in nightclubs, classrooms and living rooms, even on city streets; strangers who meet in a glance across a crowded room must first find themselves in the same crowded room. The addresses of brides and grooms illuminate the patterned encounters of city life, telling us how people came together, or at least where they had come from. In a context where Italians overwhelmingly married other Italians – as they did in Toronto's Little Italy and Italian South Philadelphia – marriage registers illuminate how ethnicity worked as an urban social bond. At the same time, marriages themselves recreate urban ethnicity. Young people marrying their neighbours (as they did in South Philadelphia) reinforce locality as the context of ethnic association. Young people marrying co-ethnics dispersed across the city (as they did in Toronto) fashion an ethnicity that operates on a metropolitan scale. Marriages both reflect and animate patterns of ethnic association. In the case of Italian Toronto and Philadelphia, I would come to argue that ethnicity operated as a different kind of social bond in each locale – people *did* ethnicity differently in accordance with their urban surroundings.

In the course of my work, I experimented with a variety of ways to present this data so that they would tell the story that I hoped to convey. My first impulse was to write 'capsules' about individuals who exemplified the larger trends within the data. These were eventually replaced by oral histories, which

---

[8]   This final speculation might be tested by pairing the addresses in the registers with street addresses drawn from another source, such as a city or telephone directory.

were able to serve that purpose but also to do much more, but these early efforts nonetheless suggest the spatial relations that can be mapped on the basis of data in marriage registers, especially as they are supplemented by other sources. For example, these two capsules position two marriages in 1980 within other information that I had gathered in tax registries and city directories:

> Native South Philadelphians of Italian origin, Cheryl Panzarella and Richard Di Biagio married at Annunciation BVM in 1980. They had been baptized six-tenths of a mile apart, each within blocks of the houses they inhabited as young adults. Cheryl's street offered a daily reminder of the stability of the neighbourhood. In the area surrounding her home on Tasker, most residents had been in place for over a decade, and a quarter had resided in their homes for at least 30 years. Like generations of young people who preceded them to marriage at Annuciation church, Cheryl and Richard were neighbours, residing less than a mile apart at the time of their marriage.

> When Teresa Galati and Francesco Spinelli took their vows in St Francis church in Toronto, they celebrated connections of a different sort. The two lived quite a distance from one another in Toronto. Teresa resided near the church, on Manning Street, and Francesco some 11 miles away, in the northwestern corner of the city at the far end of the large post-war Italian settlement. As they had a generation earlier, residents of Toronto's Little Italy lacked the local roots of South Philadelphians. Less than half of Teresa's neighbours on Manning had been in place for a decade, and scarcely any for the extended durations common in South Philadelphia. Rather than a stable neighbourhood, the two spouses shared a history of migration. Like many other Italian immigrants in Toronto, Francesco had been baptized in Cosenza, a seaside province in Calabria. Teresa took her first rite at an unknown location in Italy.

Marriage registers detail individual choices and communal patterns. In Toronto, then flush with thousands of recent Italian immigrants, newcomers like Teresa and Francesco did something surprising. Rather than forging social lives rooted in the security of a heavily Italian enclave, they participated in, and forged, social networks that spanned the metropolitan area. Italians in Toronto were connected to the College Street 'Little Italy' at the heart of the city – they returned there for commerce and for major cultural and religions events – but they were not turf-bound. Participating in multigenerational efforts to improve their material lives, they sought to benefit from the prosperity and opportunity of post-war Toronto, rather than establishing or defending a neighbourhood. In Philadelphia, people like Cheryl and Richard inhabited a shrinking neighbourhood in a dividing city. Many South Philadelphians departed for the suburbs, but those who remained behind closed ranks. Rather than preserving social contact with former residents who had left the area, South Philadelphians developed social lives that stopped at the boundaries of the neighbourhood.

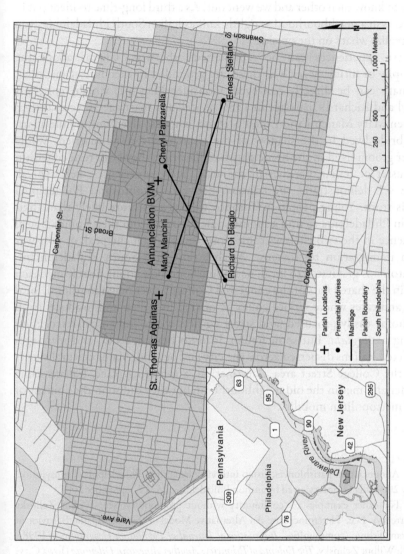

Map 4.1   Marriages in Annunciation Parish, Philadelphia, 1950 and 1980

Map by Jordan Stanger-Ross and Jacqueline Clare.

One South Philadelphian described the intensity of the local ties that brought young people together: 'you all knew their mothers and fathers and aunts and uncles, you didn't have to be introduced'. Another gestured with her hands: 'I lived on this corner, and if you went to the next corner was my husband, and we got to know each other and we went out'. As a third long-time resident put it, after years in a neighbourhood as tightly knit as Italian South Philadelphia, 'you don't realize what's on the outside'.⁹

These experiences can be represented otherwise. Claims about the geography of intimacy, such as these, are grounded in exercises of mapping, and maps can be directly conveyed. Consider Map 4.1, which represents Cheryl and Richard's marriage in 1980, as well as a marriage 30 years earlier, between Mary Mancini and Ernest Stefano, who also lived only a mile apart. Each bride lived in the shadow of the church where she married. While neither groom lived in the home parish of his bride, they both resided within the cluster of Italian parishes in the area. These experiences were typical. Figure 4.1 demonstrates the contrast between Toronto and Philadelphia on this front. Young people in Toronto were always more likely than their peers in Philadelphia to find a spouse some distance from their homes. Social experience in the two enclaves came closest in 1970, at the peak of post-war Italian immigration to Toronto. At that time, like South Philadelphians, Torontonians gravitated to local, neighbourhood ties. Young people met each other in the shared flats of the congested College Street neighbourhood, local shops and cafes where service could be offered in Italian and products from back home easily procured, and street corners where Italians lingered in an evening *passeggiata*. But soon Italian Toronto branched out, and marriages connected Italians dispersed across the city and beyond. Major cultural events made the College Street area a destination, a gathering place. Italians came together and met in the old neighbourhood, but they did so in the context of larger metropolitan mobility.¹⁰

---

⁹ Annunciation parishioners, group interview by author, Philadelphia, Pennsylvania, 10 May 2004; Ida G., interviewed by author, Philadelphia PA, 17 September 2007.

¹⁰ For other examples of 'community without propinquity', see: Wilbur Zelinsky and Barrett A. Lee, 'Heterolocalism, An Alternative Model of the Sociospatial Behavior of Immigrant Ethnic Communities', *International Journal of Population Geography* 4 (1998): 281–98; Wilbur Zelinsky, *The Enigma of Ethnicity: Another American Dilemma* (Iowa City: University of Iowa City Press, 2001); Kenneth A. Scherzer, *The Unbounded Community: Neighborhood Life and Social Structure in New York City, 1830–1875* (Durham: Duke University Press, 1992); Melvin M. Webber, 'Order in Diversity: Community without Propinquity', in Lowdon Wingo Jr, *Cities and Space: The Future Use of Urban Land* (Baltimore: Johns Hopkins University Press, 1963), 23–54.

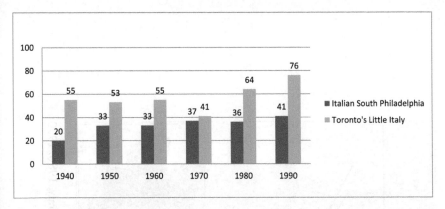

Figure 4.1   Per cent of couples separated by more than one mile at date of marriage, Toronto and Philadelphia, 1940–90 (n = 775)

This dynamic can also be represented graphically in a map of straight-line distances between spouses married at the Little Italy church in 1980/1990 (Map 4.2). Here we can see the parish as a hub, as a centre rather than a boundary in Italian communal association. The old neighbourhood, with its commercial and religious institutions, attracted Italians living throughout the metropolitan area. The young women living in the parish had ongoing social connections with Italians dispersed across Toronto. The College Street Little Italy was a celebratory and invitational space, rather than an exclusive one. In Philadelphia, by contrast, marriage choices continued to be rooted in and to reinforce the boundaries of the neighbourhood. Two final maps (Maps 4.3 and 4.4), these already published in *Staying Italian*, present the final contrast. Here only the addresses of grooms are represented. Since most Catholic brides married in their home parish, the addresses of grooms provide a legible representation of the spatial boundaries of intimate networks. In Philadelphia, Italian ethnicity remained a neighbourhood practice; intimate life choices were bound up with the territorial splintering of the struggling post-war city. In Toronto, meanwhile, Italian ethnicity bore the footprint of mobile people seeking opportunity in a prosperous city while maintaining connections with one another. Italians maintained ethnic networks in both places, but in the choreography of their daily lives residents of Toronto's Little Italy and Italian South Philadelphia gave expression to the intimate reverberations of urban change and to the creative possibilities of social experience.

These claims are based on quantitative analysis. This part of my research involved the collection and analysis of just over 1,000 marriages taken from registers spanning the years 1940 and 1990 in both cities. Using GIS, data sets of this kind can be readily mapped. Connections among sites and people can be plotted and measured. Using GIS, historians can trace the footprints of urban

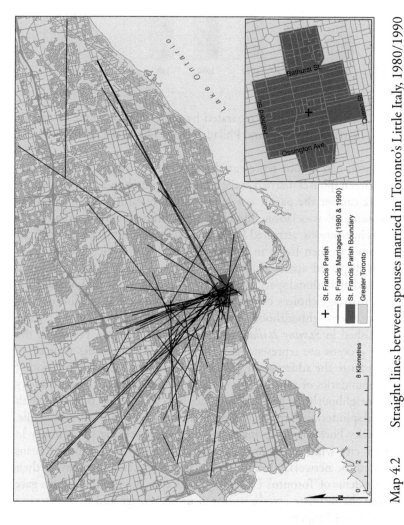

Map 4.2   Straight lines between spouses married in Toronto's Little Italy, 1980/1990
(74 marriages)

Map by Jordan Stanger-Ross and Jacqueline Clare.

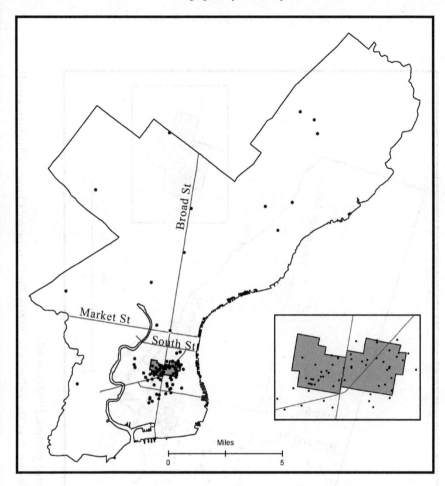

Map 4.3   South Philadelphia grooms, 1980/1990 (n = 100)

social relations. We can tell not only where people lived but also where they went when they left their houses and how they were connected to one another.

Such data answer qualitative questions. My argument focused on the character of ethnic bonds, rather than their extent. And it is this point of emphasis, I think, that gives the methods some prospect of reaching outside of their subfield. The question of *how* analytic categories – race, gender, class – actually operate in urban space is of broad comparative concern. Are race, gender and class different kinds of urban practices in different cities? Can the methods that I used in *Staying Italian* also be applied in these and other contexts?

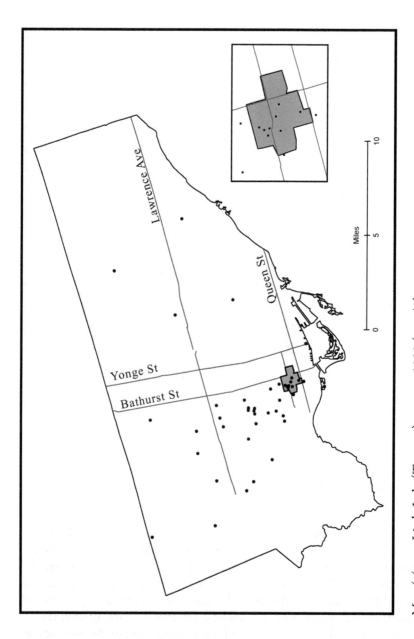

Map 4.4   Little Italy (Toronto) grooms, 1990 (n = 42)

Map originally published in Jordan Stanger-Ross, *Staying Italian* (© 2009 by The University of Chicago. All rights reserved).

Alternative Applications

Other dimensions of social life seem very likely to bear the imprint of urban environments in ways not unlike Italian ethnicity. Spatial analysis of this kind might be most useful to scholars working on categories of connection within urban environments (networks, communities, associations) and those working on categories of power and inequality (gender, class, race). In addition, scholars who are using concepts that are inherently spatial in character (segregation, neighbourhood, slum) might ask how these designations of *place* relate to everyday uses of *space* by urban inhabitants.

In each of these areas of inquiry, systematic empirical research might yield surprises and demonstrate urban variation. *Staying Italian* focused on a category of connection (ethnic community) and demonstrated its variations. Similarly, categories of power may carry unpredictable ramifications for uses of urban space. Although economic marginalization often entails isolation, it also compels regular movement across the city, particularly in search of income. Relative privilege may also express itself in both isolation and movement. Along similar lines, 'neighbourhood' carries varied implications for social practice, depending on historical circumstances, and residential segregation may have unpredictable results in the lives of urban residents, once they leave their houses and move about the city. In such realities of spatial practice researchers will find novel and unanticipated histories.

This kind of analysis can emerge out of a wide range of sources. Any data that illuminate *social geographic relations* – that is, the movement of people across space in their connection to one another – might be used to chart historical spatial practice. Any data that permit linkages between pairs of addresses – sites of work and residence; institutional and associational membership lists; business advertisements, ledgers, customer accounts – can be used to map linkages among urban dwellers, often across long periods of time.

This approach is not without methodological challenges. Especially as historians reach further back in time, and local geographies shift, the plotting of addresses onto city maps becomes more complicated and specialized. Nonetheless, GIS software opens novel opportunities to map and analyse hundreds, even thousands, of data points. With relatively accessible training and increasingly available software, historians are positioned to provide unprecedented analyses of the choreography of social life, and we'll most easily interpret the patterns that we find from comparative perspectives.[11] Just as

---

[11]   In my research I used ESRI's ArcView, which most North American Universities make available to their communities by site license. Much of the training necessary to the use of this software is available online. In addition, high quality open source alternatives are increasingly available.

analyses of change over time require some temporal sweep, social histories of urban space benefit from multiple sites of study.

Gender history seems a particularly apt context for this approach. Like historians of ethnicity, those working on gender know that place (like space) matters. Christine Stansell and Sarah Deutsch, among others, have interwoven histories of urban space and gender, demonstrating that movement across urban space has a gendered history.[12] What might be revealed in systematic comparisons of gender and geographic mobility in different urban settings and across time? Returning to my own research, two stories strike me as particularly suggestive.

The first story travels across Toronto by streetcar. A recent immigrant to Canada in the mid-1960s, Mirella Borsio was seven months pregnant when she learned that her husband had been injured at work and admitted to a hospital far from where the couple had settled in the west end of the city. Mirella set out to see him in the darkness of night:

> Since I couldn't speak a word of English I gave him [a streetcar operator] a little note with the address ... I had to change ... he actually stopped: he took me by the hand, he took me down the three steps of the streetcar ... he waited there until a bus arrived and then he talked to the driver of the other bus.[13]

The story is a striking portrayal of gender and urban mobility. It is a story of what a young woman, recently arrived and very pregnant, could do in post-war Toronto. The city was the kind of place that could be navigated; Toronto space could be traversed, even by young women who could scarcely speak English. And yet, the streetcar driver plays the role of a chaperone, and an intimate one at that ('he took me by the hand'). Men enabled travel across Toronto at night. Mirella's movement across the city required performances of both independence and dependence.

Meanwhile in Italian South Philadelphia, a story of a very different spatialization of gender. In the mid-1960s, after she graduated from high school and entered the workforce full time, Cathy S. began living what she later remembered as 'a wild life', going to bars and clubs outside of the neighbourhood where she lived. By this time, Cathy's father had died ('that would have never happened if my father was alive ... no, no, no, not when my father was alive'), and she lived alone with her mother. Cathy's mother, 'a woman before her time', had worked in her youth in the cigar factories of North Philadelphia, eventually

---

[12] Christine Stansell, *City of Women: Sex and Class in New York 1789–1869* (Champaign, IL: University of Illinois Press, 1987); Sarah Deutsch, *Women and the City: Gender, Space, and Power in Boston, 1870–1940* (New York: Oxford University Press, 2002).

[13] Mirella Borsoi, interviewed by Doreen Rumack, Toronto, ON, 24 March 1988, Folklife Fonds, Archives of Ontario, Toronto.

becoming a union organizer, a role that required her to employ a live-in domestic to tend to her children while she worked.

Nonetheless, Cathy's wanderings outside the orbit of South Philadelphia sparked conflict with her 'liberal' mother. 'She knew that everybody [on the block] used to sit out [on their stoops]', Cathy recalls, 'and if they saw me leaving all dressed up to go on the bus or something like that they knew I was going out some place'. Her mother warned that the neighbours would 'talk', but Cathy chaffed against gendered spatial restrictions imposed by neighbourhood mores, drawing the two into escalating conflict:

> I would come back at her with, well 'you did what you wanted to do when you were young, why are you all over me?' And she'd say, 'well I was married and I wasn't living at home'. And I'd say, 'well if you were married you should have been at home with your kids'. And then I would get hit, I would always get slapped with that line. I would get slapped in the face with that ... 'Don't you judge me ... I gave you birth and I'll take you out' ... that was the gist of that.[14]

Deviation from local customs came at a steep cost; Cathy's movement across the city was violently resisted. And in this intergenerational dispute over urban mobility, Cathy deployed gendered norms of her own – mothers should stay home with their children. Masculinity hovers in the exchange; an absent father opens an opportunity for mobility, a husband at home is presumed to constrain it. How typical are these stories, and what are they typical of? Did boys face reproof when they left the boundaries of South Philadelphia? How were spatial and gender norms interwoven in Toronto? As in the case of ethnicization, these questions can be answered comparatively, and they will bear rich fruit as scholars explore *how* gender and space interacted, as opposed to *how much*. As gender mapped onto the streetscapes of places like (and unlike) Toronto and Philadelphia, gender likely emerged as a variable spatial practice.

As comparative urbanists undertake such studies, they will make important contributions to both the wider history of cities and to the practice of GIS history. Whereas urbanists of previous generations often analysed, in the words of Richard Wade, a 'common metropolitan ... environment' that characterized the modern Western world, more recent syntheses urge scholars to focus on the varieties of urban experience.[15] Past president of the American Urban History Association, Michael Katz, warns that historical accounts of urbanism

---

[14]   Cathy S., interviewed by author, Philadelphia, PA, 17 September 2007.

[15]   Richard Wade, 'Urbanization', in C. Vann Woodward, ed., *The Comparative Approach to American History*, rev. ed. (New York: Oxford University Press, 1997), 187–8.

have often been 'singular' when they should have been 'plural'.[16] Historians increasingly seek not a history of 'the city' but rather of many cities, with the most sophisticated accounts drawing together both transnational linkages and local variation.[17] Even as common ideological, economic, and political forces touched cities the world over, their effects varied on the ground. Social historical accounts of the 'choreographies' of urban life can make distinctive contributions to this new history of cities. Comparative histories of everyday experiences, of the practices and paths of everyday urban life, will illuminate the similarities and differences among cities in as yet unanticipated ways.

In using digital mapping to tell new histories of cities, urbanists will also push GIS history in new and important directions. As Sam Griffiths writes in a recent and provocative essay on historical GIS, the scholarship in this area has suffered from an 'epistemological blind spot for historians wishing to access and substantively describe "spaces of practice" produced by everyday activity'.[18] 'Histories of the embodied spaces of everyday life', he continues, 'are noticeable by their absence'.[19] Similarly, David J. Bodenhamer suggests that scholars have struggled to use GIS to convey the kinds of 'meaning' sought in humanistic inquiry; GIS, with its quantitative and positivist trappings, he argues, stands in tension with efforts to 'explore, challenge, and complicate – in sum to allow us to see, experience, and understand human behavior in all is complexity and to view its deep contingency'.[20] Marianna Pavlovskaya sees a similar problem, as critical geographers seek to free GIS from its origins as a tool of policing and commerce. She urges scholars to understand GIS as a fundamentally mixed method, well capable of supporting critical and qualitative social analysis. To achieve such ends, she suggests, GIS historians will have to turn to the mapping of 'complex relationships, nonquantifiable properties, unpriviledged ontologies,

---

[16]   Michael Katz, *Why Don't American Cities Burn?* (Philadelphia: University of Pennsylvania Press), 19.

[17]   See, for example: Carl Husemoller Nightingale, *Segregation: A Global History of Divided Cities*, Historical Studies of Urban America (Chicago; London: The University of Chicago Press, 2012).

[18]   Sam Griffiths, 'GIS and Research into Historical "Spaces of Practice": Overcoming the Epistemological Barriers', in Alexander von Lünen and Charles Travis, eds, *History and GIS Epistemologies, Considerations and Reflections* (Dordrecht: Springer, 2013), 154, http://link.springer.com/openurl?genre=book&isbn=978-94-007-5008-1.

[19]   Griffiths, 'GIS and Research into Historical "Spaces of Practice"', 157.

[20]   David Bodenhamer, 'Beyond GIS: Geospatial Technologies and the Future of History', in Alexander von Lünen and Charles Travis, eds, *History and GIS Epistemologies, Considerations and Reflections* (Dordrecht: Springer, 2013), 6, http://link.springer.com/openurl?genre=book&isbn=978-94-007-5008-1.

and fluid human worlds'.[21] Comparative histories of the movement of people through urban space will answer these theoretical questions with empirical studies. The sources to do so are ready at hand to social historians. Addresses littered throughout the archives can provide a window into 'spaces of practice', illuminate 'fluid human worlds' and convey the complexity and contingency of human experience. Histories of urban practice can push GIS history beyond analysis of representations (plans and maps) and past the distribution of people and goods (censuses, city directories, tax registers) and into the history of social practice.[22]

Finally, comparative analysis of this kind speaks directly to transnational questions. By examining social practice from a comparative perspective, historians will simultaneously interrogate the transnational portability of the concepts and categories with which we understand urban life. Following Rogers Brubaker, historians will be able to observe when and where given categories mattered (that is, when and where analytic 'categories' have generated social 'groups') and when and where they did not.[23] We will explore categories with transnational significance (for example, gender) in their local variations, answering questions about both the mechanisms of their portability and their variation. As historians carry concepts across the globe, comparative social historical analysis will draw them back down to the ground of local contexts.

Comparative social histories of urban spatial relations have never been more feasible. Well beyond the field of immigrant history, such analyses promise to fill-in important 'stuff of history'. If historians recognize the abundance of sources available and seize the tools increasingly at our disposal, we will discover new comparative histories of the city that demand telling.

[21] Marianna Pavlovskaya, 'Theorizing with GIS: A Tool for Critical Geographies?', *Environment and Planning A* 38 (2006): 2016.

[22] For a good survey of the recent scholarship in historical GIS, see: Anne Kelly Knowles and Amy Hillier, eds, *Placing History: How Maps, Spatial Data, and GIS Are Changing Historical Scholarship*, 1st ed. (Redlands, CA: ESRI Press, 2008).

[23] Rogers Brubaker, *Ethnicity without Groups*, 1st Harvard University Press (Cambridge, MA; London: Harvard University Press, 2006).

Chapter 5
Rebuilding the Cities Destroyed in the Second World War: Growing Possibilities for Comparative Analysis

Jeffry Diefendorf

When I began researching the reconstruction of West Germany's bombed cities around 1980, there was surprisingly little scholarship on that topic. A decade later, scholarship existed on post-war urban reconstruction in West Germany and a few other Western European countries, but a great deal remained to be done. Since then important new work has appeared on rebuilding cities that experienced wartime damage in Eastern Europe, the former Soviet Union, Japan, France and Great Britain. This now makes it possible to compare this process across a broad spectrum and use comparisons to identify and evaluate the key variables that shaped reconstruction. Demographic, economic, legal and political conditions, considerations of appropriate architectural forms, issues of heritage and historic preservation and urban planning were all important in shaping reconstruction.[1] This chapter will use a range of examples, drawn from existing research, to focus on the ways in which the relationship between urban planning and urban reconstruction can be explored through comparative research.

Why comparative history? Comparative studies can help reveal critical variables that have facilitated and hindered reconstruction.[2] This can not

---

[1]   Often the term 'reconstruction' is used to refer to post-war political, economic and international structures rather than physical rebuilding. For example, see the special issue by Mark Mazower, Jessica Reinisch and David Feldman, eds, 'Post-War Reconstruction in Europe. International Perspectives, 1945–1949', *Past and Present* 210 (2011), 9–367.

[2]   An example of comparative work is Nick Tiratsoo, Junichi Hasegawa, Tony Mason and Takao Matsumura, eds, *Urban Reconstruction in Britain and Japan, 1945–1955: Dreams, Plans and Realities* (Luton: University of Luton Press, 2002). In July, 2011, the Technical University of Berlin hosted a conference on 'Architecture and Urban Planning of the Postwar Era in Europe'. The German version of the conference title refers to 'Nachkriegsmoderne', or post-war modernism, rather than the 'Post-war Era'. Presumably there was much comparative discussion, though the papers were case studies from all parts of Europe, including cities that were not damaged in the war.

only point the way for scholars to work on as yet relatively understudied cities damaged in the Second World War, but perhaps also help inform decision-makers in cities that have in recent years also suffered wartime destruction. It can also provide insights for cities seeking to rebuild after major natural disasters or for cities suffering from flawed peacetime development. Although wars cause different kinds of damage, citizens and officials in cities today might learn from histories of reconstruction planning and the challenges of implementing those plans.[3]

It is surely the case that transnationalism is a powerful tool for breaking out of the conceptual (and real) confines not only of the nation-state, but also of intensely local, self-limiting perspectives. In certain fields of enquiry, temporal as well as spatial flows and processes clearly defy any purported limits of nationhood. Moreover, moving beyond the confines of the nation-state can provide the practical potential of encouraging interdisciplinary, comparative and collaborative research and opening windows for new audiences for that work.[4] However, it is important to recognize that elements of local urban culture and identity have provided continuities that have resisted transnational trends.

In terms of planning, there are several key elements for a comparative matrix, though there is not time to examine all of these in detail. Comparisons might include: (1) planning models and motifs; the relationship between general or master plans; plans limited to a part of a city, war-damaged or not, and regional plans; whether reconstruction plans were produced by a local planning office, hired consultants, participants in an open or limited competition or authorities in a central/national bureau; the extent to which reconstruction plans were essentially utopian fantasies based on the premise of starting with a *tabula rasa*;

[3]   See Lawrence J. Vale and Thomas J. Campanella, eds, *The Resilient City: How Modern Cities Recover from Disaster* (Oxford and New York: Oxford University Press, 2005); and Jeffry Diefendorf, 'Reconstructing Devastated Cities: Europe after World War II and New Orleans after Katrina', *Journal of Urban Design* 14 (2009): 377–97. A similar example can be found in a paper presented at the 2012 meeting of the European Association for Urban History: Carola Hein, 'Werner Hebebrand and Edmund Bacon: A comparative analysis of post-war urban renewal in Hamburg and Philadelphia'.

[4]   For a good discussion of recent transnational histories of planning, see Stephen V. Ward, Robert Freestone and Christopher Silver, Centenary paper: 'The "new" Planning History. Reflections, Issues and Directions', *Town Planning Review* 82 (2011): 231–62. At the 2012 meeting of the European Association for Urban History, papers examining town planning as a transnational phenomenon included: Clément Orillard, 'Urban Design: The Building of a Transnational Field in the English-Speaking World', and Phillip Wagner, 'The Transnational Lobby for Postwar Planning? The International Federation for Housing and Town Planning in the 1940s and 50s' (papers presented at the 11th International Conference in Urban History, European Association of Urban History, Faculty of the Arts, Charles University, Prague, August 2012).

(2) planners, as individuals and members of a profession; (3) planning processes: the provisions of planning laws, if extant, and the way they defined the planning process; organization and size of planning offices; the role played by local, provincial or national officials in implementing or hindering reconstruction planning; (4) the relationship between reconstruction planning and memories of pre-war urban characteristics; and (5) the degree to which these variables reveal long- or short-term continuities from the pre-war and war periods and how long reconstruction planning continues after the war's end.[5]

This chapter will focus primarily on the need to consider post-war reconstruction in terms of longer continuities between pre-war planning, wartime planning, immediate post-war planning and later modifications to these plans; and then the need to look at reconstruction planning in terms of transnational, national and local inputs. The transnational 'turn' receives much attention today, with some scholars brashly accusing others of being too timid to abandon 'anachronistically national paradigms'.[6] I will argue that one must be careful not to let this new interest in transnationalism obscure the real importance of the local and the national in shaping reconstruction, especially since reconstruction planning in many cities began already during the war.[7] First, however, a few words about the issue of continuities.

Often there were continuities in personnel from the pre-war into the post-war period.[8] This in turn suggests that reconstruction historians must pay attention to how one employs the planning process in time. When implementation of a

---

 5 Leo Grebler long ago stressed continuity, but he considered the desires of populations to return to old places and buildings, the power of existing property ownership and the fact that in spite of vast destruction, much remained undamaged, even in city centres. He did not consider continuities in planning. Leo Grebler, 'Continuity in the Rebuilding of Bombed Cities in Western Europe', *The American Journal of Sociology* 60 (1956): 463–9. A valuable new comparative study of collective and individual memories of the destruction of cities in the Second World War, a study that includes post-war reconstruction planning, is Jörg Arnold, *The Allied Air War and Urban Memory. The Legacy of Strategic Bombing in Germany* (Cambridge: Cambridge University Press, 2011). Arnold compares the history of Kassel, a city in West Germany, and Magdeburg, a city in East Germany.

 6 Russell Berman, 'Colonialism, and No End. The Other Continuity Thesis', in Volker Langbehn and Mohammad Salama, eds, *German Colonialism. Race, the Holocaust, and Postwar Germany* (New York: Columbia University Press, 2011), 165.

 7 An excellent new book on wartime planning is Jörn Düwel and Niels Gutschow, eds, *A Blessing in Disguise. War and Town Planning in Europe, 1940–1945* (Berlin: Dom Publishers, 2013).

 8 Key studies of this for Germany are Werner Durth, *Deutsche Architekten. Biographische Verflecthugnen 1900–1970* (Braunschweig and Wiesbaden: Friedrich Vieweg & Sohn, 1986) and Werner Durth and Neils Gutschow, *Träume in Trümmern. Planungen zum Wiederaufbau zerstörter Städte im Westen Deutschlands 1940–1950*, 2 vols (Braunschweig and Wiesbaden: Friedrich Vieweg & Sohn, 1988).

plan was delayed, for whatever reason, or when planning personnel changed, did this open the door to major changes, and from what source? At what point can one say that post-war planning was no longer shaped by the opportunities presented by wartime destruction and was part of the normal planning process, at which point one stops speaking of reconstruction and uses other terminology? Did the 'post-war' period end a decade or more after 1945, or has it continued to the present?

This issue can be illustrated with two cases: Berlin and Warsaw, both capital cities. Warsaw became the capital of the newly formed Polish state in 1919, and in 1928, a new chief urban planner, Stanislaw Rozanski, began work on a master plan. This plan, based on functional zoning, contained new garden city suburbs, radial roads, a north-south axis, new green wedges for better air circulation and a new industrial area to the northeast. Another large-scale plan with functional zoning but a different alignment of transportation corridors was prepared by Jan Chmielewski and Szymon Syrkus in 1934.[9] Horribly damaged in the German assault and conquest of 1939, the suppression of the Warsaw ghetto uprising in 1943 and the Warsaw uprising of 1944, reconstructing the capital posed a huge challenge for Poland. Throughout the period of German occupation, Polish architects and planners, including Chmielewski and Syrkus, had engaged in 'semi-legal, semi-conspiratorial town-planning', so when the Bureau for Rebuilding of the Capital was created in January 1945, it could immediately draw upon the pre-war and wartime planning.[10] Foreign planners, including Patrick Abercrombie, William Holford, and Hans Bernoulli, visited to observe rebuilding and offer advice. Though the Bureau for Rebuilding was dissolved in 1949, work on a master plan continued until it was finally approved in 1956. In other words, pre-war planning blended with reconstruction planning and was thus a continuous activity from the 1920s through the 1950s, not something determined solely by the vast destruction experienced by the city.[11]

In Berlin, large-scale, long-term planning during the Weimar Republic, particularly under the leadership of Martin Wagner, was based on modernist ideas. During the Third Reich, urban redesign on a monumental scale was in the hands of Albert Speer. During the early post-war years before the division of the city, Hans Sharoun produced reconstruction plans that reverted to modernist models for decentralization. In the divided city there were elements of both Western modernism and Soviet models for monumental avenues and massive new housing districts. Reunited in 1990 and declared the new capital in 1991,

---

[9]   Anna Jozefacka, 'Rebuilding Warsaw: Conflicting Visions of a Capital City, 1916–1956' (PhD diss., New York University, 2011), 57ff, 74ff, and 94ff.

[10]   Stanisław Jankowski, 'Warsaw: Destruction, Secret Town Planning, 1939–44, and Postwar Reconstruction', in Jeffry Diefendorf, ed., *Rebuilding Europe's Bombed Cities* (Houndmills and London, Macmillan, 1990), 81–2.

[11]   Jozefacka, 'Rebuilding Warsaw', 244ff, 268.

Berlin engaged in a new round of reconstruction planning to heal the wounds caused by the Second World War *and* the Cold War. Here reconstruction planning lasted 50 years and involved continuities and discontinuities.

Now to planning and the transnational perspective. Urban planning was a new profession, one that grew out of architecture and engineering in the late nineteenth and early twentieth centuries, and it quickly became a transnational phenomenon. Its practitioners read each other's publications, undertook study visits to other cities and attended meetings of new organizations such as the International Garden Cities Association, which later became the International Federation of Housing and Planning and the Congrès International d'Architecture Moderne (CIAM), the famous proponent of modernism.[12] Planning ideas were also spread through participation in or visits to city planning exhibitions, such as the famous Berlin exhibition of 1910, designed by Werner Hegemann and featuring planning ideas not only from Germany but also from the United States and other countries.[13] Moreover, in the decades prior to the Second World War, some planners succeeded in winning contracts to apply their ideas in cities beyond their own national boundaries. In the early 1930s, Ernst May and other German planners worked in the Soviet Union planning new cities. Other planner/architects, like Walter Gropius and Martin Wagner, chose to or were forced to emigrate to escape a hostile political environment, and they carried their ideas to new locales. Information exchange and personal contacts continued right to the eve of Hitler's assault on Poland. In August 1939, there was an International Congress on City and Regional Planning in Stockholm. The chief German delegate presented a study of local traffic planning issues based on information gathered from all over Europe and the United States.[14]

The international exchange of planning ideas continued even during both World Wars. During the First World War, neutral countries like the Netherlands and Denmark facilitated contacts between planners. During the Second World War, French planners visited German cities.[15] It is not surprising, then, that the exchange of ideas continued, even accelerated, after 1945, when the vast wartime

[12]   Stephen V. Ward, 'A Pioneer "Global Intelligence Corps"? The Internationalisation of Planning Practice, 1890–1939', *The Town Planning Review* 76 (2005): 119–41.

[13]   Ursula von Petz, 'Städtebau-Ausstellungen in Deutschland, 1910–2010', *disP – The Planning Review* 174 (2008): 24–50. Hegemann had studied in Berlin, Munich, Paris and Philadelphia and was acquainted with leading American planners and architects, such as Daniel Burnham.

[14]   Reinhold Niemeier, *Städtebau und Nahverkehr* (Berichte zur Raumforschung und Raumordnung. Bd 8, 1941). Niemeier was the president of the Deutsche Akademie für Städtebau, Reichs- und Landesplanung.

[15]   Danièle Voldman, 'Èchanges Culturels et Techniques entre Reconstructeurs', in Dominique Barjot, Rémi Baudouï and Danièle Voldman, eds, *Les Reconstructions en Europe (1945–1949)* (Brussels: Éditions Complexe, 1997), 326.

destruction of urban areas presented the urgent need for reconstruction and the possible opportunity to implement planning models that had been evolving over decades. Patterns of exchange reappeared after the war. For example, the 1957 Internationale Bauausstellung in Berlin was visited by architects' delegations from Denmark, Sweden, Switzerland, South Africa, Poland and Israel, along with teachers and students from foreign cities, including Istanbul, Krakow, Pretoria and Brno, where they examined how war-damaged West German cities were dealing with issues such as housing, traffic flow, functional zoning and renewal of old urban neighbourhoods.[16]

Post-war reconstruction planning certainly drew upon internationally known pre-war models and motifs. These included: garden cities, garden suburbs and satellite cities which were intended to reduce congestion in big cities; new forms and citing of housing with ample access to light and air; new inner and outer city ring roads and new wide through and tangent arteries to facilitate the flow of motor vehicles; new or enlarged green spaces for city lungs and recreation; decentralization of urban activities; and functional zoning that would separate housing, industry, cultural and administrative activities. In these models one can see a mixture of motifs from the garden city movement and CIAM modernism.[17] One could also point to pre-war German, Italian and Soviet planning models that stressed monumental architecture and broad axes and squares for staging political demonstrations, the construction of which would require the redesign of inner city streets and neighbourhoods and the relocation of residents to new suburbs.[18] When applying these different models to post-war reconstruction, planners might focus on the bombed areas (especially city centres), the entire city, including more distant suburbs, or entire regions.

One area where post-war reconstruction planning was transnational concerned how to deal with the growth of automobile traffic, both between cities and within cities. During the 1920s, planners and civil engineers from Western Europe and America had been studying the construction of parkways around New York City and *autostrade* in Italy. In this decade, Le Corbusier and modernists in CIAM were also making proposals for new highways into or through cities, broad arteries with few or no crossings that would facilitate rapid movement between distant suburbs in the inner city. Starting in 1933, Hitler and his engineer Fritz Todt drew everyone's attention with the program of Autobahn construction between German cities, but as I mentioned earlier, German

---

[16]   Josef Walter Hollatz, 'Einleitung', in Edgar Wedepohl, ed., *Deutscher Städtebau nach 1945* (Essen: Richard Bacht, 1961), v–x. Städtebau can be translated as urban development and urban planning.

[17]   Konstanze Sylva Domhardt, 'The Garden City Idea in the CIAM Discourse on Urbanism: A Path to Comprehensive Planning', in *Planning Perspectives* 27 (2012): 173–97.

[18]   Aristotle Kallis, 'The 'Third Rome' of Fascism: Demolitions and the Search for a New Urban Syntax', *The Journal of Modern History* 84 (2012): 40–79.

planners like Reinhold Niemeyer, while drawing upon information from other countries, also continued to develop ideas for improving transportation within their cities.[19] When Albert Speer created the 'Working staff for rebuilding war-damaged cities' in 1943, he called upon the planners to meet the challenge of the growth of automobile traffic in cities and avoid the problems that this traffic created in cities like New York and London.[20]

After the war, some reconstruction planners did manage to introduce inner city highways or major arteries in the ruined cities. An example of the former is the elevated highway into Düsseldorf planned by Friedrich Tamms and the broad north-south and east-west avenues in Cologne, the latter being completions of streets initially planned during the Third Reich. Kurt Leibbrand, the best-known German transportation planner during the 1950s and 1960s, was a strong advocate for broad inner city arteries to facilitate automobile traffic.[21] The planning models here all reflected continuities with pre-war transnational planning.

On the other hand, in many cities these plans met considerable resistance from a citizenry that sought to rebuild the city as it had been in order to preserve something with which they closely identified. Instead of such arteries, they preferred retaining the historic street pattern and creating pedestrian zones that valued foot traffic over motor vehicle auto traffic. In cities like Munich and Cologne, the local prevailed over the transnational. And whereas Leibbrand argued that pedestrian zones were bound to kill inner cities by denying access to them, it is interesting that the famous and influential British study of urban traffic, commissioned by the British Ministry of Transport and largely composed by Colin Buchanan, insisted that 'Closely associated with the quality of the environment is freedom of pedestrian movement'.[22] Buchanan praised Cologne,

---

[19] See the articles in the 'Netzwerk Autobahn' issue of *Werkstatt Geschichte* 21 (December 1998). For a detailed study of German planning regarding autos, see Barbara Schmucki, *Der Traum vom Verkehrsfluss. Städtische Verkehrsplanung seit 1945 im deutsch-deutschen Vergleich*. Deutsches Museum, Beiträge zur Historischen Verkehrsforschung, vol. 4 (Frankfurt and New York: Campus Verlag, 2001).

[20] Jeffry Diefendorf, *In the Wake of War. The Reconstruction of German Cities after World War II* (Oxford and New York: Oxford University Press, 1993), 172.

[21] Kurt Leibbrand's ideas can be found in *Transportation and Town Planning*, trans. Nigel Seymer (Cambridge, MA. and London: MIT Press, 1970). [Simultaneous publication by Leonard Hill books, London. The German version appeared in 1964.] This was based on an earlier book, *Verkehrsingenieurwesen* (Basel: Birkhäuser, 1957). For my comments on Leibbrand's work and career, see Jeffry Diefendorf, 'Urban Transportation Planning Influences and Legacies: Kurt Leibbrand, Germany's Acclaimed Postwar Traffic Planner', *The Journal of Transport History* 35 (2014).

[22] Ministry of Transport, *Traffic in Towns. A Study of the Long Term Problems of Traffic in Urban Areas. Reports of the Steering Group and Working Group appointed by the Minister of Transport* (London: Her Majesty's Stationery Office, 1963), 38. This government-issued

Essen and Bremen for their pedestrian zones and criticized Hannover for its inner ring road, a ring that allowed crossings and damaged the environment.[23] Here is an example of transnational thinking about planning that stood out by praising the local.

While there is thus no question that planning ideas crossed national borders, one must be careful not to exaggerate transnational influences. Specifically national and local concepts and concerns were equally important. It is tempting to assume that central direction prevailed in authoritarian regimes like those in the Soviet block, but centralized planning was also found in democratic, capitalist countries like France and Japan. Moreover, even where centralized planning existed, in some cases local initiatives and concerns succeeded in resisting or modifying planning models or planners dispatched from the national capital.[24]

After the 1917 revolution, the Soviet confiscation of all urban land along with the institution of a centrally planned economy potentially opened the way for massive urban change directed by Moscow-based planners, and Soviet planners were influenced by Western modernist planners, ranging from Ludwig Hilbeseimer and le Corbusier to the German planners who worked in the USSR in the 1930s.[25] During the Second World War, some 500 cities or towns were totally or partly destroyed, and reconstruction planning began under central direction in 1943.[26] In the case of Leningrad, a new general plan, based on a pioneering plan for Moscow, had been created in 1935–36 by the Leningrad's official city architect Nikolai Baranov. In 1947 Baranov converted this into a reconstruction plan that emphasized new housing, victory parks and a new

---

report received such attention that it was quickly published in an abbreviated paperback version, *Traffic in Towns* (Harmondsworth: Penguin Books, 1963). For a recent evaluation of the Buchanan Report, see Simon Gunn, 'The Buchanan Report, Environment and the Problem of Traffic in 1960s Britain', *Twentieth Century British History* 22 (2011): 521–42.

[23]   Ministry of Transport, *Traffic in Towns*, 174–5.

[24]   For Soviet influences on rebuilding in East Germany after 1945, see Jorn Düwel, *Baukunst voran! Archteiktur und Städtebau in der SBZ/DDR* (Berlin, Schelzky & Jeep, 1995) and Werner Durth, Jorn Düwel and Neils Gutschow, *Architektur und Städtebau der DDR*, vol. 2 *Aufbau. Städte, Themen, Dokumente* 2nd ed. (Frankfurt and New York, Campus Verlag, 1999).

[25]   Milka Bliznakov, 'Urban Planning in the USSR: Integrative Theories', in Michael F. Hamm, ed., *The City in Russian History* (Lexington, Kentucky: University Press of Kentucky, 1976), 246, 253.

[26]   Serguei V. Mironenko, 'La Restauration et la Reconstruction des Villes de Russie Endommagées pendant la Seconde Guerre Mondiale (1943–1955) d'après les Matériaux des Archives d'État de la Fédération Russe', in Dominique Barjot, Rémi Baudouï and Danièle Voldman, *Les Reconstructions en Europe (1945–1949)* (Brussels: Éditions Complexe, 1997), 109–11.

stadium.[27] However, as Blair Ruble argues, '... the final document – as with all Soviet general city plans of the period – largely ignored major social and economic trends then shaping the city's destiny. These forces rendered Chief Architect Baranov's plans fanciful and obsolete almost as soon as they left is drawing board'.[28] The victory parks were built, but local architects and city officials prioritized the rebuilding of public buildings in a neo-classical style, paying homage to the 'Leningrad tradition'. This was an effort at restoring local identity and asserting 'local self assertion'.[29] In other words, even in a strongly centralized and authoritarian regime, local traditions and interests could prevail.

Karl Qualls' study of the rebuilding of Sevastopol similarly shows how local architects and political leaders managed to resist the imposition of a Moscow-developed reconstruction plan, thereby recreating the traditional identity of the city as a Russia naval centre (not a Soviet city.) In the pre-war USSR, planners combined modernism with some elements of the garden city model in producing the Moscow Plan of 1935, a plan to guide the transformation of the capital and other cities. The goal was to have Soviet cities become socialist cities and shape new lives within an industrialized state. This continued to be the post-war theme from Moscow, but local planners sought to transform it in ways intended both to satisfy their superiors in Moscow and to accommodate local needs and wishes. After the war, competing plans were developed in Moscow, but they were resisted in Sevastopol, where locals sought more to recreate the pre-revolutionary and pre-war city than to produce a new, modern city. In this they enjoyed considerable success in resisting Moscow, showing that even in an authoritarian regime, the centre does not always dominate the periphery.[30] In contrast to Leningrad and Sevastopol, centrally directed planners rebuilt the devastated formerly Prussian city of Königsberg into the Soviet city of Kaliningrad, a process made easy by the fact that the native, ethic German population that might have defended local urban traditions had fled the Soviet forces.[31]

---

[27]   Blair A. Ruble, *Leningrad: Shaping a Soviet City* (Berkeley, Los Angeles, Oxford, University of California Press, 1990), 2–3, 43–5; and Denis J.B. Shaw, 'Planning Leningrad', *Geographical Review* 68 (1979): 183.

[28]   Ruble, *Leningrad*, 51.

[29]   Lisa A. Kirschenbaum, *The Legacy of the Siege of Leningrad, 1941–1995: Myth, Memories, and Monuments* (Cambridge, Cambridge University Press, 2006), 124, 128.

[30]   Karl Qualls, *From Ruins to Reconstruction. Urban Identity in Soviet Sevastopol after World War II* (Ithaca and London, Cornell University Press, 2009), Chapter 3, 'Local Victory over Moscow: Planning for the Future'.

[31]   For this city, see Bert Hoppe, *Auf den Trümmern von Königsberg. Kaliningrad 1946–1970* (Schriftenreihe der Vierteljahrsheft für Zeitgeschichte, 80, Munich, Oldenbourg Verlag, 2000).

Whereas the West German state did not try to shape post-war rebuilding, leaving that to local authorities, the East German state did seek to dictate how cities other than Berlin should be rebuilt. In 1950, a year after the founding of the German Democratic Republic, the Communist state proclaimed the 'Sixteen principles of urban planning', principles derived from discussions with Soviet planners in Moscow. These principles called for building socialist cities, whether they were to be new cities or rebuilt cities, and local plans had to be approved in Berlin. While there was some local protests against this centralized planning based on transnational models that could erase local identity, they did not succeed in the same measure as in West Germany. However, in both German states, it was common for reconstruction planners to seek to modernize their cities in one way or another, and these plans frequently blocked the rebuilding of historic structures.[32]

In both Japan and France, new agencies of the central government were given responsibility for post-war reconstruction planning, though neither country's government had the same kind of authoritarian power as did the USSR. In Japan, urban planning had been the responsibility of the central government since 1918. The Great Kanto Earthquake of 1923 that destroyed Tokyo resulted in reconstruction agencies, plans to modernize the city and laws intended to further the use of Land Readjustment, the main planning device. In 1945 and 1946, new national laws and reconstruction agencies, including the War Damage Rehabilitation Board were created, using the 1923 model, and that agency was charged with guiding the rebuilding of the 116 most-badly damaged cities. As André Sorensen has argued, 'postwar Japanese planners saw the destruction of their cities as an opportunity to start again, freed of the constraints of the existing urban fabric which had been conveniently burned away by American bombs', and they hoped the new agency would make this realizable.[33]

Japanese planners had been influenced by European models, including the garden city movement, since early in the century. Japanese planners had visited Berlin in 1936 to see how the Germans prepared the capital for the Olympics. They also became acquainted with Nazi ideas for monumentalized

[32] For the comparison of Kassel and Magdeburg, see Arnold, *The Allied Air War and Urban Memory*. Another useful comparative study is Michael Meng, *Shattered Space: Encountering Jewish Ruins in Postwar Germany and Poland* (Cambridge: Harvard University Press, 2011). Meng examines several cities in both German states as well as in Poland.
[33] André Sorensen, *The Making of Urban Japan. Cities and Planning from Edo to the Twenty-First Century* (London and New York: Routledge, 2002), 164. See also Ishida Yorifusa, 'Japanese Cities and Planning in the Reconstruction Period: 1945–55', in Carola Hein, Jeffry M. Diefendorf and Ishida Yorifusa, eds, *Rebuilding Urban Japan after 1945* (Houndmills, Basingstoke, Palgrave Macmillan, 2003), 18 and 25ff.

cities representing that country's grandiose ambitions.[34] Here again we see the transnational currency of planning ideas. Faced with rebuilding their bombed-out cities, planners, both centrally and locally, sought to control urban sprawl, build trunk roads and create new parks and green belts. Widened arteries were to carry traffic and act as fire breaks in case of future urban disasters.[35] Japan's most influential planner was Ishikawa Hideaki, the director Tokyo's metropolitan planning office, and he produced a reconstruction plan for the capital by 1946. For the most part, the 1946 Tokyo plan was not realized, primarily due to financial shortages but also due to opposition from landowners and existing property patterns.[36] One important district, Kabuki-cho, was redesigned and rebuilt on the initiative of local property owners and businessmen, though with approval from Hideaki.[37] Opposition from property owners was one of the most frequent reasons that ambitious centralized plans for large-scale urban transformations had to be scaled down or set aside.

In Hiroshima, the issue was not only the scale of the damage but also the desire to commemorate this tragedy, a desire shared internationally and that led to competing priorities. Was the city to be foremost a monument to the bomb or a living city for survivors and future residents? Rebuilding reflected both disagreements and cooperative efforts between the War Damage Rehabilitation Board, the prefecture and the local planning office. Ishikawa Hideaki visited Hiroshima that year, as did the architect Kenzo Tange, both representing the War Damage Rehabilitation Board. Because of Hiroshima's symbolic significance, foreign planners, including Americans and Australians, also offered suggestions about how to rebuild and memorialize the impact of the atomic bomb. In addition to the famous Peace Memorial Park with its modernist museum designed by Kenzo Tange in 1949, the city built a 100-metre wide central avenue, other broad streets and new green spaces along the river running through the city. The major features of this mixed bag of plans were completed by the end of the 1950s.[38] The point here is that while there were both transnational inspirations and national guidance, as in the USSR, in Japan

34 Sorensen, *Urban Japan* 137; Junichi Hasegawa, 'Reconstruction Planning of Tokyo after the Second World War', in Peter J. Larkham and Takashi Yasuda, eds, *Reconstruction, Replanning and the Future of Cities in Japan and the UK* (Working Paper series no. 1, Faculty of Law, Humanities, University of Central England, Birmingham Institute of Art and Design, 2005): 6. On German influences, see Carola Hein and Ishida Yorifusa, 'Japanische Stadtplanung und ihre deutschen Wurzeln', in *Die alte Stadt*, 3 (1998), 189–211.
35 Sorensen, *Urban Japan*, 159; Yorifusa, 'Japanese Cities', 27–9.
36 Sorensen, *Urban Japan*, 165–7.
37 Ichikawa Hiroo, 'Reconstructing Tokyo: The Attempt to Transform a Metropolis', in Hein, Diefendorf and Yorifusa, *Rebuilding Urban Japan after 1945*, 57–64.
38 Ishimaru Norioki, 'Reconstructing Hiroshima and Preserving the Reconstructed City' in Hein, Diefendorf and Yorifusa, *Rebuilding Urban Japan after 1945*, 91–100.

local initiatives and officials played key roles.[39] The same was true for France, where the Ministry for Reconstruction and Urbanism, created in November 1944, also ran into opposition when trying to impose its models for rebuilding.[40]

German bombs began to hit British cities in the autumn of 1940. In several cities, reconstruction plans were soon prepared that reflected modernist, transnational models, and bold planning was encouraged by the new Minister of Works and Planning, Lord John Reith. These plans called for decentralization, relocation of people to suburbs or satellite cities, improved road systems based on ring roads and broader arteries, better functional zoning and green belts. Such features appeared in Sir Patrick Abercrombie's County of London Plan of 1943 and Greater London Plan of 1944, but also plans for cities like Birmingham, Coventry and Plymouth. The Town and Country Planning Act of 1944 required cities to gain London's approval of their plans in order to obtain funding, something essential for the land acquisition needed for redesigning these cities.

And yet here too the appearance of the dominance of centralized planning is misleading. Donald Gibson, Coventry's city architect, had already developed a plan for the redevelopment of the city centre by May 1940. The subsequent bombing and then funding difficulties led to some reductions in the scope of Gibson's plan, but it remained the basis for rebuilding once the war ended.[41] The situation in Birmingham was similar: here the key player was city engineer Herbert Manzoni, who in the 1930s developed plans for renewing 'middle-ring slum housing areas'. In 1939 the town decided 'to prepare a similar plan for 12,638 acres of the city's central area'.[42] Although the bombing was not concentrated in the centre, Mazoni remained focused on building an inner city ring road and redeveloping poor housing areas. Because it took a long time to obtain funds and then acquire property, actual construction of the ring road

---

[39]   Case studies of rebuilding Osaka, Nagaoka, and Okinawa can also be found in Hein, Diefendorf and Yorifusa, *Rebuilding Urban Japan after 1945*.

[40]   See Rémi Baudoui, 'Between Regionalism and Functionalism: French Reconstruction from 1940 to 1945', in Jeffry M. Diefendorf, ed., *Rebuilding Europe's Bombed Cities* (Houndmills and London: Macmillan, 1990); Danièle Voldman, *La reconstruction des villes françaises de 1940 à 1954: histoire d'une politique* (Paris: L'Harmattan, 1997); and Hugh Clout, 'Place Annihilation and Urban Reconstruction: The Experience of Four Towns in Brittany, 1940 to 1960', *Geografiska Annaler* 82 (2000): 165–80.

[41]   Tony Mason and Nick Tiratsoo, 'People, Politics and Planning: the Reconstruction of Coventry's City Centre, 1940–53', *Rebuilding Europe's Bombed Cities*, 96–112. See also Phil Hubbard, Lucy Faire and Keith D. Lilley, 'Remembering Post-war Reconstruction: Modernism and City Planning in Coventry 1940–1962', *Planning History* 24 (2002): 7–20.

[42]   Peter J. Larkham, 'Replanning Birmingham: Process and Product in Post-War Reconstruction', Faculty Working Paper series no. 2, Faculty of Law, Humanities, Development and Society, University of Central England, Birmingham (2007): 3.

began only in 1957. The first section opened in 1960 and the rest was completed in 1971.[43] In both cities, continuities in local planning were thus key elements in rebuilding.

In Plymouth, the mayor, the minister of works and planning, Lord Astor, was a friend of Lord Reith, and in 1941, after the bombing, the city hired Abercrombie to prepare a rebuilding plan. The plan that resulted from collaboration between Abercrombie, James Paton Watson, the city engineer, and William Crabtree, the city architect, was radically modernist. Stephen Essex and Mark Brayshay have declared that 'There is no doubt that the post-war reconstruction of the city along radical lines was a remarkable and unprecedented achievement. Plymouth was a pioneer in post-war urban reconstruction planning and had often been an unofficial test case in the framing of national policy.'[44] Transnational models were thus important here. Disagreements among the key planners and complaints from local property owners nevertheless resulted in significant changes in the original plan.

It is also worth noting that the consultant most frequently hired to advise on rebuilding in Britain was Thomas Sharp. Starting in the 1930s, Sharp was notable for 'the advocacy of an alternative modernist strand to the planning of town and country that was distinct and different from the prevailing planning garden city ideology or the radical modernism associated with Le Corbusier'.[45] Sharp's alternative, known as 'townscape', sought neither the rejection of existing cities for small garden cities, which would destroy the countryside, nor radical modernization, which would destroy the traditional and cherished character of English towns. He advocated renewal and improvement while retaining traditional architectural forms and small, crooked streets, features which made each town distinct. His ideas appealed to local officials and citizens who wanted some change but not the bold urban transformations advocated by Lord Reith.[46]

---

[43] Larkham, *Replanning Birmingham*, 36–46; see also David Adams, 'Everyday Experiences of the Modern City: Remembering the Post-War Reconstruction of Birmingham', *Planning Perspectives* 26 (2011): 237–60.

[44] Stephen Essex and Mark Brayshay, 'Vision, Vested Interest and Pragmatism: Who Re-made Britain's Blitzed Cities?' *Planning Perspectives* 22 (2007): 435.

[45] John Pendlebury, 'Thomas Sharp and the Modern Townscape', *Planning Perspectives* 24 (2009): 3. The entire issue of this journal is devoted to Sharp. See also Ceci Flinn, '"Exeter Phoenix": Politics and the Rebuilding of the Blitzed City', *Southern History* 30 (2008): 104–27.

[46] Clement Orillard, 'Urban Design: The Building of a Transnational Field in the English-Speaking World', notes how Sharp's concept of 'Townscape' did move beyond British borders after the war and became part of transnational discussions (paper presented at 11th International Conference in Urban History, European Association of Urban History, Faculty of the Arts, Charles University, Prague, August 2012).

Comparing these cases of post-war reconstruction shows how transnational models faced multiple obstacles, which is why I am here arguing that historians should not be carried away by the transnational turn. While planning models might be national or transnational, that did not mean that national, state or city laws existed that would enable implementation. The imposition of centralized planning directed by national governments, particularly where national governments controlled the allocation of the financial and material resources needed for implementing plans, could challenge the place of both transnational and local models. Local politics and local economic conditions could tip the orientation of planning from one model to another. We must be aware of cases where native residents of bombed cities argued that only natives should guide reconstruction and that guidance should be shaped by cultural and architectural traditions particular to each city. While some cities hired outside planning consultants or staged planning competitions open to national or international experts, others restricted competitions to local architects/planners. We must consider the extent to which the production of plans was purely the work of experts, and when, if at all, was input from the public solicited and influential. Another important factor was the personality of the planners and how they interacted with officials on all levels and with the public.[47] All of these things could also support or disrupt continuities in planning on all levels.

At the beginning of this chapter, I suggested that comparative studies could provide guidance for historians of rebuilding in cities not yet studied. In a 1948 essay, one scholar stated that Italian law required creation of a Master Plan and open competitions as a basis for rebuilding and that young architects were involved in this process all over the country.[48] However, at least in the literature I have found, historians of reconstruction in Italian cities like Florence have mostly focused narrowly on architecture in damaged areas rather than contextualizing rebuilding within a larger urban vision.[49] Much is yet to be learned about reconstruction in Eastern Europe, including the former USSR, where there was a great deal of war damage. The same is true for China, where

---

[47]   Leo Grebler, *Europe's Reborn Cities* (Washington, DC: Urban Land Institute, 1956), 69, describes planners unfairly as 'a motley group' that took a second seat to civil engineers and local politicians. He saw August Perret of France and Rudolf Hillebrecht of Germany as exceptions.

[48]   Eugenio Giacomo Faludi, 'Reconstruction: Italy', *Task* nos 7–8 (1948): 37–8.

[49]   See the essays in Carlo Cresti et al., *Firenze 1945–1947. I Progetti della 'Ricostruzione'* (Florence: Alinea, 1995). Judi Loach, 'QT8: A Neglected Chapter in the History of Modern Town Planning', in Thomas Dekker, ed., *The Modern City Revisited* (New York: Spon Press, 2000) examines a modernist garden suburb built after 1947 in a Milan suburb partly on an artificial hill made from the ruins of buildings destroyed in the war.

fighting continued after 1945 as a civil war.[50] There are language barriers here for me, but perhaps comparative studies could bring both Chinese and Eastern European scholars into the dialogue about reconstruction.

While aware of the interactions between transnational, national and local planning models, processes and relevant laws, there are some other things that historians researching new cases of post-war urban reconstruction and renovation should keep in mind. In seeking to determine the bases of planning decisions, it is important to learn about the role played in each case by local social structures, culture and politics in defining key values and identities sensed collectively and individually by residents.[51] Paradigm shifts from political, intellectual, social and cultural history can influence the selection of sources and the changing character of urban history. Another challenge in understanding past decisions is investigating not just the nature of officially endorsed plans but also all rejected entries that had been submitted in a competition or prolonged planning process. Unfortunately, much too often the characteristics of unsuccessful proposals were not presented to the public, and the proposals themselves were not saved in archives, although they can perhaps be found in the records of private companies or architects. Moreover, it would be good to try to discover the essential ideas and tendencies of planners but also of agency heads, members of town councils, competition jurors and so on.[52] Were these individuals influenced primarily by transnational ideas or by local traditions? Historians must answer this question.

---

[50] For a recent study on Chinese rebuilding, see Toby Lincoln, 'The Rural and Urban at War: Invasion and Reconstruction in China during the Anti-Japanese War of Resistance', *The Journal of Urban History* 38 (2012): 114–32.

[51] The most recent collection of essays on post-war planning is John Pendlebury, Erdem Erten and Peter J Larkham, eds, *Alternative Visions of Post-War Reconstruction* (London: Routledge, 2015). This contains chapters on Italy, Britain, Japan, Poland, France and the United States, and a common subject is the interaction of local and transnational concepts of urban design.

[52] For example, in the city of Boston, a major planning competition was staged in late 1944 to encourage modernization, even though that city had not been bombed. Given the academic appointments in the late 1930s of Walter Gropius, the founder of the Bauhaus, and Martin Wagner, the pre-war planner of Berlin, at the new School of Design at Harvard University, transnational models were certainly present. There were 90 entries, and a book containing the three top prize winners and items from those receiving honourable mention awards was published in 1945. The prize winners, chosen by a conservative jury, combined some elements of modernization and some suggestions on how to maintain Boston's traditions. Radical elements were not implemented. The complete entries of all but the top three were not saved, nor were minutes of the jury meetings. For information on this, see my introduction to a new facsimile edition the *Boston Context* in Jeffry M. Diefendorf, *The Boston Contest of 1944* (London: Routledge, 2015).

PART II

Chapter 6

Urban Governance and Prostitution in Eighteenth-Century Port Cities in France and England

Marion Pluskota*[1]

Initiated by social sciences and studies on urbanization, comparative methodology in historical studies has been primarily used by contemporary historians, who tend to have access to larger, sometimes more comparable amounts of data than early modern historians. The non-systematic archival of documents and the complexity of national and regional legal and socio-economic organizations are also common obstacles to neat comparisons between countries, cities and culture in the pre-modern period. Nevertheless, sociologists and historians have been concerned with issues linked with comparative methodology in social history for more than a century: Marc Bloch, for instance, claimed that comparative studies were necessary, as they are *'seules capables de dissiper le mirage des fausses causes locales'.*[2] In other words, by adding different levels or systems to the comparative process (that is, from local to transnational), comparative methodology should allow us to define more thoroughly the influence of each variable on a precise phenomenon and therefore challenge arguments which prioritize the role of local governance.

Theoretical research, over the past 20 years, has focused on the most reliable manner to use comparative methodology, in order to find patterns that can be applied to different societies or different cultures.[3] Working first on quantitative

* The author would like to thank Rebecca Madgin and Nicolas Kenny for their comments, as well as the colleagues who attended our sessions at the European Urban History Association in Prague (2010) and at the Urban History Association in New York (2012) and held a very fruitful discussion.

[1] This chapter is based upon a larger study on prostitution and social control in eighteenth-century ports, see Marion Pluskota, *Prostitution and Social Control in Eighteenth-Century Ports* (Abingdon: Routledge, 2015).

[2] Quoted in Robert Binion, 'Marianne au foyer. Révolution politique et transition démographique en France et aux États-Unis', *Population* 55 (2000): 81–104, 87.

[3] For extensive bibliographical references, see Thomas Denk, 'Comparative Multilevel Analysis: Proposal for a Methodology', *International Journal of Social Research Methodology* 13 (2010): 29–39.

data, historians gradually integrated qualitative research and more empirical data to back up their arguments and to get a deeper understanding of the influence of the environment surrounding the subject studied.[4] However, comparisons based on qualitative data remain rare among urban historians of the pre-modern period. Economic developments, demographic increase and even crime rates have been the subject of comparison, but more abstract concepts such as urban governance are by nature more difficult to compare. Thus, the question remains of a possible comparative methodology that encompasses and goes beyond the issues of missing data and background differences. This chapter is therefore an attempt to show how urban governance and daily policing of the city were influenced by different systems, from local specificities to transnational trends and international events. The focus is set on the response of the municipalities of Bristol and Nantes to increasing concerns over prostitution between approximately 1750 and 1830. By comparing these two cities, I aim to point out the variables which influenced the elites' response to prostitution and how their attitudes changed, revealing a complex relationship between different levels of urban governance. This chapter will start with a brief reflection upon the process of comparison in social history before analysing the various levels of influence in the response of the municipalities to growing concerns over prostitution. The conclusion will emphasize the importance of local context and underline the strengths and weaknesses of comparative history in understanding urban governance.

How to Compare Urban Governance?

The decision to articulate my research with a comparison results from questioning the social organization of these cities and the evolution of attitudes towards prostitution. Schutt highlighted four necessary stages to build a systematic qualitative comparative historical study: (1) to develop the premise of the investigation, identifying events and concepts that may explain the phenomena; (2) to choose the case(s) (location, nation, region) to examine; (3) to examine the similarities and the differences; (4) based on the information gathered, propose a causal explanation for the phenomena.[5] I aim to demonstrate that there existed common cultural and moral values that transcended national differences, determining the attitude of contemporaries towards prostitution. I posit that the end of the eighteenth-century saw the gradual imposition of

---

[4]   David A. Smith, 'Method and Theory in Comparative Urban Studies', *International Journal of Comparative Sociology*, 32 (1991): 39–58, 39.

[5]   Russell K. Schutt, *Investigating the Social World* (University of Massachusetts: Sage, 2012).

a stricter control over prostitutes, leading eventually to a listing of prostitutes and a criminalization *de facto* but that the means put in place to increase this control were largely determined by the local environment and local context. The comparative process, however, must be done at different levels in order to perceive the contrasts between cases. This means that what happened at a sublocal level, in the subsystem of community control, must be compared to the actions taken at the local and national levels, in relation to the subsystems of municipal legislation and the national legal system. In order to do this, it is important to focus on the 'connective story':[6] for Bristol and Nantes, moral panic and fears linked to the American war of Independence, the French Revolution and later on the Napoleonic wars were push factors towards a reinforcement of the structures of social control.

Research Design

Building a research plan on early modern cities with a comparative and qualitative approach in mind demands careful research on what can be compared. Indeed, the legal structures of the early modern period varied considerably from one city to another, let alone between two countries. The various layers of legal systems at work in early modern cities (at a community/neighbourhood level, by the police and eventually by the courts) mean that a strict comparison of systems is not possible, and thus the choice of subjects must be done at a meta-level. Nantes and Bristol appeared as interesting objects of research to study changes in urban governance because of their comparable socio-economic development. Legal and cultural settings were different but the cities' fundamental structures in place at the start of the period, in 1750, were similar. The economy of the city was turned towards the port and therefore a large number of male migrants regularly came ashore. Similarly, female migration towards eighteenth-century urban centres is well documented.[7] Both cities were socially mixed and the process of social segregation, which appeared in the nineteenth century, was still largely inexistent. Finally, municipal governance in both cities was dominated by rich merchants.[8] Differences in the legal

---

6   See Carl H. Nightingale, in this volume.

7   For instance, Pamela Sharpe, ed., *Women, Gender, and Labour Migration: Historical and Global Perspectives: Routledge Research in Gender and History* (London: Routledge, 2001).

8   Guy Saupin, *Nantes au XVIIe siècle, vie politique et société urbaine* (Rennes: Presses Universitaires de Rennes, 1996), 85; Alfred Harvey, *Bristol, a Historical and Topographical Account of the City* (London: Methuen and Co., 1906), 220; Peter Fleming, 'The Emergence of Modern Bristol', in Madge Dresser and Philip Ollerenshaw, eds, *The Making of Modern Bristol* (Tiverton: Redcliffe Press, 1996), 1–24, 13.

system and juridical organization were significant but the similarities in the socio-economic development outweighed these discrepancies: these were two port cities facing similar problems, but possessed different means to deal with the development of prostitution. Indeed, for both municipalities, issues with public order, population's morality and risks of infectious diseases were prevalent when touching upon the subject of prostitution. Because the core of the comparison focuses on the evolution of abstract concepts, similar tangential socio-economic developments need to exist to allow the comparison to work.

A wide range of sources needs to be collected to define and compare evolutions in urban governance. Prostitution, like many other areas of research, has produced limited data, which is often not easily comparable. Only once the corpus of archives has been created is it possible to categorize the documents by type: because of the specificity of the subject, and indeed the provincial locations, focusing only on one type of archives would be detrimental to the research, as the material available would rarely be sufficient. The details in the archives differ according to the institutional and social rank of the producer and this must be kept in mind whilst researching urban governance: the closer to the street, the better the view on the practice. As Arlette Farge argues, the necessary formal language of judicial archives forms a barrier between the historian and the reality of the *mentalités*.[9] Therefore, both official (legal texts) and non-official sources (newspapers, correspondence) must be used and compared to judicial practice. The qualitative research must be backed up by quantitative findings in order to root the evolution of *mentalités* in daily practices and customs. This relates especially to the police and officials on the streets who usually dealt with prostitutes. The top-down approach to legal changes can only be applied with restrictions to the work of police and watchmen on the streets. A new, more dynamic understanding of urban governance arises when daily practice and official documents are compared and when the dialectic in place at different levels, between the national discourse and the local response, between municipal regulations and daily practice of the lower officials, is highlighted.

Transnational Discourses, Local Aspirations

The historiography of Bristol and Nantes shows that much work is still needed to understand the social construction of these cities and the relations between the inhabitants and the elites, their perceptions and beliefs regarding urban social control and the imposition of new policies to tackle growing social problems.

---

9   Arlette Farge, *La Vie Fragile: Violence, Pouvoirs et Solidarités à Paris au XVIIIe siècle* (Paris: Seuil, 1986), 8.

In this chapter, social control refers to the concerns of the inhabitants over certain categories of people and the formal and informal means put in place to supervise these people and prevent them from behaving in a manner contrary to common beliefs and practices (loud, disorderly behaviour) and against the common good (economic or moral).[10] Prevention can be done through criminalization and regulation at an official level or in a more informal way by neighbours and close relations.[11]

Socio-economic developments in Bristol and Nantes during the eighteenth century were comparable: both cities had mercantile elites, seconded by provincial nobility and influential religious figures. Their economies were thriving until the second third of the century when they started to decline, despite having developed small industries within the city. The concerns of the middling sort in Bristol and Nantes were mainly focused on the protection of the city's economic interests, by encouraging trade and by making the city safer and favourable to commercial exchange, but also by managing a constant flow of migrants. As Barry observed while analysing the urban legislation concerning the poor, 'such aspirations are normally described as "social control", aimed at the unruly poor, but they were also important as an affirmation of civic, bourgeois identity'.[12] As such, both municipalities kept an eye on the development of prostitution in their city. Though Bristol and Nantes never communicated directly on the subject of prostitution, information on social control and prostitution passed between the two cities thanks to national and transnational networks. Indeed a common understanding of the risks linked with these women emerged, via international debates and publications but also through common values that transcended cultural and structural differences.[13]

The discourse of the elites on prostitution in the eighteenth century was not uniform and to a certain extent reminds us of the hesitations of nineteenth-century social commentators upon labouring women's sexuality.[14] Firstly, in Bristol, the discourse on moral issues, reminiscent of previous campaigns against prostitution and immorality such as the ones led by the Societies for

---

[10]   For an in-depth discussion of the concept of social control, see Clive Emsley, Eric Johnson and Pieter Spierenburg, *Social Control in Europe v2: 1800–2000* (Ohio State University Press, 2004), 1–21.

[11]   Robert Muchembled, *Une histoire de la violence* (Paris: Seuil, 2008), 387–8.

[12]   James Barry, 'Bristol pride: Civic Identity in Bristol c. 1640–1775', in Dresser and Ollerenshaw, *The Making of Modern Bristol*, 25–47, 35.

[13]   This idea of common understanding or shared beliefs can be seen in many of the articles published in this collection. See for example Polasky, Nightingale, Platt and Couperus and Ewen in this volume.

[14]   Frank Mort, *Dangerous Sexuality: Medicomoral Politics in England since 1830* (London: Routledge, 2000), 37.

the Reformation of Manners,[15] appeared in every legal text published by the municipality. Indeed, the threat of immorality and of setting bad examples for children is continuously presented as an argument to reduce prostitution or, if its suppression was not possible, to confine prostitution and hide it from the eyes of the citizens.[16] The moral discourse on prostitution was not specific to Bristol and Nantes: this was part of a transnational discourse, in London and Paris, but also in Amsterdam and Seville showing, at the macro-level, the interplay of local and international factors.[17]

Secondly, the health risk carried by these women appeared constantly in the writings of the heads of the army and navy.[18] The role of syphilis and sexual diseases in weakening soldiers and sailors is not to be ignored: though death was rarely the result of such infection, the number of men needing days off in the hospital remained important all along the century.[19] With the Revolution and Napoleonic wars, the issue became even more acute, officials blaming prostitutes for the spread of the disease.[20] But parallel to the discourses on immorality and diseases, literary commentators and romantic writers drew a more sensitive picture of the young prostitute: from the mid-century onwards, the 'wretchedness' of a woman's life was increasingly discussed to explain a woman's fall into prostitution.[21] The common description, following the literary conventions of the time, focused on a poor single woman who had no family or help and found refuge in prostitution to survive. Under this frame of mind, the upper-middle class tended to focus on the young and 'saveable' girls, these 'young creatures', who could be re-educated and after some time, as the Grand jurors of Bristol expressed it, 'might be restored to their families and friends'.[22] The common discourse that existed in France and England at that time led to an interesting exchange between capital cities (where the main discourse was

---

[15]   Edward Bristow, *Vice and Vigilance, Purity Movements in Britain since 1700* (Dublin: Gill and Macmillan, 1977), 4.

[16]   Bristol Record Office (BRO), JQS/Friendly Societies/13–14; 08823/1a – Asylum for Poor Orphan Girls; Archives Municipales de Nantes (AMN), FF 291.

[17]   Lotte van de Pol, *The Burgher and the Whore* (Oxford: Oxford University Press, 2011); Mary E. Perry, *Crime and Society in Early Modern Seville* (University Press of New England, 1980).

[18]   Stanislav Andreski, *Syphilis, Puritanism and Witch Hunts* (New York: St Martin's Press, 1989) and AMN, 1D8.

[19]   Jean-Pierre Goubert, 'Le phénomène épidémique en Bretagne à la fin du XVIIIe siècle', *Annales. Économies, Sociétés, Civilisations*, 24 (1969), 1562–88, 1577–8.

[20]   Linda E. Meriens, *The Secret Malady, Venereal Disease in Eighteenth-Century Britain and France* (University Press of Kentucky, 1997).

[21]   See John Fielding, *A Plan for a Preservatory and Reformatory for the Benefit of Deserted Girls and Penitent Prostitutes* (London, 1758).

[22]   BRO, JQS/P/95.

forged) and provincial cities, which adapted London and Parisian policies to their own environment. As such, this chapter, whilst focusing on the local level in Bristol and Nantes, is also informed by broader international considerations and indeed sees local determinants as a key part of the transnational discourse on prostitution.

National Trends and Local Contexts

National legislation in both England and France on eighteenth-century prostitution remained extremely vague. Prostitution in itself was not an offence, however legislators were aware of the existence of a network surrounding these women that needed supervision. They also became aware over the century of the close link between territorialization and the practice of prostitution. Indeed the 1751 *Act for the better preventing Thefts and Robberies, and for regulating Places of publick Entertainment, and punishing Persons keeping disorderly Houses (sic)*, which was introduced in response to the riots sparked off in the bawdy houses of the Strand in London, is an example of legislation regulating the network and places of prostitution. Fines on tenants of disorderly houses were meant to prevent the gathering of disorderly people: in the records of charges brought against tenants, they were accused of encouraging tippling, whoring and illegal games.[23] Interestingly, this legislation did not target prostitutes directly, as a specific category: they were not considered as a specific group needing specific legislation, as it was the case a century later. Henderson argues that the majority of demands for new legislation concerning prostitution in England did not ask for toleration but encouraged stricter rules against prostitutes and their networks.[24] These demands reflected the extent of the understanding of prostitution and disorderly behaviour in general: in order to maintain the peace, the locations where disorderly behaviour could develop had to be supervised, suggesting that the focus of the regulation shifted from the disorderly persons to the disorderly places. This shift of focus towards the location rather than the person was apparent in both countries: in France, the royal declaration of 1778 denounced the publicity of prostitutes in the streets, quays, alleys and windows of French cities.[25]

Thus, concerns for the morality of urban citizens and focus on spaces of prostitution arose in both countries and had a certain impact mid-century on the daily policing of the two port cities. Though only London watchmen and

---

[23] Parliament Records, HL/PO/PU/1/1751/25G2n28.
[24] Tony Henderson, *Disorderly Women in Eighteenth-Century London* (London: Longman, 1999), 100.
[25] AMN, FF 291.

Parisian *commissaires* were specifically asked to look out for prostitutes in their districts, Bristol and Nantes police actions against prostitutes followed a similar trend.[26] In 1749, 1750 and 1752, disorderly houses on Tower Lane in Bristol were raided by watchmen and constables. The aim was to arrest the prostitutes for the night, hoping that they moved to other places after being released. These stings had very little success over the long term but the tendency to target places instead of people remained. Watchmen kept an eye on disorderly houses, sometimes even looking through the keyhole to find evidence.[27] Watchmen or night constables were often called as witnesses in trials against tenants of disorderly houses and their knowledge of the district and therefore of what occurred in these houses could work against tenants. This territorialization and focus on the location of prostitution also occurred in France. Catherine Denys has shown that the territorialization of the police in France occurred in the eighteenth century and a more thorough division of the urban environment led to a better control and supervision of the population. Since 1722, the *commissaires* of Nantes were assigned a district to supervise. Though they were supposed to shift district every two to six months, it seems that this rule was quickly forgotten. Whilst local conditions dictated the manner in which prostitution was policed, the impetus for territorialization came from London and Paris. Though the policing systems were clearly distinct from each other, territorialization became a general trend in both countries. As we have seen above, the Disorderly House Act was a response to riots that occurred in London. In France, historians of the police have shown that the Parisian model was often used in provincial cities to organize a (semi-) professionalized police: Parisian *commissaires* were working from a city plan since the end of the seventeenth century.[28] The interplay of local and national factors in France and England ensured that whilst policies emanating in the capital cities became a key aspect of change, they were inextricably connected to both international ideas and local specificities.

Lastly, to understand the changes in attitudes towards prostitutes, it is essential to look at the evolution of the international context. After the war of independence in the American colonies and the return of the soldiers on land, a crime wave hit England and fears of criminals roaming the country and civil unrest were propagated through newspapers and hearsay.[29] In 1783, Bristol

---

[26]   Susan Conner, 'Politics, Prostitution, and the Pox in Revolutionary Paris, 1789–1799', *Journal of Social History* (1989): 713–34, 729.

[27]   BRO, JQS/P/63.

[28]   See Vincent Milliot, dir., *Les mémoires policiers, 1750–1850. Écritures et pratiques policières du Siècle des Lumières au Second Empire* (Rennes: Presses Universitaires de Rennes, 2006).

[29]   Elaine Reynolds, 'Sir John Fielding, Sir Charles Whitworth, and the Westminster Night Watch Act, 1770–1775', *Criminal Justice History, Policing and War in Europe* 16 (2002), 1–20, 11.

elites also had to face a riot over bridge taxes. Before the feeling of panic could subside, the political turmoil on the continent affected the English population. Indeed the French Revolution and the Empire had a great influence on English attitudes: the fear of invasion and of popular riots was widespread amongst the English population.[30] As Wilson explains, 'invasion anxieties manifested themselves in other worries: of health and morality and religion'.[31] These worries did not spare Bristol inhabitants and it directly influenced the development of charities to increase social control over the labouring classes.[32] The last decade of the century in Bristol saw a rise in the number of charitable societies organized by women from the elite or middle class, in an attempt to control the morality of the labouring sort and make the poor less susceptible to be influenced by radicals.[33] The asylum for the poor orphan girls, opened in 1794, aimed to 'rescue them from this danger [moral corruption] by a proper education, instilling early principles of religion, morality and industry'.[34] The hatred and fear of immorality, which historians suggest was born from an end-of-the-century 'moral panic', were constantly at the core of the debate. Hannah More's *Cheap Repository Tracts*, published between 1795 and 1798 were another form of social control 'imposed' upon the poor. These tracts repeated moral condemnations of the beginning of the century: they denounced drunkenness, debauchery, idleness,

---

[30]   On moral panic and crime waves see Peter King, 'Moral Panics and Violent Street Crime 1750–2000 : a Comparative Perspective', in Barry Godfrey, Clive Emsley and Graeme Dunstall, eds, *Comparative Histories of Crime* (Cullompton: Willan Publishing, 2003), 53–71; David Lemmings, *Moral Panics, the Media and the Law in Early Modern England* (Basingstoke: Palgrave, 2009), especially 195–266.

[31]   Ben Wilson, *Decency and Disorder* (London: Faber, 2007), 9.

[32]   Steve Poole, 'Popular Politics in Bristol, Somerset and Wiltshire, 1791–1805' (PhD diss., University of Bristol, 1992); Philip Jones, 'The Bristol Bridge Riot and its Antecedents: Eighteenth-Century Perceptions of the Crowd', *Journal of British Studies* 19 (1980):74–92; Steve Poole, 'To be a Bristolian: Civic Identity and the Social Order, 1750–1850', in Dresser and Ollerenshaw, eds, *The Making of Modern Bristol*, 76–95, 83–4.

[33]   Mary Fissel, *Patients, Power and the Poor* (Cambridge: Cambridge University Press, 2002), 91; John Cranidge, *A Mirror for the Burgesses and the Commonality of the City of Bristol* (Bristol, 1818); Some earlier charities: the Somersetshire charity for blind boys and poor lying-in women existed since 1774, as well as Mrs Ann Thurnston's charity for the relief of nine poor pregnant women per year, founded in 1754: BRO, AC/JS/13/8 Smyth Family of Ashton Court, Jarrit Smith Papers, Personal miscellanea, Annual report of the Somersetshire Society; BRO, 04190 – 04191, Mrs Ann Thurston's charity; after her death, the sum was to be managed by the mayor and mayoress, which emphasizes once again the close link between charity and municipal governance.

[34]   BRO, JQS/Friendly Societies/ 13–14 (PPV and Female Clubs); 08823/1a – Asylum for Poor Orphan Girls.

gambling and riotous assembly.[35] To respond to these anxieties, one establishment was created and directed solely at prostitutes in Bristol: the Female Penitentiary, which opened in 1801. The committee of the Female Penitentiary was designed to rescue prostitutes and approved without reservation the fact that the inmates 'were considered the outcast of the society' but that they would eventually be reinstated within the community as industrious women and not as consuming agents.[36]

In 1804, the Bristol Female Penitentiary counted 168 subscribers: 20 of them were from the clergy, seven subscribers were ladies (three single or widowed and four married to a subscriber), but the bulk of subscribers consisted of upper-middle-class women (77) and the rest of the subscribers were men.[37] Based on their titles, it appears that the Bristol penitentiary attracted members of the gentry, as did the London Magdalen Hospital when it opened: 54 gentlemen (esquires) and gentlewomen donated to the hospital, which accounts for 32 per cent of the subscribers.[38] However of the men and ladies' committees which supervised the Penitentiary, each being respectively composed of 28 men and 17 women, the gentry was represented only by four men and one lady. Relatively speaking, the only Bristol charity for prostitutes was mainly supervised by the merchant upper-middle class, as was the London Magdalen Hospital 40 years earlier. The official director of the penitentiary was the mayor, and the two sheriffs were chosen as vice-presidents: Bristol common council, in this charitable institution, as in many others, was clearly represented by its official members and by the families of merchants who shared official and charitable positions. This institution remained their main tool to impose control over these disorderly people: incapacitated by a disreputable police and an overcrowded workhouse, the governing elite followed this path to facilitate the supervision of these women.

The initiatives taken by the upper-middle classes to increase control over the labouring classes reflect Couperus and Ewen's argument developed in this book.[39] Parallel to the individuals promoting the Urban Internationale and relying on their networks to succeed, Bristol elites were influenced by their networks within and without Bristol. Daily contacts occurred between London and Bristol, through commercial transactions and local publications, as proved

[35] Susan Pedersen, 'Hannah More Meets Simple Simon: Tracts, Chapbooks, and Popular Culture in Late Eighteenth-Century England', *Journal of British Studies* 25 (1986): 84–113.

[36] BRO, 17567 (7) – Bristol Female Penitentiary; Jenny Batchelor, 'Industry in Distress: Reconfiguring Femininity and Labor in the Magdalen House', *Eighteenth-Century Life* 28 (2004): 1–20, 10–11 on London Magdalen hospital's aims.

[37] BRO, 17567 (7).

[38] Donna T. Andrew, *Philanthropy and Police, London Charity in the Eighteenth Century* (Princeton: Princeton University Press, 1989), 117.

[39] See Stefan Couperus and Shane Ewen in this volume.

by the length of the columns on London political news in Bristol newspapers. Material and immaterial exchanges with London were being reinforced by the situation of Bristol as an international port, directly influenced by the political and economic upheavals of the Empire. Thus the extent of elites' and middle-classes' networks went far beyond the boundaries of the city, but eventually the initiatives taken by these people revealed their own political and social agenda, based on very personal motives. They used their network's knowledge of subsystems, what was done in London against prostitutes, poor pregnant women, to modulate the system in their own city.

Local Specificities

The reactions to prostitution and the social control imposed over prostitutes at the end of the century in Nantes differed greatly from the means put in place by Bristolians, although the initial concerns were similar. The upheavals of the Revolution and the civil war that surrounded Nantes during the last decade of the century led to a different approach to the understanding of the 'risks' linked with prostitution. Nantes suffered from the replacement of its municipality by delegates from Paris and time was needed until the upper-middle class recovered supervision of the municipality. Instead of implementing national laws and national ideas through local organizations, as was the case in Bristol, governance in Nantes during the Revolution favoured the transplantation not just of ideas but also of officials. These differing approaches did however have one thing in common: the idea of national control over local contexts was constant in both France and England. Through this example, the urban historian can understand the spatial complexities involved in the process of urban governance in Britain and France during this period.

With the start of the Revolution, the city elite gradually lost its prerogatives and direct influence over the control and policing of the city to the new administration and more importantly to the lower officials. Indeed, little information on day-to-day governance of the city remains for the first years of the Republic and war against the Chouans, but it seems that the delegates relied heavily on lower officials to keep the city running. These lower officials remained in charge throughout the Revolution and Empire: a certain structural continuity in the police remained, given that out of six *commissaires* in 1792, two had already been in charge before 1789 and a *commissaire-inspecteur* was chosen in 1790, after a career of 20 years as a *commissaire*.[40]

---

[40]   Vincent Danet, 'Les commissaires de police de la ville de Nantes au XVIIIe siècle (1720–1792)', *Annales de Bretagne et des Pays de l'Ouest* 116 (2009): 39–72, 57–8.

There were structural differences between both police forces in Bristol and Nantes: cities in England, except London, did not develop a professional police force until the mid-nineteenth century whereas Nantes had one since the beginning of the eighteenth century.[41] The role of the municipal police had become essential in the urban governance of the port city. In France, the police system was based on a (semi-)professionalized police force, with officials – *commissaries* – seconded by the *garde bourgeoise* who worked under the same system as the watchmen. This police followed the order of the *lieutenant général de police* (Parisian model) who worked in partnership with the *procureur du roi* and the city council to promulgate and implement the laws. The *commissaires* had extensive functions in the eighteenth century such as 'inventorying properties, hearing criminal complaints, conducting searches' and they could also act as a judge if necessary.[42] Their knowledge of the urban territory and its inhabitants was determinant in the effective supervision of the population.

Before the turmoil of the Revolution, the *commissaires* were mostly 'reactive' towards prostitution, arresting prostitutes only if they committed an offence, but the constant state of war, the violent Chouans uprisings in Brittany and the civil war in Vendée, were the starting point in Nantes for a campaign of suspicion against prostitutes, which eventually led to the official regulation of prostitution. Despite continuity in the officials in charge, the number of arrests and interrogations of prostitutes increased. The municipality claimed that they feared people coming from outside the city would organize riots and targeted those 'foreigners' as a potential danger. The condemnation of prostitutes for disorderly behaviour intensified, the need for control was made more and more explicit, and supervision of prostitutes was gradually implemented. The evolution of the listing of prostitutes corresponded with an increasingly suspicious attitude but also a more methodical approach to the control of the population by the administration and the police.[43] In 1804, the first real attempt to list prostitutes by districts was made: 68 names were recorded in the busy port district of La Fosse and was followed by others, for most districts, and on a yearly

---

[41] Clive Emsley, *Crime and Society in England, 1750–1900* (London: Longman, 1996), 64.

[42] Alan Williams, *The Police of Paris 1718–1789* (Baton-Rouge: University of Louisiana Press, 1979), 120–21.

[43] On the evolution of the administration under the Revolution and Empire: Robert Badinter dir., *Une autre justice: contributions à l'histoire de la justice sous la Révolution* (Paris: Fayard, 1989); Emmanuel Berger, *La justice pénale sous la Révolution: les enjeux d'un modèle judiciaire libéral* (Rennes: Presses Universitaires de Rennes, 2008); Jacqueline Lafon, *La Révolution française face au système judiciaire d'Ancien Régime* (Genève: Droz, 2001).

basis.[44] The specific experience in Nantes was that the momentum was given by the inspector and the *commissaires* themselves, without recorded incentives from the municipality or from the national government (neither the Empire nor the Restoration).[45]

Comparing the discourses and practices at different levels in these two cities shows the essential barriers preventing the implementation of new legislations, but it also highlights the means put in place to diffuse new ideas and practices. The lack of well-organized infrastructure could weaken the application of certain measures. In Bristol, the watchmen and constables did not arrest more prostitutes despite pleas by the elite to reduce public debauchery. In Nantes, the breaking down (for some years) of the traditional municipal organization slowed down the exchange of ideas and propelled lower officials in charge of policing the city, despite attempts from the national government to supervise urban governance. The revolutionary context meant that some traditional power relations became obsolete and, in terms of urban governance and the disappearance of the *lieutenant général*, opened the path to lower officials to implement new organizational structures. Furthermore, the implementation of Parisian officials and their failure in controlling the city also shows how knowledge of the local context is necessary for sound urban governance. Clear, simple transpositions of officials or practices from the capital cities to provincial ones rarely led to a successful control of the city. However, at the same time the success of local policies allowed the development of a national pattern in prostitution control, through the development of a system of regulation in France and charities in England. By comparing each system, it clearly appears that it is the dialogue between the national and the local that leads to the evolution of policies and urban governance. This focus also shows how national policies trickled down to the lower officials and the streets: from an idealized image of the poor prostitute that needed help, the encounters with prostitutes and their representations were influenced by the social and spatial distance between officials and these women. National discourses rarely represented the reality of the situation, many adaptations were needed at the local level, and the daily practice of the law was built according to the lower officials' prerogatives. The role of urban institutions, especially during troubled times, was taken over by lower officials, the backbone of urban governance. Ultimately, by using a comparative methodology, this research demonstrates the existence of

---

[44]   It is unclear if only the *commissaires* of these two districts of the city had to do it or each *commissaire* was asked to do so, but their lists subsequently went missing. Sections 13 and 14 of Nantes were close to the port and were known to be very populated and with many lodging-houses.

[45]   See Michel Vincineau, *Proxénétisme, débauche ou prostitution depuis 1810* (Bruxelles: Bruylant, 2006) for an analysis of the Code Penal of 1810 and its impact on prostitution.

interconnections between multi-level governance and individual agency, the two not being mutually exclusive.

Conclusion

The methodology followed in this chapter highlights the relationship between provincial and capital cities (two subsystems) and the extent to which these port cities were able to act autonomously. It is evident that Bristol and Nantes were influenced by Paris and London (for example, the Magdalen Hospital) but their independence in terms of legislation and social control appears conspicuous when studying prostitution. Despite two different political contexts at the end of the century, the same fears invaded the officials in charge. However, the autonomy of officials and the importance of personal initiatives in the treatment of prostitution show that Nantes and Bristol were responding to prostitution in a manner that they judged more adequate to the local problem. They used national legislation, often constructed with the capital cities in mind, as a very loose framework for their own practice. A common understanding of the difficulties of the poor and unruly existed in Nantes and Bristol: interconnections between systems had an impact on the local level, but it differed qualitatively, according to the organizational structures in place in these cities.

The role of *commissaires* and of personal initiatives in urban governance is essential in this shift of attitude, as was the Bristol upper-middle-classes' desire to improve the morality of the poorest and guarantee their own safety. The police system in France was more developed than in England and it became an efficient tool to impose social control. By contrast, in England, the elites relied more systematically on their abilities to strengthen their networks by organizing charitable associations and multiplying establishments to help or confine the poor and potentially disorderly people. This was particularly the case at a provincial level, where the means employed to develop a police system were far less important than in London. By adding to the analysis of the 'vertical process'[46] (from national to sublocal), an intrasystem comparison[47] (study of the relations between the different levels), it is possible to improve our knowledge of the history of urban governance in both France and England. Personal initiatives and local specificities proved to be as important as the national and legal framework and international events in the understanding of the gradual regulation of prostitution: they responded to a transnational discourse over prostitutes, which asked for more caution and better supervision of these women.

---

[46] Bas Denter and Karen Mossberger, 'Building Blocks for a Methodology for Comparative Urban Political Research', *Urban Affairs Review* 41 (2006): 550–71, 555.

[47] Denk, 'Comparative Multilevel Analysis', 29.

Thus, the intrasystem comparison is a methodology that leaves enough space to study the effects of context over the relation between variables at a subsystem level.[48] Only a thorough analysis of Nantes and Bristol representations of prostitutes, concerns and means of action can highlight the motivations and the role of the different social actors in the evolution of social control over prostitutes.

The nineteenth century saw multiple correspondences and exchanges of statistics concerning urban problems between municipalities and experts at an international level.[49] From 1835 onwards, the Nantes Royal Society of Medicine regularly organized congresses on venereal diseases and the means to prevent its spread. These meetings were paralleled with intense correspondence between provincial societies of medicine, creating and reinforcing strong network ties between scientists, whose debates and conclusions reached an international level.[50] This however was not a new phenomenon: already in the eighteenth century urban governance was influenced by general trends noticeable at a European level (increasing concerns over prostitution, territorialization of the police force, gradual differentiation between prostitutes and the poor). Local contexts were determinant in modelling the municipalities' response to social problems but external factors had a real impact upon urban governance. A comparative approach shines new light on the interplay between systems and the influences of each variable on changing attitudes towards prostitution.

[48]   Denk, 'Comparative Multilevel Analysis', 30.

[49]   Robert Nye, *A Mad, Mad World, Crime, Madness and Politics in Modern France: The Medical Concept of National Decline* (Princeton: Princeton University Press, 1984) on the rise of scientists as experts in policy making.

[50]   For instance, the conclusions of one of the meetings are discussed in *British and Foreign Medical Review*, 5 (1838).

Chapter 7
Comparing Urban Reform in London and Brussels

Janet Polasky

The overcrowding of London and Brussels, the capitals of the first two industrialized nations, deeply troubled nineteenth-century urban reformers. Industrial production required a concentrated labour force, but the workers inundating London and Brussels who sheltered nightly with their families in the teeming rookeries and shadowy impasses threatened to disrupt the urban centres of the very nations they were building. This urban chaos spawned by industrialization called out for comparison across national borders, as urban reformers acknowledged their common plight. Historians have not been as ready to address questions posed by transnational social forces or to compare local political contingencies evolving within two different national contexts.

In the capitals of their industrializing societies, both undergirded by a strong foundation of laissez-faire principles, the Belgians watched the British who in turn observed the Belgians as they pioneered strategies of government intervention to domesticate the labour force in their capitals. On both sides of the Channel, reformers adopted residential dispersion as the solution to urban overcrowding at the end of the nineteenth century. They harnessed the railway, the symbol of the industrial revolution itself, to induce workers to follow the middle class, already commuting to rural villages and suburbs beyond the urban centres. In response to the transnational phenomenon of industrialization, local planners in Brussels as in London redesigned their congested city centres as they reformed their labouring citizenry.

By contrast, ever since the turn of the twentieth century, historians studying urban housing and mobility have worked in isolation, constrained by the bounds of national historiographies. Most have pursued research agendas formulated within their own national context. Even as the European Commission issues White Papers on Sustainable Transport, adopts Green papers on the New Culture for Urban Mobility and confers on the topics of homelessness and housing rights, twenty-first-century scholars overlook the interlocking agendas of the nineteenth-century reformers who set masses of commuters into motion.[1] British historians probe the development of council housing either before or after the First World War while Belgians analyse the evolution of the labour force and patterns of migration across their internal linguistic divide. It is not only languages, but also the cultivation of distinct historiographies on the two sides of the English Channel that separate Belgian from British urban historians.

More than 70 years ago Marc Bloch compared European history to 'a Tower of Babel' with British, German and French historians all asking different questions in ignorance of the work of their neighborus.[2] Raymond Grew introduced the first of two comparative issues of *The American Historical Review* in 1980, by acknowledging that 'among professional historians, comparison is more widely admired than consciously practiced'.[3] In the *Annales, Economies, Sociétés, Civilizations*, Nancy Green suggested that despite the appeals for comparative history issued with renewed urgency each decade, few practitioners had emerged.[4] Comparative history that required spanning distinct historiographical traditions and pursuing research in geographically dispersed archives in a multitude of languages proved too daunting. Few historians have accepted Marc Bloch's challenge to move beyond familiar stories and across national boundaries while focusing on the municipality as the unit of comparison.

---

[1]   Commission of the European Communities, White Paper. *European Transport Policy for 2010: Time to decide* (Brussels, 12.9.2001): http://ec.europa.eu/transport/themes/strat egies/doc/2001_white_paper/lb_com_2001_0370_en.pdf; Commission of the European Communities Brussels, Green Paper. *Towards a New Culture for Urban Mobility* (Brussels, 25.9.2007), http://eur-lex.europa.eu/legal-content/EN/TXT/PDF/?uri=CELEX:52007 DC0551&from=EN; Commission of the European Communities, White Paper. *Roadmap to a Single European Transport Area. Towards a Competitive and Resource Efficient Transport System* (Brussels, 28.3.2011), http://eur-lex.europa.eu/legal-content/EN/TXT/PDF/?u ri=CELEX:52011DC0144&from=EN; and Communication from the Commission to the European Parliament, the Council, the European Economic and Social Committee and the Committee of the Regions, *Together Towards Competitive and Resource-Efficient Urban Mobility* (Brussels, 17.12.2013), http://ec.europa.eu/transport/themes/urban/doc/ump/ com(2013)913_en.pdf.

[2]   Marc Bloch, 'Pour une histoire comparée des sociétés européennes', *Melanges historiques* (1928) 1 (Paris, EHESS, 1983), 1–9. In his presidential address to the International Congress of Historical Sciences, Henri Pirenne also called on his colleagues between the two World Wars to move beyond national traditions. Henri Pirenne, 'De la méthode comparative en histoire', *Ve Congrès international des sciences historiques*, eds G. Des Marez and F.L. Ganshof (Brussels: Weissenbruch, 1923), 19–23; and Lucien Febvre, 'Une esquisse d'histoire comparée', *Revue de Synthèse historique* 37 (1924): 151–2.

[3]   Raymond Grew, 'The Case for Comparing Histories', *The American Historical Review* 85 (1980): 768.

[4]   Nancy Green, 'L'histoire comparative et le champ des études migratoires', *Annales Economies, Sociétés, Civilisations* 45 (1990): 1335–50.

Therein lies the promise of the convergence of transnational and comparative history for the study of urban centres. Marc Bloch counselled comparing the history of 'two neighbouring, contemporaneous societies ... that continuously influenced each other'.[5] The city, he advised, made for closer comparisons than the unwieldy nation-state. At the local level, informed by archival research, historians could ask how transnational social movements traversed varied political terrain. Crossing the national borders made rigid by generations of historians, they could compare responses to similar or related phenomena. Comparative urban historians focused on the municipalities where networking urban reformers practiced could analyse the various strategies, shaped by global mentalities and movements and buffeted by national politics that unfolded pragmatically at a municipal level.

My comparative, transnational study of urban reform began when I followed my interest in what had been cast as a uniquely Belgian scheme of workmen's trains. I was living in Leuven, the university town 20 minutes by rail from my research at the Royal Library in Brussels, located almost on top of the train platforms of the Central Station. Each evening, hordes of commuters shoved past me to board their trains departing every few minutes for cities and villages throughout the Belgian provinces. Research in the Royal Library revealed that this apparently exceptional pattern of national commuting originated in 1869 when the Belgian Parliament established half-price fares on workmen's trains. Why, I wondered, as a student well-steeped since graduate school in Belgian history, would the parliament of the industrializing society characterized by Marx as 'the hell of the proletariat' for its lack of regulation and oversight, subsidize rail fares for the workers? This national story of workmen's trains seemed to raise more questions than it answered. Why did the Belgian government intervene to encourage urban workers to live throughout the countryside?

As the Belgian story went, in 1869 when Joseph Kervyn de Lettenhove, a Catholic deputy and medieval historian from the village of Ekloo, proposed subsidizing rail service for 'the industrious classes', he explained that substantially reduced railway fares for workmen's trains would put an end to the migration of working families from the countryside to the 'large cities where they fall prey to the habits of corruption and disorder'. Labourers employed in urban centres would instead leave these cities at the end of each work day, travelling by rail to 'what the English call "home"', to the moralizing influence of their wives and children in the countryside'.[6] The Liberal minister of public works, Alexandre Jamar, not an obvious ally for the Catholic deputy, listened and pledged that the government would organize 'trains that will permit workers living in the

---

5   Bloch, 'Pour une histoire comparée des sociétés européennes', 1–19.

6   M. Kervyn de Lettenhove, *Annales parlementaires. Chambre des représentants* 1868–69 (21 April 1869), 735.

countryside to return each evening to their residence and thus avoid the immoral influences of the large population centres'.[7] Ernest Mahaim, the sociologist who studied the organization of workmen's trains, admitted there might be an international dimension to the scheme, but chose 'to isolate the phenomenon and to consider it uniquely within its own milieu'. Within Belgium, the problem was 'sufficiently complex'.[8]

Studying the Belgian parliamentary debates and political tracts revealed that Belgian Liberals and Catholics alike were terrified that their rapidly expanding capital would fall prey to the vices already rampant in the cholera-infested dens of the East End of London. They realized that as industrialization scaled national borders, so too did the social discontent left in its wake. Contemporary sources suggest that this 'complex' problem was international from its inception. To understand why the workforce commuted from dispersed housing located beyond their industrial capital called for comparison at the municipal level where individual reformers interacted and their projects entangled. The urban reformers shared a common understanding of the crisis of overcrowding as a problem that transcended national borders, the foundation of what Nancy Green labelled 'comparison as similarity'.[9]

Reformers in both London and Brussels pioneered national legislation and municipal construction to transport and house the workers outside of their capitals. It was not only that the Belgians watched the British who had industrialized before them. The comparison worked both ways, because the British, trying to figure out how to relieve overcrowding by building out rather than up, eyed the innovative Belgian railway scheme. The study of urban reform in London and Brussels before the First World War seemed an ideal fit for Marc Bloch's model – 'two neighboring, contemporaneous societies', that 'continually influenced each other'.[10]

I worked simultaneously on both sides of the comparative study, bringing Belgian questions to the London archives and British questions to the Brussels archives. Like all other comparative historians, I undertook research in unfamiliar archives and libraries, posing questions at inquiry desks set up for scholars interested in topics very different from the ones that I carried across the Channel. In the end, the rich and continuous interchanges between the reformers in Brussels and London enabled me to write a comparative history with a single narrative line, rather than setting national case studies in distinct chapters as comparative historians more typically have done.

[7]   M. Jamar, *Annales parlementaires. Chambre des représentants 1868–69* (22 April 1869), 765.
[8]   Ernest Mahaim, *Les abonnements d'ouvriers sur les lignes de chemins de fer belges et leurs effets sociaux* (Brussels: Misch & Thron, 1910), ix.
[9]   Green, 'L'histoire comparative', 1342.
[10]   Bloch, 'Pour une histoire comparée des sociétés européennes', 1–19.

There were some obvious differences separating the two cities. Reformers in London, unlike Brussels, were interested in workmen's trains, not to keep the workers out of the British cities, because they were already there, but to induce the urban workers to move out to the suburbs with their families. Members of the Locomotion Subcommittee of the London County Council nevertheless repeatedly cited the ever expanding workmen's service provided by the Belgian state-owned railway as they despaired at the reluctance of the competing private British railways to carry more workers. At the same time, Belgian mayors and architects visiting garden cities constructed by British industrialists and philanthropists and by the London County Council returned home with drawings of model cottages to instruct their colleagues sitting on communal councils and in parliament of what was possible. The divergence in their strategies designed to reach similar goals intrigued the reformers in Brussels and London. Just as the British, inspired by Belgian reformers, asked what regulations would be required to get their private railways to serve the public interest, the Belgians, inspired by the British, wondered at the lack of charitable institutions invested in housing the poor in their cities.

Neither the Belgian nor the British reformers expected the problems plaguing their capitals to go away or new residential patterns that might alleviate the overcrowding to develop on their own. Reformers on both sides of the Channel assumed that governments, both municipal and national, had a new and significant role to play in reshaping the workers' environment. They saw themselves as pioneers in a newly industrialized world. That the reformers watched each other as they experimented opened up the seemingly disparate municipalities to comparative analysis.

Throughout Europe, political leaders observed the widely reported massing of the poor, or in London journalist Jerrold Blanchard's words, the 'vanguard of the army of Labour who are to ... add a new story to a new terrace; the cornerstone to another building; bulwarks to another frigate; another station to another railway; and tons upon tons of produce from every clime, to the mighty stock that is forever packed along the shores of the Thames'.[11] In his comparative study of housing the poor published in 1887, the Russian economist Arthur Raffalovich, described the 'unimaginable misery that hides in the alleyways and culs-de-sacs that we would not ordinarily penetrate'.[12] The first and worst case was London, especially the East End. As reported by the London Congregational minister Andrew Mearns in *Outcast London*, 'poisonous and malodorous gases arising from accumulations of sewage and refuse' choked all Londoners, not

---

[11] Gustave Doré and Blanchard Jerrold, *London. A Pilgrimage* (London: Grant & Co., 1872), 114.
[12] Arthur Raffalovich, *Le logement de l'ouvrier et du pauvre, Etats Unis, Grande Bretagne, France, Allemagne, Belgique* (Paris, Librairie Guillaumin et Cie., 1887), 46.

Figure 7.1   Gustave Doré, 'Over London by Rail' (1890). Railway trestle over London slum housing

Source: Gustave Doré and Blanchard Jerrold, *London. A Pilgrimage*, London: Grant & Co., 1872, 121.

just the so-called residuum hunkered down in the hidden alleys, where 'the sun never penetrates'.[13]

Belgian observers reported industrial disorder overtaking their capital, as it had London. The worker turned editor of the official Belgian *Moniteur*, J. Dauby, cautioned the Brussels bourgeoisie who ventured into the lower city that if they opened the door from their boulevards into these *impasses*, then they would find 'a veritable anthill of human beings' crammed into every inhabitable space between the attic and the cellar.[14] The problem of density, of overcrowding, was all pervasive. As nations industrialized, they ran the risk of following the lead of London into hell.

---

[13]   Andrew Mearns, *The Bitter Cry of Outcast London. An Inquiry into the Condition of the Abject Poor* (London: James Clarke & Co., 1883), 6.

[14]   J. Dauby, *La question ouvrière en Belgique. Causes de nos crises ouvrières; remèdes possibles* (Brussels: Librairie de A.-N. Lebègue et Cie., 1871), 10. On Dauby, see: Jean Puissant, 'Le bon ouvrier, mythe ou réalité au XIXe siècle. De l'utilité d'une biographie. J.F.J. Dauby (1824–1899)', *Revue belge de philologie et d'histoire* 56 (1978): 879–929.

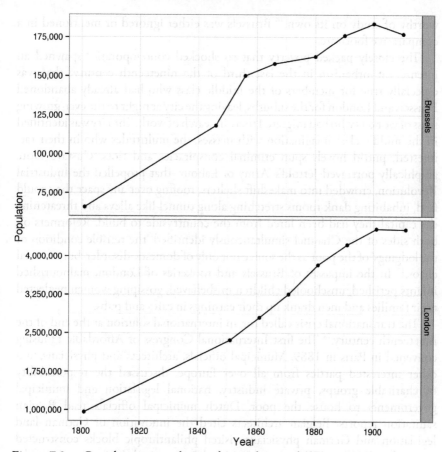

Figure 7.2   Population growth, London and Brussels[15]

These industrial cities into which workers and their families were flooding at an ever intensifying rate loomed as an increasingly unnatural habitat for civilized men and women wherever they were located. In the last decades of the nineteenth century, reformers noted that their urban centres harboured populations at a density almost double that of the first ring of their suburbs. Even though the rates of growth were quite similar, the vastly different size of the two industrializing capitals – London's population of 2,633,341 dwarfed Brussels at 150,244 in 1856 – convinced historians to see London as unique,

---

[15]   Data from *Royal Commission appointed to inquire into and report upon the means of locomotion and transport in London* (London, 1905–06), 126; and *Les recensements de 1910*, 2. Graph by Marta Lyons.

worthy of study on its own.[16] Brussels was either ignored or mentioned in a comparative footnote.

The closely packed poverty that so shocked contemporaries spawned an intense anti-urbanism in the last third of the nineteenth century: that was especially true for members of the middle class who had already abandoned Brussels and London for the suburbs, leaving the city at night to the ever-growing mass of workers who had migrated there in search of work. The city was identified in the middle-class imagination with masses, the multitudes who in their rat-infested, putrid hovels spun criminal conspiracies and riots. Gustave Doré graphically portrayed Jerrold's 'Army of Labour' that propelled the Industrial Revolution, crowded into makeshift shelters, roofing over any space they could find, inhabiting dank rooms stretching along tunnel-like alleys and threatening the capital they had been lured from the countryside to build. Reformers on both sides of the Channel simultaneously identified 'the terrible condition of the lodgings' of the poor as the source not only of domestic disorder, but of social chaos.[17] In the impasses of Brussels and rookeries of London, malnourished infants perished, unschooled children misbehaved, gossiping women neglected their families and men drank up their earnings in cafes and pubs.

The transnational crisis called for an international solution at the end of the nineteenth century.[18] The first International Congress of Affordable Housing convened in Paris in 1889. Municipal officials, architects and physicians, and other interested parties from all over Europe, discussed the responsibility of charitable groups, private industry, national legislation and municipal governments to house the poor. Dutch municipal officials read Belgian sanitation reports, Belgian architects cited the innovation of German land legislation and German physicians visited philanthropic blocks constructed in London. William Thompson, a British delegate, cited the investment of the Belgian National Savings Bank in housing schemes while Charles De Quéker, a Belgian delegate, suggested that his compatriots emulate the efficient housing designs of the British. Their comparative discussions had practical effects. For example, the housing committee of the Brussels commune of St Gilles used de

---

[16]   *Les recensements de 1910* (Brussels: E. Guyot, 1912) and J.N. Tarn, 'French Flats for the English in Nineteenth-Century London', *Multi-Storey Living: the British Working-Class Housing*, ed. A. Sutcliffe (London: Croom Helm, 1974), 19–40.

[17]   Doré and Jerrold, *London. A Pilgrimage*, 114.

[18]   Among the many comparative transnational studies of the period written by reformers, see: Charles De Quéker, *Rapport sur les logements à bon marché à l'étranger* (Brussels: Wormhout, 1906); Leonce du Castillon and Fernand Bansart, *La question des habitations et des logements à bon marché en Belgique et à l'étranger* (Brussels: Etablissmeents Généraux d'imprimérie, 1914); H. Garnier, *La législation et la réglementation anglaise en matière de salubrité de l'habitation* (Paris: Giard et Brière, 1902); and Adolf Rutten, *Het Samenwonen in Steden. Een maatschappelijk Vraagstuk* (Ghent: A. Siffer, 1902).

Quéker's comparison as support in their call for municipal intervention, noting tellingly that the London County Council had spent 74 million francs to build housing for 38,000 people.[19]

To buttress these reports, social surveyors in Brussels and London such as Charles Booth and Emile Hellemans measured and mapped the housing of the poor. On both sides of the Channel, they distinguished the regularly employed workers who could be educated to be good citizens from the unemployed residuum that would be abandoned to stew in 'the hell of savagery'.[20] These meticulous and pragmatic social scientists from both sides of the Channel came up with strikingly similar diagnoses of this 'problem of all problems'.[21]

Although Booth and Hellemans agreed that housing the working class held the key to reform, their compatriots diverged in their initial strategies for accommodating the poor. In London, philanthropists built voluminous blocks; the Peabody Trust alone constructed 5,017 rental dwellings, typically two-room flats lining a central corridor with communal laundries and baths on the top floor of the four story buildings, washing facilities and sculleries on the landings and a caretaker to monitor the comings and goings of tenants. Disillusionment followed among both the urban reformers and the displaced poor. The British planner Raymond Unwin disparaged what another reformer called 'brick boxes with slate lids'.[22] He complained in a 1905 report to the International Congress on Affordable Housing, 'It is impossible in such blocks to give any expression to homeliness'.[23] The British author and lecturer on housing and transportation reforms, Ernest Dewsnup added: 'Block dwellings common enough in some places ... never appealed to the English'.[24]

---

[19] Comité officiel de Patronage de St Gilles, 1902.

[20] Robert A. Woods cited by Harold James Dyos, 'The Slums of Victorian London', *Victorian Studies* 9 (September 1967): 18.

[21] Charles Booth cited by Phillip J. Waller, *Town, City and Nation. England 1850–1914* (Oxford: Oxford University Press, 1983), 44. See: Charles Booth, *Life and Labour of the People in London* (London: Macmillan, 1902–03); Mary Catherine Booth, *Charles Booth: A Memoir* (London: Macmillan and Co., Ltd., 1918); Emile Hellemans, *Enquete sur les habitations ouvrières en 1903, 1904, 1905* (Brussels: Imprimerie des institutions de prévoyance, 1905); Thomas Spensley Simey and Margaret B. Simey, *Charles Booth. Social Scientist* (London: Oxford University Press, 1960).

[22] Henry Adridge, Report of the Society for National Housing Reform Council for England and Wales, *Actes du VIIme Congrès International des Habitations à bon Marché tenu à Liège, du 7 au 10 Août 1905* (Liège: Imprimerie industrielle et commerciale, M. Thone, 1906).

[23] Raymond Unwin, *Actes du VIIme Congrès international des habitations à bon marché tenu à Liège, du 7 au 10 août 1905* (Liège: Imprimerie industrielle et commerciale, M. Thone, 1906), 81.

[24] Ernest Dewsnup, *The Housing Problem in London* (Manchester: Manchester University Press, 1907).

IMPASSE DU MUGUET

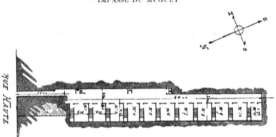

Figure 7.3   Impasse du Muguet. One of many dead-end alleyways at the centre of Brussels

Source: Emile Hellemans. *Enquête sur les habitations ouvrières en 1903, 1904, 1905.* Brussels: Imprimerie des Institutions de Prévoyance, 1905.

Some British reformers suggested that large blocks of flats belonged on the continent, rather than in Britain. The Bruxellois, less inclined to large-scale philanthropic projects, were not so sure. The Brussels mayor and urban reformer Charles Buls replied that perhaps multi-story urban dwellings had their place in Paris, but definitely not Brussels.[25] 'Like the Anglo-Saxon, whose cousins we are, we love our home, the family fireside', he answered the British with whom

---

[25]   Edouard Van der Linden, *Etude sur l'amélioration des habitations ouvrières et sur l'organisation du domicile de secours* (Brussels: Librairie Polytechnique Decq & Duhent, 1875), 26–7; and H. Langerock, *De arbeiderswoningen in Belgie* (Ghent: Boekhandel J. Vuylsteke, 1894), 10.

he often compared his compatriots.[26] 'Building up' was soon rejected on both sides of the Channel, even though that appeared to be the only way to construct housing inside their capitals with their escalating land costs.

The *Railway Register* proposed an alternative to the existing sites within the densely populated city: they must 'plant out in the vicinage'.[27] Outside the overcrowded capitals, in the suburbs and the countryside, land was cheap. In contrast to the 'barbaric cities that seemed to have sprung from the earth to cut down human life', reformers envisioned a future when 'the face of the whole land may be made merry with colonies of cottages and with smiling gardens and orchards, verdant meadows and waving corn, happy village workshops, and beautiful buildings'.[28] The privacy assured by greenery would prevent the spread of epidemics, the scourge of urban life. More than that, cottages with a mother at their centre would enhance home-life for families of respectable workers. In the evenings, workers' families would tend the gardens of half-timbered cottages set along winding roads that romantically followed the contours of the land. This suburban life would afford the workers, as it did the middle class, a retreat from the tumult of the city.[29]

In Belgium, workmen's trains were organized to take the labourers back and forth between the city and the countryside. Over the course of the last three decades of the nineteenth century, the Belgian government oversaw the construction of branch railroad lines, employers adapted their shifts to train schedules and additional worker cars lined with wooden benches were coupled onto the trains leaving each morning for the industrial and mining centres of their new nation at the crossroads of European trade and industry. But how to get London workers out of the city? The answer lay in trusting 'modern inventions, and modern improvements in locomotion for abolishing time', Charles Booth explained, quoting Lord Balfour in a 1901 tract, *Improved Means of Locomotion as a First Step towards the Cure of Housing Difficulties of London*.[30] 'That the question of transportation has an influence on that of housing is one of those truisms, one of the axioms that no one debates', Charles Didier, the Belgian editor of *Le Cottage*, informed his readers.[31]

---

26   Charles Buls, *Esthétiques des villes* (1894) (Brussels: Sint-Lukasdossier, 1981), 28.

27   Railway Register 2 (1845): 495, as cited by Harold James Dyos, 'Railways and Housing in Victorian London', *Journal of Transport History* 2 (1955): 114.

28   Robert Williams, *London Rookeries and Collier's Slums: A Plea for More Breathing Room* (London: W. Reeves, 1893), 12.

29   A. De T'Serclaes de Wommerson, *La condition du logement de l'ouvrier dans la ville de Gand* (Ghent-Paris: H. Engelcke, 1889), 23.

30   Arthur Balfour, quoted in Charles Booth, *Improved Means of Locomotion as a First Step towards the Cure of the Housing Difficulties of London* (London: Macmillan, 1901), 2.

31   Charles Didier, 'Notre programme', *Le Cottage* (July 1903).

If the Belgians at the time were aware of how unique was their national workmen's railway scheme, it is not evident in the parliamentary records that document the introduction of the subsidized fares that would redefine demographic patterns in industrial Belgium. Thirty years later, one of every five Belgian workers was commuting by train. Belgian Socialist, Emile Vandervelde, credited the workmen's trains as the origin of 'a profound social revolution', one that made of workmen commuters.[32]

The contrast with the British is telling. Railway acts passed by the British Parliament in 1868 required the railways to provide the working families they had displaced with affordable means of travelling between their work in London and new residences to be constructed in the suburbs. The persistent requests by commuting workers and strikes for more frequent and earlier train services, however, testify to the inadequacy of workmen's trains to London. In 1883, the British Parliament passed the Cheap Trains Act that required the railways to run a 'proper and sufficient' number of workmen's trains between 6 p.m. and 8 a.m., but the protests continued. They were often backed by reformers on the London County Council who compared British rail service with that of the Belgians.

Belgian deputies, too, noted the difference between Belgium, with its national railway, and Britain, 'the country with which we are always compared', and which other Europeans were emulating.[33] British reformers picked up the comparative refrain, observing as did James Hole, that: 'Few social questions have been more warmly contested than this: whether the State should own the railways of a country, if not own them, to what extent it should control them'. As opposed to the share-owner obsessed British railways, 'the Belgian Government has not tried to make a large profit for the State, but rather to develop commerce and industry by cheap transit'.[34] Belgian reformer Ernest Mahaim cautioned the British that they would not convince their railway managers to serve the interests of the state as long as the railways remained in private hands. The low fares and convenient service that set the Belgian trains apart from Britain, he argued, 'must be understood as a natural consequence of State management, which aims less at a profit than at furthering the public good'.[35]

Direct statistical comparison between the two rail networks is as difficult for historians now as it was for reformers and planners then. The Belgian state railways counted passengers on the national network, concentrating on employment hubs, for parliament; the British railways recorded the number of

---

[32] Emile Vandervelde, *L'exode rural et le retour aux champs* (Brussels: A. Vromant & Co., 1901), 155.

[33] Minister Van Hoorebeke cited by Joseph Pauly, *Le chemin de fer et le parlement 1835–1860* (Brussels: H. Wauthoz-Legrand, 1935), 125.

[34] James Hole, *National Railways, An Argument for State Purchase* (London: Caswell & Co. 1893), 373 and 260.

[35] Ernest Mahaim, *The Belgian Experience of State Railways* (London, 1912).

trains, not passengers, for their shareholders. Piecing together the data collected by British railways surprisingly reveals that by 1912, approximately 25 per cent of all suburban London passengers were travelling with workmen's tickets. Within the six to eight mile zone of the centre of London, 40 per cent of the suburban railway passengers were workmen.[36] By 1907, one of every five Belgian workers was commuting by train and 43 per cent of all travellers on the Belgian national railway used worker tickets in 1907.[37] Despite the reluctance of British railways to cater to the workmen, they did achieve roughly the same results as the Belgian railways.

The most striking difference between the two commuting patterns was that British workers travelled shorter distances from the suburbs to the capital than did the Belgians from their rural villages to jobs dispersed throughout their much smaller country. That is not surprising: the Belgians were trying to root unskilled, marginally employed workers on land they already owned in the countryside, while the British were transplanting skilled workers from the city to new houses constructed in the suburbs.

Belgian and British social scientists at the turn of the twentieth century noted the emergence of different demographic patterns. 'Nothing is more striking for the visitor who goes from London to Brussels than the contrast between the deserted pastures of Kent and the animated fields bordering our major cities', the Belgian Socialist and author of an often-cited study of rural exodus, Emile Vandervelde, noted on his own journey by rail from London to Brussels. On the Belgian side of the Channel, he observed, workmen's trains each evening delivered their 'human cargo to the red-roofed cottages after a day's work in the factory.'[38] Vandervelde bolstered these personal observations with interviews of land-owning Belgian labourers. Dispersed through the countryside, they often walked two kilometres back and forth to their village rail stations and spent upwards of two or three hours a day on the train, foregoing a quieter agrarian life for the good wages industrial work afforded. They explained that beyond the city, in their ancestral villages, their families lived in four-room houses surrounded by gardens with potatoes, chickens, a pig and a cow. Belgium, the president of the Second Socialist International asserted, based on his comparative study, was exceptional among industrial societies.

The British reforming social scientist Benjamin Seebohm Rowntree, urged on by David Lloyd George, crossed the Channel in the other direction, travelling to Belgium to observe, explain and extend the lessons of this second industrial

---

[36]   Anthony S. Wohl, 'The Housing of the Working Classes in London, 1815–1914', in Stanley D. Chapman, *The History of Working Class Housing* (Newton Abbot: David and Charles, 1971), 35.

[37]   Mahaim, *Les abonnements*, 38.

[38]   Vandervelde, *L'exode rural et le retour aux champs*, 138.

nation to Britain. Rowntree described the Belgian labouring commuters as hybrids, half urban, half rural. Residing in the countryside where 'the life is healthier for his wife and children, he gets a larger house, probably for less rent, and he has the advantage of a plot of land where, besides growing vegetables, he can keep a pig, a goat, and a few hens'. The workmen's trains had alleviated the urban overcrowding that typically accompanied industrialization, Rowntree concluded, equalizing wages between town and country. 'If we follow the lead of Belgium in these matters, and in various others which are dealt with in this volume, we may expect to see the rural districts of Britain repeopled and her agriculture once more prospering', he optimistically advised his countrymen.[39]

In London, Lord Salisbury, citing the success of rural housing schemes on the continent, urged local British governments to acquire land and build 'enough good cottages to satisfy the demand'.[40] They did. The London County Council (LCC), spurred on by its Progressive majority, resolved to buy land in Wandsworth, just inside the county line, and then proceeded to construct Totterdown Fields Estate, followed by Norbury Estates near Croydon, White Hart Lane in Tottenham, and finally, in 1912, Old Oak Estate. An LCC study in 1910 revealed that 81.3 per cent of heads of families on these first three estates constructed outside the county line commuted to work in central London.[41] Advertisements to promote these garden estates depicted robust children romping in greenery surrounding the stucco cottages tended by attentive mothers.[42]

Belgian reformers contrasted the 'workers' barracks, less healthy than prisons' with the 'small well-aired houses lodging one family surrounded by a corner of greenery'.[43] Flats in the city had unnaturally constricted their lodgers. These 'cubes of masonry, rental machines constructed by the devil', lacked a soul, the editor of the Belgian journal, *Le Cottage* complained in his call for *l'exode urbain* – the return to the countryside.[44] With the exception of a few Socialists in Brussels who defended the right of the workers to remain in the city rather than being shunted off to reservations like the American Indians, British and Belgian reformers shared this dream of a bucolic residential future. Echoing the British Garden City visionary, Ebenezer Howard, who feared that the further

---

[39]   Benjamin Seebohm Rowntree, *Land & Labour. Lessons from Belgium* (London: Macmillan, 1911), 593, 434, 292, and 544.

[40]   *The Housing Journal* 1 (August 1900).

[41]   London County Council, *Housing of the Working Classes in London* (London: Oldhams Ltd., 1913), 104.

[42]   London County Council, *Workmen's Trains and Trams, with Particular of the Council's Dwellings for Workmen* (2 February 1914), Greater London Records Office, London.

[43]   *Moniteur des Comités de patronage et des sociétés d'habitations ouvrières* (25 October 1900).

[44]   Didier, *Le Cottage* (June 1903).

degeneration of urban life spelled doom for civilization, housing reformers expected to transform society by radically changing the physical environment in which people lived.

British and Belgian housing strategies for workers on the land beyond the city though differed as dramatically in implementation as did the schemes for locomotion. In contrast with British reformers who sought to expand affordable rental options for the working poor, expecting to domesticate them by controlling their environment, most Belgian reformers argued that frugal, hard-working labourers ought to aspire to home ownership. The British Housing of the Working Classes Act of 1890 and the Reform of Local Government Acts of 1888 and 1894 enabled British municipalities in general, and the London County Council in particular, to intervene directly in clearing land and constructing affordable housing for rental. Belgian housing legislation passed by parliament in 1889, the year the London County Council was organized, established Official Patronage Committees for Workmen's housing to encourage building housing for purchase by workers throughout the countryside. A semi-private savings and loan bank, the CGER extended loans to these private societies, revitalizing the all-but-moribund housing construction in Belgium, especially in rural areas. Ernst Mahaim, the Belgian reformer who had studied the workmen's trains, pointed to the 1889 housing legislation as 'perfectly conceived to fit the Belgian spirit'.[45] The Belgian state had eased the way for private enterprise to tackle the social problem, he explained, in conscious contrast to the British.

Meanwhile, other Brussels reformers enviously studied the success of the London County Council with its mandate to establish a municipal identity for London and to tackle the urgent social problems not resolved on a national level. Two years after the International Congress of Affordable Housing met in Liège in 1905, they gathered in London where they trekked out to the housing estates and garden cities on the periphery of the British capital. Belgian, Dutch, German and French delegates returned from London full of admiration for the activism of their British counterparts. The Belgians built one 'inexpensive self-standing house' for the Exposition Universelle de Bruxelles in 1913. With obvious allusions to the garden city cottages of Britain, the Brussels model boasted ivy-covered balconies, bow windows and a white brick facade to contrast with the overhanging red roof.[46] Only after the First World War would Brussels planners adapt stucco cottages to housing schemes for workers in the Brussels suburbs.

Municipal leaders in both capitals had complained over the course of the nineteenth century of fragmentation and powerlessness, but only London was finally allowed to organize itself as a unified municipal entity at the turn of the

---

45   Ernest Mahaim, *La législation sociale en Belgique, 1869–1919* (s.n., s.d.), 167.

46   Caisse générale d'épargne et de retraite, *Une habitation a bon marché* (Brussels, 1910).

century. Repeated attempts to annex the 18 communes surrounding the central pentagon-shaped commune of Brussels failed, leaving them as autonomous villages. Brussels mayor Charles Buls despaired at the lack of coordination across administrative jurisdictions. 'Look how easily the problem [of housing] is resolved in London, Berlin, Vienna, and even Paris given the availability on the periphery of the city of spacious, inexpensive grounds and inexpensive public transportation', he sighed.[47] A unified Catholic government in Belgium stood in the way of such municipal reform. Urban reformers on the London County Council did not worry that Conservatives controlled the British Parliament during these years of Progressive control in London. Prime Minister Lord Salisbury smugly noted, 'I rather look to the new London County Council to play the drunken helot for our benefit'.[48] In Belgium where politicians sat on communal councils at the same time that they served as parliamentary deputies, national political agendas tended to overwhelm local affairs.

It was hopeless, one of Buls' successors, Liberal Brussels mayor Adolphe Max realized. He prefaced an urgent call for action in response to the housing crisis with the admonition: 'On such questions, there should be no parties'.[49] Instead, a debate at the communal council of Brussels over the height of a proposed municipal block of flats aroused Liberal muttering of the dangers of collectivism (four stories), countered by Socialists' denunciations of capitalist oppression (two stories). A Socialist councillor responded to Liberals' obstruction of housing construction with the threat of proletarian revolution in the Belgian capital.[50]

In the adjacent commune of Schaarbeek, alderman and national Socialist leader, Louis Bertrand admonished councilors to 'look at what is happening in England, the classic site of *laissez faire* and of *laissez passer*', citing the 25 million spent by the LCC on workers' housing.[51] The head of the Housing Committee of the London County Council had justified municipal activism in 1900, as they launched clearance schemes, appointed medical investigators, and planned blocks of flats for the 'vast population of toilers' by explaining that there was more than enough work for both municipal action and private development.[52]

---

[47] Charles Buls, *Bulletin Communal de Bruxelles 1899*, 274, cited by Marcel Smets, *Charles Buls. Les principes de l'art urbain* (Brussels: Pierre Mardaga, 1995), 91.

[48] Lord Salisbury cited by Ken Young and Patricia Garside, *Metropolitan London* (London: Edward Arnold, 1982), 62.

[49] Adolphe Max, Conseil Communal, *Moniteur des Comités de Patronage*, 25 April 1911.

[50] M. Rochette, 27 March 1899, *Bulletin communal de Bruxelles* (1899), 487.

[51] Louis Bertrand, Commune de Schaerbeek, *Construction d'habitations à bon marché par la commune* (Brussels: Becquart-Arien, 1898), 38 and 45.

[52] London County Council, *Housing of the Working Classes in London* (London: Oldhams, 1913), 27.

In Brussels, unlike London, national and municipal politics got hopelessly intertwined as politicians operated on both levels of government.

Urban historian Anthony Sutcliffe notes that only 'rarely do we fully appreciate the extraordinary ambition of specifically urban modes of intervention in economic and social processes during a century in which the informed public was generally unsympathetic to administrative limitations of individual freedom.'[53] The strident campaign of the London County Council for workmen's trains and the pioneering construction of affordable rental housing first within the County and then on its periphery appears all the more extraordinary in juxtaposition to Brussels. In this new Belgian nation, in contrast to Britain, local governments were dismissed as sites of corruption and influence peddling. Similarly, the Belgian workmen's trains, when compared with the British railways, appear more clearly as an extraordinary governmental scheme engineered in a prosperous young country where the railways were organized on a national level to promote industry. Comparing urban reform across the Channel demonstrates the unique strength of the London County Council at the turn of the twentieth century as it disrupts the long-standing Belgian image of their national government as a weak overseer of the quintessential *laissez-faire* entrepreneurial society composed of strong municipalities.

Comparative history is yet more disruptive of the two national histories. Both Belgian and British historians have typically portrayed reform at the end of the nineteenth century as a pitched battle that pitted government intervention against private enterprise. Set in comparative context, however, it appears rather that the dynamic of the divergent strategies for housing reform and the building of a transportation infrastructure pitted national versus local governments, not private enterprise. Governments cooperated, collaborated and at times competed with the market in response to transnational forces. In Brussels, as in London, relationships between municipal and national authority were evolving in this critical period marked by the 'politicization of social policy.'[54]

The similarities highlight the national differences. On both sides of the Channel, encouraged by national legislation, municipal programs and industrial initiatives, labourers in ever increasing numbers commuted from jobs in urban centres out to the greenery of suburbs and the countryside. The outward migration of these respectable workers following the bourgeoisie and the razing of their crowded, chaotic neighbourhoods allowed urban planners to restructure their capitals around the stately monuments for which they are known today.

---

[53] Anthony Sutcliffe, 'The Growth of Public Interventions in the British Urban Environment during the Nineteenth Century: A Structural Approach', *The Structure of Nineteenth-century Cities*, eds, James H. Johnson and Colin G. Pooley (London: Croom Helm), 107.

[54] Susan Pedersen, *Family Dependence, and the Origins of the Welfare State* (Cambridge: Harvard University Press, 1993), 47.

In no time at all, as the Belgian Vandervelde had foreseen, William Morris' visionary suggestion in *News from Nowhere* that 'one meets in the cities, but lives in the countryside' would hold as true for the Bruxellois as for the Londoner.[55] By different routes, inspired by similar fears and ideals, reformers in London and Brussels reordered the first two industrial capitals and their inhabitants. Their gaze extended across the national borders that have been built up by the practice of generations of historians.

---

[55] William Morris cited by Vandervelde, *L'exode rural*, 318.

Chapter 8

Town Planning and Municipal Growth in Late Colonial Bombay: Towards a Transnational Perspective

Nikhil Rao

Introduction

As the historian Gyan Prakash has pointed out, South Asian historiography has only relatively recently taken an 'urban turn'.[1] For the leaders of the anti-colonial struggle such as Gandhi and Nehru, it was the countryside, rather than the city, that represented the authentic India. Even modernists such as Nehru had little interest in actually existing cities, seeking instead to build new cities that could project India's emergence from both colonial servitude as well as from rural backwardness.[2] Since Indian historiography, following the concerns of nationalist leaders, had focused principally on the nation, the emphasis of this historiography had been on the countryside or on the city and urbanization as a *telos* of development. It has only been in the last 15 years or so that Indian historiography has considered the city as an enduring and important locus of Indian society, and permitted a perspective on 'spaces of power and difference suppressed by the historicist discourse of the nation.'[3]

The 'urban turn' in Indian historiography has not yet yielded many efforts to compare Indian cities or to locate Indian cities in wider, transnational contexts. South Asian urban history can look to another, still more recent turn within other subfields of the South Asian historiography towards global and transnational history.[4] While this recent work represents a move away from

[1]   Gyan Prakash, 'The Urban Turn' in Sarai Reader 2002, *The Cities of Everyday Life*, eds Ravi Vasudevan et al. (Delhi: Centre for the Study of Developing Societies, 2002), 2–7.

[2]   Prakash, 'The Urban Turn', 4–5.

[3]   Prakash, 'The Urban Turn', 6.

[4]   Some works include Chris Bayly, *The Birth of the Modern World* (Hoboken: Wiley-Blackwell, 2003), Sugata Bose, *A Hundred Horizons: The Indian Ocean in the Age of Global Empire* (Cambridge: Harvard University Press, 2009), Sugata Bose and Kris Manjapra, *Cosmopolitan Thought Zones: South Asia and the Global Circulation of Ideas* (Basingstoke:

Indian historiography's long-standing emphasis on particularities of Indian experiences to consider the movement of ideas across oceans, it also represents an attempt to write a global or transnational history that was not just a variation on imperial history. Scholars such as Kris Manjapra have moved outside the Britain-India-colonies framework within which non-national history had previously been written, seeking to unearth 'entanglements' between German and Indian intellectuals.

This chapter is an initial effort to elaborate some transnational dimensions of Indian cities. Specifically, it seeks to distinguish between such transnational dimensions and other, more familiar kinds of connections that resulted from the colonial relationship between England and India. While there has been a wealth of literature on South Asian cities in the past several years, these have sought principally to complicate the category of 'colonial city' by showing that cities like Delhi, Calcutta, Lahore or Bombay were not simply built expressions of colonial ideology. Rather, they were the result of collaborative ventures between the British and various Indian, usually elite, groups.[5] An important insight of this more recent body of literature has been to note that a variety of imperatives other than the colonizer-colonized dynamic – ranging from commercial incentives to the desire of some Indians to distinguish themselves from others – went into the building of South Asian colonial cities. Such efforts, while complicating our understanding of colonial urban history by showing varying motivations among Indian actors, remain within the England-India context. The transnational connections of Indian cities went beyond the England-India colonial axis, however, and not all connections between England and India in the context of urban history were 'colonial' as such.

The city in the late colonial period of the 1910s to the 1940s presents an especially challenging analytic object to a historiography dominated by the framework of the nation-state. Understanding the emergence of the independent nation-state out of the colonial frame has been until relatively recently the principal organizing rubric of Indian historiography and thus the nation-state has dominated Indian historiography perhaps even more than it has the historiographies of other regions of the world. Yet this period was

Palgrave, 2010), Kris Manjapra, *Age of Entanglement: German and Indian Intellectuals Across Empire* (Cambridge: Harvard University Press, 2014) and Samuel Moyn and Andrew Sartori eds, *Global Intellectual History* (New York: Columbia University Press, 2013).
    5   Some works in this vein include Jyoti Hosagrahar, *Indigenous Modernities: Negotiating Architecture and Urbanism* (London: Routledge, 2005), Swati Chattopadhyay, *Representing Calcutta: Modernity, Nationalism and the Colonial Uncanny* (London: Routledge, 2006), William Glover, *Making Lahore Modern: Constructing and Imagining the Colonial City* (Minneapolis: University of Minnesota Press, 2007), and Preeti Chopra, *A Joint Enterprise: Indian Elites and the Making of British Bombay* (Minneapolis: University of Minnesota Press, 2011).

also one when cities expanded greatly and Indians gained greater control than ever before over municipal governance, establishing patterns that endured well into the postcolonial period. Most significantly, as a result of the Montagu-Chelmsford reforms of 1919, the colonial state distanced itself from urban intervention and local self-government became a subject 'transferred' to Indian control.[6] Especially in the 1910s and 1920s, the urban sphere was where Indians tested their newly won rights to self-determination, often at odds with the nationalist agenda. The nationalist lens of Indian historiography has thus proven to be exceptionally distorting for those seeking to understand the histories of cities in the late colonial period. As cities grew larger and more complex and as Indians grew more assertive within this expanded context, urban problems and concerns were only imperfectly, if ever, aligned with nationalist concerns, often until remarkably late into the nationalist struggle.[7]

Following up on these arguments, this chapter examines transnational aspects of efforts to transform and urbanize Salsette, a large, agrarian island lying just to the north of Bombay city and island, in the period between 1910 and 1925.[8] Attending to such transnational perspectives locates Bombay within a larger, often shared, history of urban growth among the large cities of the world. As Bombay city industrialized and grew rapidly in the late nineteenth and early twentieth centuries, and especially in the aftermath of a plague epidemic in the city at the end of the nineteenth century, residents and administrators looked to settle and urbanize Salsette. Such efforts entailed two forms of change. In a very material sense, the physical landscape of Salsette, with irregular plots and scanty road networks, needed to be replaced by an urban cityscape with regular plots and a street pattern. In an administrative sense, the district and provincial level colonial government, which concerned itself principally with land revenue, needed to be supplemented and eventually replaced by municipal

---

[6] For more on the implications of these reforms for Indian cities, see Douglas E. Haynes and Nikhil Rao, 'Beyond the Colonial City: Re–evaluating the Urban History of India, ca. 1920–1970', Introduction to Special Issue of *South Asia* co-edited by Haynes and Rao, *South Asia* 36 (2013): 317–33.

[7] Elsewhere I have discussed instances where imperatives of class, caste, and community were at odds with the nationalist imperative in the context of the franchise and municipal elections in Bombay. See Nikhil Rao, 'Community, Urban Citizenship and Housing in Bombay, ca. 1919–1980', *South Asia* 36 (2013): 415–33.

[8] The literature on Bombay is growing. Some recent works in addition to that of Chopra cited earlier include Prashant Kidambi, *The Making of an Indian Metropolis: Colonial Governance and Public Culture in Bombay, 1890–1920* (Aldershot: Ashgate, 2007), Gyan Prakash, *Mumbai Fables* (Princeton: Princeton University Press, 2010), Mariam Dossal, *Theatre of Conflict, City of Hope: Bombay/Mumbai 1660 to Present Times* (New Delhi: Oxford University Press, 2010), and Nikhil Rao, *House, but No Garden. Apartment Living in Bombay's Suburbs* (Minneapolis: University of Minnesota Press, 2013).

governance that was equipped to deal with the needs of increasingly complex urban formations.

For the first of these goals – the physical transformation of Salsette – authorities turned to Town Planning.[9] Shortly following the passage of the English Town Planning Act of 1909, Bombay's administrators and residents debated the adaptation and subsequent adoption of this act in the Bombay context, which finally resulted in the Bombay Town Planning Act of 1915. Crucial to the Bombay Act was the experimentation with certain German legislations for land acquisitions. For the necessary administrative changes, authorities considered a variety of measures for municipalization, especially from the 1920s onward. This chapter will consider the response to one such initiative, the recommendations of the Committee appointed in 1924 to 'consider the reorganization of local self-government in Salsette', known as the Bell Committee after its Chairman Robert D. Bell.[10] Central to this discussion was the question of whether or not to restructure Salsette in the form of an English county, with a governing County Council and a Central Board.

Salsette and its urbanization and subsequent annexure to Bombay has not been much studied, which is surprising considering that the annexed portions of Salsette constitute the greater portion of the present-day city of Greater Mumbai, both in terms of land mass as well as in terms of population.[11] Further, this process of physical and administrative expansion proved to serve as an important model for future instances of urban growth. One reason for the absence of consideration of Salsette's growth is that the period considered here – from about the 1910s to the mid 1920s – is the very period when nationalism and the anti-colonial struggle gained momentum and came also to subsequently dominate the historiography. Thus the specific histories of cities from this period onward tend to get assimilated into the story of Indian independence,

---

[9]   As used then and here, the term Town Planning refers not to urban planning generally, but rather to a very specific mode of land use conversion through which agrarian lands could be transformed into urban plots.

[10]   The recommendations of the committee were published in *Report of the Committee Appointed to Consider the Reorganization of Local Self-Government in Salsette* (Bombay: Government Printing, 1925). Not much actually happened in the wake of this committee's report, but the response it provoked was interesting and will be analysed here. The most significant changes to Salsette's administrative organization came much later when, in two stages in 1950 and 1957, large sections of Salsette were annexed to Bombay to form the present-day city of Greater Bombay.

[11]   C. Rajagopan's *The Greater Bombay: A Study in Suburban Ecology* (Bombay: Popular Book Depot, 1962) is one study, especially interesting as it was undertaken in the immediate aftermath of the annexure of Salsette to Bombay and thus offers a contemporary perspective.

and the emergence of Greater Bombay becomes a corollary to the emergence of independent India out of colonial rule.[12]

In fact, neither Town Planning nor debates over local self-government can easily be yoked to the narratives of colonialism and the emergence of the nation from it. Both emerged in the context of transnational conversations about urban planning and governance. Both Town Planning and debates over local self-government in Salsette looked to models from Germany and England as offering possible solutions to the challenges in Bombay. Such transnational conversations were interwoven with – but distinct from – the changing perception of the colonial relationship between England and India. In this sense, this chapter seeks to disengage the transnational aspects of urban history from the colonial history of cities (and thus also from the history of the nation). In so doing, it affords a perspective on the transnational contexts for urban change in India. However, it also suggests that such a transnational perspective on urban change could also offer new insights into nationalism as well, specifically on the links and articulations between the urban scale and the national scale.

Urban Expansion and Town Planning

Beginning in the early twentieth century, colonial authorities turned to suburbanization as an indirect mode of urban transformation in Indian cities such as Bombay. Early suburbanization schemes undertaken in the 1900s by colonial planning authorities such as the Bombay Improvement Trust featured a strong and aggressive colonial state. In developing the first suburbs such as Dadar, Matunga and Sion in the island city, the still-confident Trust sought to impose its overarching vision on lands newly colonized by the expanding city. Most importantly, the Trust sought to physically acquire all the land envisioned for the suburb and then lay out an orderly street pattern, with each plot subject to strict building regulations, designated open spaces and reserved spaces for schools and public institutions.

From the middle 1910s, however, facing greater resistance from increasingly empowered local elites and diminishing support for urban development from the provincial and central governments, city authorities turned to Town Planning –

---

[12] Thus Sandip Hazareesingh's excellent book on Bombay dismisses Town Planning as nothing more than 'a means of enabling colonial agencies to bring suburban land suitable for building to the market', and argues further that 'it [Town Planning] did not mark a break with the piecemeal colonial approach to urban development'. Sandip Hazareesingh, *The Colonial City and the Challenge of Modernity: Urban Hegemonies and Civic Contestations in Bombay City 1900–1925* (Bombay: Orient Longman, 2008), 53. In fact, Town Planning was quite different from earlier colonial approaches, not least because, as will be shown, it entailed a sympathetic appreciation of German practices.

as elaborated in the context of the English Town Planning Act of 1909 – as a better mechanism for transforming agrarian lands into urban plots. Town Planning appeared more suitable in the context of reduced intervention in urban affairs by the state because it did not entail wholesale acquisition of lands by the state. Within the framework of the English Town Planning Act of 1909, the state did not have to actually purchase lands from agrarian landowners. Rather, when these groups, in conjunction with local authorities, sensed the need or potential to convert their agricultural lands into urban lands, they temporarily relinquished their lands to the local authority which, using the provisions of Town Planning legislation, reconfigured the agrarian lands into an urban streetscape with even-shaped house plots, a network of streets and provision for other urban infrastructural needs. Once the lands were thus reconfigured, the original landowners received plots in the new cityscape that were smaller in size, but presumably enhanced in value due to their potential for urban use.

The growing numbers of applications to convert agricultural plots into building sites in Salsette – and the imperative of administrators to control the pattern of building – led the provincial government in 1908 to appoint an Indian Civil Service officer by the name of P.J. Mead to conduct an extensive survey of Salsette's potential for suburban development.[13] The problem in Salsette was that there existed only a very weak legislation to handle the impending urbanization of the large island. This was the 1901 District Municipalities Act, promulgated to allow for the creation of municipal bodies to regulate growth in newly urbanizing areas.[14] Most importantly, this latter legislation contained no effective provision to regulate building on private lands. While byelaws could be framed, the penalty for infringement of byelaws was so low as to be irrelevant.

Mead's ambitious and wide-ranging study provides an extraordinary portrait of Salsette in its early stages of urbanization, with descriptions of the various villages and townships scattered across the island, now recognizable as large urban neighbourhoods. Beginning with an account of the topographical features of Salsette, Mead's detailed assessment of the various infrastructural assets and liabilities in the development of Salsette emphasized the problem of water supply and the malaria-prone lands on the eastern parts of the island.[15] However, significant obstacles to the orderly development of Salsette presented themselves. First, the lack of developed street patterns meant that little back land had been developed, while congested ribbon development took place along the existing street frontages. Second, the absence of any suitable mechanism to

---

[13]   P.J. Mead, *Report on the Possibilities of Development of Salsette as a Residential Area* (Bombay: Government Printing Press, 1909).

[14]   Mead, *Report on Possibilities of Development of Salsette*, 7.

[15]   Mead, *Report on Possibilities of Development of Salsette*, 1–5.

pool lands – especially small or irregularly shaped plots – served as a severe disincentive to permitting lands coming to market in an orderly fashion.[16]

Mead's influential report recommended the formulation of Town Planning legislation on the lines of the English Town Planning legislation then under discussion before parliament, but with some key differences. Noting that the English Bill under discussion left much of the work of redistribution of land to the Local Government Board (the central authority), in Germany, on the other hand, 'where Town Planning has been an accomplished fact since 1875', the local authority was given the power to pool and redistribute lands in the event of failure of the owners to privately negotiate amongst themselves.[17] Mead maintained that 'certainly in Salsette nothing short of this will be wholly effective'.[18] His report contained extracts of two important German urban planning legislations that, according to Mead, were excellent models to adapt for the proposed development of Salsette: the Prussian *Fluchtliniengesetz* of 1875 (which determined the street lines for undeveloped lands) and the *Lex Adickes* of 1902, first legislated for Frankfurt, and named after Franz Adickes, an energetic urban thinker and mayor of that city.[19] Mead also included a draft of what he called the Salsette Development Act, which incorporated elements of the German legislations into the principles of English Town Planning to create what he considered to be a stronger legislation for Salsette.[20]

In recommending German legislation, Mead was reflecting a broader interest among British urban thinkers of the early twentieth century in German urban planning, independent of the Bombay context.[21] The German legislations provided mechanisms for four important aspects of urban expansion. In crucial

---

[16] Mead, *Report on Possibilities of Development of Salsette*, 7. The previous two paragraphs on the appointment of P.J. Mead to conduct a survey of Salsette are taken from Rao, *House, but No Garden*, 214.

[17] Mead, *Report on Possibilities of Development of Salsette*, 10. See Dennis Hardy, *From Garden Cities to New Towns: Campaigning for Town and Country Planning* (London: E & FN Spon, 1991), 56–7 for an account of the way in which local authorities worked under central authorities in the form of Local Government Boards within the framework of the English Act of 1909.

[18] Mead, *Report on Possibilities of Development of Salsette*, 10.

[19] Mead, *Report on Possibilities of Development of Salsette*, 25–33. The extracted text of the *Lex Adickes* is from 25–32 and a synopsis of the *Fluchtliniengesetz* is on 33. Robert Home has noted the link between the Bombay Town Planning Act and the *Lex Adickes*, but does not pursue the connection. Robert Home, *Of Planting and Planning: The Making of British Colonial Cities* (London: Routledge, 2011), 179.

[20] Mead, *Report on Possibilities of Development of Salsette*, 33–40.

[21] Brian Ladd, *Urban Planning and Civic Order in Germany, 1860–1914* (Cambridge: Harvard University Press, 1990), 8. Ladd notes that for the British, the 'secret of German success' in the field of urban planning lay in the great freedoms granted to local authorities as against regional and central authorities.

ways, these legislations permitted local authorities – or municipalities – to assert themselves over against central and regional authorities. The first two were provisions of the Prussian *Fluchtliniengesetz*: a right for municipalities to appropriate lands for the purposes of building streets and roads; a right for these same municipalities to assess property owners for the cost of buildings streets and roads and subsequently regulate building along these streets and roads.[22] The second two were features of the *Lex Adickes*: a protocol whereby growing municipalities could articulate and share sovereignty with regional administrative authorities; and, critically, a means whereby landowners could pool their lands and receive equivalent parcels after the completion of the proposed improvements to the lands. This provision was especially important for landowners who had odd-shaped lands, or lands that were too small in size themselves, both common features of landholding in parts of Germany. (And of Salsette, it turned out.)

The power of local authorities in 'reparceling' (*Umlegung*) lands by combining and redistributing plots was promoted by Adickes and his supporters as a way to benefit both private property owners and the general public by bringing land to market for urban use in efficient fashion.[23] Such a balance between private property rights and general community interest was reiterated by Mead in his endorsement of the *Lex Adickes*.[24] Bombay's landowners, of course, were not convinced that their interests were adequately protected by the draft bill. The franchise in this period was restricted to owners of property, and property owners therefore dominated the Bombay Municipal Corporation, which vehemently opposed the Town Planning legislation as it was being debated in the Bombay Provincial legislature. Dinshaw Wacha, the Bombay Municipal Corporation's representative on the Board of the Improvement Trust, argued that the draft bill was 'confiscatory in its character and calculated to destroy all just and fair rights and interests in private property'.[25] A founding member of the Indian National Congress and its one-time President, Wacha's critique of the colonial administrative establishment could occasionally slide into the discourse of nascent anti-colonial nationalism. Yet more often than not, Wacha spoke as a landowner, and on behalf of other landowners whose property rights were threatened by such legislation.[26] Wacha and his colleagues fought hard to sink the Town Planning bill, but were only partly successful. They were able to

---

[22] Ladd, *Urban Planning and Civic Order in Germany*, 91.
[23] Ladd, *Urban Planning and Civic Order in Germany*, 200.
[24] Mead, *Report on the Possibilities of Development of Salsette*, 16.
[25] *Proceedings of the Bombay Improvement Trust* (henceforth PBIT), 15 March 1910, 133.
[26] For more on how the domination by landowners of the Bombay Municipal Corporation affected the latter body's critique of the Bombay Improvement Trust, see Hazareesingh, *The Colonial City and the Challenge of Modernity*, especially 30–31.

restrict the applicability of the Town Planning legislation to urban areas outside Bombay City. Only with the consent of the landlord-dominated Bombay Municipal Corporation could Town Planning be made applicable to areas within Bombay city.

In drawing upon German legislations and empowering municipalities to frame street plans for and facilitate 'reparceling' of agricultural lands on the verge of urbanization, the Salsette Development Act drafted by Mead departed significantly from English practice, including the Town Planning Act of 1909, which placed greater responsibility upon landowners and regional authorities for the construction of streets and the redistribution of lands. This point was emphasized in a meeting of the Trustees of the BIT to discuss the draft Town Planning bill for Bombay, where it was underscored that 'the English [Town Planning] Act contains no provision for redistribution', and that the *Lex Adickes* provided better for this important aspect of land use conversion.[27]

Since German Town Planning laws and practices were receiving such strong endorsements by civil servants and urban planners in Bombay, the Government of Bombay deputed an ICS officer by the name of B.W. Kissan to conduct a study tour of German cities and towns in 1913.[28] A fluent speaker and reader of German, Kissan spent three months in early 1913 visiting no less than 15 cities and towns in various provinces of the German Empire. On the eve of the Great War, in a context where relations between Britain and Germany were already tense, this visit by a British colonial officer to Germany must have been interesting for a variety of reasons. Strikingly, Kissan doesn't say much about this larger context, but records the kindness and graciousness of his German hosts.[29] In any case, his *Report on Town Planning Enactments in Germany* was the most comprehensive document produced by a Bombay civil servant examining the relevance of German urban practices for the Bombay setting.

Kissan helpfully spelled out the distinctions, in his view, between the German and the British legislations. The English Town Planning Act provided for a more comprehensive developmental plan for the designated region. Not only were projected roads and open spaces fixed, the number of houses that could be constructed per acre was fixed and zoning rules regulating the location of businesses and industries were also specified. In the Prussian system, on the other hand, while there was no such comprehensive planning, it had been a long-standing practice of regional police authorities to assume the right and the responsibility of framing street plans, instead of leaving this to builders or

---

[27]   *PBIT*, 8 March 1910, 117.

[28]   B.W. Kissan, *Report on Town Planning Enactments in Germany* (Bombay: Government Printing, 1913).

[29]   Kissan, *Report on Town Planning*, 27.

regional powers, as was the case in England.[30] As a result of the *Fluchtliniengesetz* of 1875, this responsibility of framing street plans was handed over by regional police authorities to local authorities. Kissan thus confirmed the German practice – of great importance for Bombay observers as noted above – of asserting stronger rights and responsibilities for local bodies, as against regional authorities and builders.[31]

Kissan also observed an important difference between landholding patterns in England versus landholding patterns in Germany, which in turn resulted in different kinds of legislation.[32] Whereas in England it would have been possible for a prospective builder or developer to acquire a large piece of land from a large landowner and then proceed to layout a street pattern, in Germany the nature of landholdings available for purchase tended to be more fragmentary. In the absence of large areas of land available for purchase, it became harder to impose uniform street patterns without making adjustments in the pattern to reflect the realities of landholdings. Since in England it was relatively more common to find large areas, reasoned Kissan, there existed only a relatively weak legislation in the form of a Liverpool Corporation Act that permitted a local body to insist that abutting landowners conduct necessary exchanges in land to permit uniform street patterns.[33] In Germany, on the other hand, where smaller and fragmented landholdings tended to be more often available for purchase, it became more important to devise effective methods of redistribution of land in order to be able to impose street patterns. This, according to Kissan, was the reason why German legislation such as the *Lex Adickes* had a superior mechanism for effecting redistribution of land, and why the power to effect redistribution was handed over to local authorities.[34] This was why P.J. Mead, recognizing that landholding patterns in Salsette more closely resembled German patterns than English patterns and that thus German-type redistribution powers were required by local bodies in the suburbs of Bombay, had declared a few years earlier that 'certainly in Salsette nothing short of this will be wholly effective'.[35]

In his Introduction to Kissan's Report, E.G. Turner, another ICS officer who was Mead's successor as Special Officer, Salsette Building Sites, gave a strong endorsement of the *Lex Adickes'* provisions for redistribution of land and of the

---

30   Kissan, *Report on Town Planning*, 5.
31   Elsewhere I have sought to demonstrate that this particular strength of local authorities vis à vis regional power, deriving from the particularities of German law that found their way into the Bombay Town Planning Act, continued to have implications in contestations over urban lands well into the postcolonial period. Nikhil Rao, 'Towards Greater Bombay. Town Planning and the Politics of Urban Growth, 1915–1964)' manuscript article.
32   Kissan, *Report on Town Planning*, 5–6.
33   Kissan, *Report on Town Planning*, 6.
34   Kissan, *Report on Town Planning*, 7.
35   Mead, *Report on Possibilities of Development of Salsette*, 10.

Fluchtliniengesetz's provisions for the laying down of street lines and the recovery of street construction costs from those landowners who gained frontage. After six years of deliberations in the Bombay Presidency Legislature and elsewhere, the Bombay Town Planning Act was finally passed in 1915. It was the first Town Planning Act in India and was followed by the Madras Town Planning Act in 1919. Other presidencies subsequently passed their own versions. From 1915 until 1964, Town Planning remained the principal mechanism through which agrarian lands at the city's edge were converted to urban use in Bombay.

After the passage of the Bombay Town Planning Act in 1915, A.E. Mirams, a surveyor active in city expansion schemes in Bombay, gave a lecture in 1919 to the Town Planning Institute in London on Town Planning in Bombay.[36] Mirams had served as Arbitrator in all of the first 10 Town Planning Schemes notified in Salsette, so he had a good perspective on the issues. Mirams adopted a somewhat servile tone and begged the indulgence of the 'august assembly of expert professional Town Planners' before him. He assured them that despite the fact that his Town Planning experience was in 'the lands of jungles and tigers', there 'were still advantages which would accrue as the result of copying the Town Planning methods of the East'. The English law was at that time being considered for amendment and Mirams was hoping to point to the advantages of the Bombay Act. The one great advantage of the Bombay Act over the English Act, according to Mirams, was the facility it offered for 'reparceling' plots. Quoting the relevant section (Section 12) of the Act, Mirams pointed out that:

> The section allows of the provision of decent building plots, and where the plots in the ownership of small owners are too small for building, it enables the Local Authorities, with the consent of the owners, to combine the interest of two or more parties and give them one or more plots to be held in ownership in common ... [I]nstead of the small proprietor having his plot bought from him under the scheme at the value it had at the date of notification of the scheme, he is able to combine with another owner and thus reap any benefits the scheme confers ... [T]hese principles are largely based on the German Lex Adickes, which originally dealt with land in Frankfort-on-Maine. [Sic][37]

In the discussion at the end of Mirams' lecture, Joshua Scholefield, a member of the British Town Planning Institute, characterized Section 12 as 'one of the most progressive and far-reaching features of the Act'.[38] Both the mechanism

---

[36] A.E. Mirams, 'Town Planning in Bombay Under the Bombay Town Planning Act, 1915', *British Town Planning Institute, Papers and Discussions*, 6, 1919–20, 43–63.
[37] Mirams, 'Town Planning in Bombay', 46.
[38] Mirams, 'Town Planning in Bombay', 57.

for redistribution as well as the powers accorded to the local authorities were enviable.

In the view of these experts, thus, the Town Planning legislation generated in the colonial Bombay context, which modified the original English law with two important German innovations, proved to be superior to the English original version. They sought nothing less than to have the original version modified accordingly, showing yet again that the directionality of innovation in laws and administration generally did not simply move from imperial metropole to periphery, but often followed complicated routes. In this instance, the road beginning in England found its way via Germany to Bombay before making its way back again.

Urban Expansion and Municipal Administration

Salsette had originally been a part of Thana district, a largely agrarian region in the late nineteenth and early twentieth centuries. As such, the administration concerned itself principally with land revenue, while also seeking to provide basic communication and other infrastructural services to residents of the villages and small towns of the district. A District Collector oversaw large tracts of agricultural lands interspersed with villages and small towns. As Salsette urbanized from the early twentieth century onward, an agrarian administrative logic driven principally by land revenue concerns was gradually replaced by a municipal administrative logic driven by the concerns of managing the infrastructure of the urbanizing area. A classification of space based on the district, *taluka*, and village was increasingly supplemented by one where the municipality and the ward were the principal organizing rubric.

Such a transition was hardly seamless. The problem was that Salsette in the first three decades of the twentieth century contained a very wide range of settlements that required different forms of governance. Much of Salsette still consisted of large tracts of agrarian land interspersed with villages. Some towns such as Kurla and Ghatkopar had developed into fairly complex urban formations with their own industrial and commercial activity. In between lay a wide assortment of settlements, some of which were dormitory communities bearing a strictly suburban relationship to Bombay while others were already beginning to resemble slums. Perhaps most importantly, the various towns and villages in Salsette had developed sufficient inter-dependency such that larger, supra-local initiatives such as water supply, sewerage, transport and public health needed to be coordinated for the region as a whole.

The problem was exacerbated by the fact that the existing mechanisms of local self-government were multifarious and, in the view of several Indians, did not truly assign adequate powers to local bodies. For instance, within the more rural parts of Salsette, some villages had *panchayats*, a traditional form of village governance. These might be supplemented by Sanitary Committees, while District Local Boards and Taluka Local Boards attempted to provide some basic supra-local services. Urban areas were governed by the District Municipalities Act of 1901. Settlements that had begun to assume an urban form were governed by Notified Area Committees: they were 'notified' by the provincial government and committees were formed, by appointment, to manage their affairs. Towns that were more developed were permitted to avail of the most advanced form of self-government: they were classified as District Municipalities and were governed by elected representatives. By the early 1920s, thus, a variety of local self-governmental bodies proliferated on Salsette Island.

In the views of many residents of Salsette, even the most advanced of these local bodies – the District Municipalities – were severely hobbled in their workings by the very limited powers accorded to them by the provincial government. While the existing legislation did permit urban areas to elect representatives to the municipal committee, the law was structured in such a way that once elected, the committee was not answerable to the people who elected it, but rather to provincial government. The electorate had no means of taking an initiative in directing municipal action, no powers of referendum were made available. The municipal committee was answerable only to provincial government and was more often than not, compelled to do its bidding. As one shrewd observer put it, the effect of this legislation was 'to substitute an unpaid agency [the elected municipal committee] in place of a Government officer, to work under such officer, to collect taxes and use them as desired by the Governor-in-Council'.[39] In other words, under the guise of 'self-governance', the colonial government was getting Indians to pay taxes for public works and also to do the work of collecting the taxes, all without any say in how that tax money was spent.

To address these classes of problems – the proliferation of various local bodies in Salsette, the perception that none of these bodies was adequate to the task before it, and determining the future administrative relationship between Bombay city and Salsette – the provincial government of Bombay appointed a committee in 1924 to 'consider the problems of Local Self-Government in Salsette'.[40] The committee – referred to as the Bell Committee after its Chairman Robert Bell – conducted its inquiries in 1924 and early 1925 before issuing its

---

[39] K.R. Daphtary's Dissenting Minute to the Bell Committee Report, reproduced in *Bombay Chronicle*, 13 August 1925, 4. Daphtary's scathing critique of the 1901 District Municipalities legislation is perhaps the most comprehensive account available of the Indian perspective on the possibilities for local self-government in Salsette.

[40] The appointment of this committee needs to also be understood in the context of the Montagu-Chelmsford reforms in the colonial administration of India announced in 1919 and the extension of greater rights of self-determination to Indians, especially in the sphere of local self-government.

report with recommendations in 1925.[41] The report provoked a substantial response among the local population. In brief, the Report's recommendations sought to tackle the challenges posed by Salsette through a threefold approach that entailed a simplification of the number of jurisdictions, consolidation of powers assigned to each jurisdiction and creating the possibility of coordinating efforts between jurisdictions.[42]

Of immediate concern here was the Committee's assessment of the problem posed by Salsette's peculiar composition described above, namely the juxtaposition of agrarian lands, villages, small towns, residential suburbs and nascent industrial centres, all affected by the proximity to Bombay city. For the Committee, this structure appeared to resemble the greater London area, and they took up the notion that Salsette should perhaps be formed into a county-like unit resembling the County Councils to be found in England. Within this model, Salsette would now have four municipalities for the larger urban areas; also, four 'urban communities' for smaller urban areas, whose jurisdiction would also encompass the villages and rural tracts lying in their vicinity; and finally, a supra-local Central Board, elected from among the residents of Salsette, whose function would be to coordinate within these various entities and, especially, to oversee the provision of district-wide services such as education, water supply, sewerage, building rules and transport. Generally, the thrust of these recommendations was to reduce the number of local bodies, especially eliminating the smaller ones such as the village *panchayats*, on the ground that the 'prevalent illiteracy' made the 'experiment of village communities ... not likely to be successful in practice'.[43]

What is striking here is how easily the structure and organization of a city like London presented itself as a model for Bombay at this moment in the 1920s. While the members of the Bell Committee were clearly aware of the differences between these two settings, they also appeared to feel that there were sufficient similarities to advance the possibility of creating for Salsette a structure similar to the one to be found in the English counties. It appeared to be a moment of transnational urbanism, an instance where the particularities of the urban condition trumped national difference and, in this instance, the fact of colonial power.

This moment did not last long, however, and literally within the very paragraph following the proposal for creating a County Council with an elected Central Board, the Report of the Bell Committee confusingly appeared to retract this

---

[41]   *Report of the Committee Appointed to Consider the Reorganization of Local Self-Government in Salsette* (Bombay: Government Printing, 1925). The Report of the Bell Committee was reproduced in *Bombay Chronicle*, 10 August 1925, 9–10. All citations to the Report will be from this reprint.

[42]   'Report of the Bell Committee', *Bombay Chronicle*, 10 August 1925, 9.

[43]   'Report of the Bell Committee', *Bombay Chronicle*, 10 August 1925, 9.

proposal, suggesting that 'the executive and coordinating functions [envisioned for the Central Board] are to a considerable extent at present already performed by the Development Department, and the immediate necessity for the authority advocated is therefore not so great'.[44] In other words, after recommending greater enfranchisement in Salsette and recommending that supra-local matters be coordinated by a Central Board elected from among the Indian residents of Salsette, the Bell Committee Report went on to say that in fact this would not be necessary for some period of time because the Development Department, a non-elected executive branch of provincial government that, moreover, as a reserved department of the provincial government was entirely under British control, could handle these affairs!

Observers, including Indian members of the Bell Committee itself, were quick to note the glaring contradiction at the heart of the Report. R.P. Masani, a member of the Committee, attacked the report in his dissenting minute.[45] Excoriating the Committee's Report for its 'half-hearted and halting approach' to the Central Board, which he felt to be essential for Salsette, Masani zeroed in on the reason advanced by the Committee Report for its waffling approach, namely that the Development Department was already performing most of the functions slated for the Board. Not only did the Development lack the means to execute these tasks, the whole notion of an executive branch of government overseeing such work was repugnant to the spirit of self-government.

Masani also debunked the Committee's proposal to create four 'urban communities' that would also be responsible for the villages and rural tracts lying within their jurisdiction. He rejected the notion that the alleged illiteracy of villagers rendered them unfit for self-government, arguing instead that 'long before self-governing institutions were evolved in Europe, the people of India, whether literate or illiterate, had their village communities for the control and management of local affairs'.[46] In his critique, he went on to make an explicit link between taking up responsibilities for small local matters such as sanitation and the greater responsibilities of citizenship and nationhood:

> The report fails to suggest any line of advance on the path of local self-government. Nor does it suggest anything practical to promote administrative efficiency. There is nothing in it likely to arouse the people to a consciousness of their solidarity, to enlighten them and stir them to active cooperation and to train them for those duties and responsibilities and qualify them for those rights and prerogatives which mark the growth of a nation.

---

44 Report of the Bell Committee', *Bombay Chronicle*, 10 August 1925, 10.
45 R.P. Masani's Dissenting Minute, reproduced in *Bombay Chronicle*, 12 August 1925, 10.
46 Masani's Dissenting Minute, reproduced in *Bombay Chronicle*, 10.

The connection made between local self-government and the 'rights and prerogatives' of citizenship suggest that in Masani's view there was more to the Report than mere ineptitude. Perhaps the Committee's recommendations were designed not to foster self-government in Salsette as was its mandate but in fact the very opposite: to staunch the upswell of local self-government that was now being seen as constituting a pathway to citizenship, nationhood and, by implication, the end of British colonial rule.

The suggestion that the Bell Committee's bumbling Report was actually part of a concerted effort by the colonial provincial government to thwart the momentum of self-government in Salsette (and, implicitly, elsewhere in India) was taken further by the *Bombay Chronicle* in its Editorial assessing the Report.[47] The Editorial argued that the Report was useless, and that this was the fault not of the Committee but of the provincial government that appointed it. Most importantly, despite the fact that Salsette's present and its future were inextricably linked to Bombay, government had inexplicably restricted the membership of the Committee to residents of Salsette and to officials. Furthermore, five out of the nine members of the Committee were linked to the Development Department, either as government officers or as civilian members of the department's suburban committee. In short, in artificially seeking to separate the problems of Salsette from Bombay, the colonial provincial government was attempting nothing less than a form of divide and rule under the guise of promoting local self-government.

What's interesting here is that the response of critics of the Bell Committee Report like Masani and the *Bombay Chronicle* quickly linked the Report's 'half-hearted' approach to an attempt by the colonial state to retain control of urban governance despite having formally handed over the right to self-determination in this domain to Indians after 1919. Yet, there was no move to reject the County Council plan on the basis of it being an English model; rather, the model was embraced or rejected on the basis of its suitability or unsuitability for the Bombay setting. Here, the consideration and embrace of the County Council model by Masani and the *Bombay Chronicle* must be understood as belonging to a transnational conversation about the city. The critique of the provincial Bombay government's method of recommending this model on the other hand – its 'half hearted and halting approach' – must be seen in the light of Salsette's residents' growing resentment of the colonial relationship between themselves and the provincial government, in other words, of nationalism.

---

[47] Editorial titled 'Greater Bombay', *Bombay Chronicle*, 11 August 1925, 8. The *Chronicle* and its readership constituted a new kind of middle class urban public realm, as argued by Hazareesingh in *The Colonial City and the Challenge of Modernity*.

Conclusion

Kris Manjapra has proposed the term 'transnational entanglement' to characterize moments such as the ones discussed in this chapter, instances where ideas and practices may cross from one setting to another without necessarily also conveying the teleology of nation or civil society.[48] For him, such a transnational history offers a corrective to forms of global history writing that '[bring] order to a messy world of change and contingency' by positing that the histories of the world ultimately come to be integrated into one or another narrative such as colonialism, nationalism or capitalism.[49] At the same time, of course, such transnational entanglements obviously take place within larger contexts of political, cultural and economic power.[50]

Manjapra's observations resonate with Carl Nightingale's injunction to be sensitive to connections, comparisons and contingencies in seeking to write transnational histories.[51] For Nightingale, urban practices don't simply appear in different places at different times. They are connected, usually through a process of transfer of knowledge that, however, doesn't always follow a pre-determined trajectory. To trace the connections, it often helps to move away from the larger institutional scale; the movement of persons bearing ideas as parts of networks offers insight into the connections between urban practices. In this respect, Nightingale's method converges once again with that suggested by Manjapra as well as that practiced by Shane Ewen and Stefan Couperus in their contribution to this volume.

This chapter has attempted to absorb some of these methodological insights in elaborating transnational aspects to Bombay's growth and expansion into Salsette. I have suggested that the narratives of 'colonialism' and 'nationalism' have structured attempts to locate Indian cities in broader contexts, in ways that sometimes distort or obscure the motivations and implications of historical actions. Yet, not all interactions and exchanges were determined by the colonial relationship. When officials in Bombay such as Mead and Kissan turned to German urban planning legislation for help in formulating a suitable land use conversion law for Bombay, they were acting more as *urban* planners and less as *colonial* administrators. When residents of Salsette such as R.P. Masani advocated for an English-type County Council, they were seeking to adapt a form of urban governance that, while developed in England, appeared to offer a

---

[48] Kris Manjapra, 'Transnational Approaches to Global History: A View from the Study of German–Indian Entanglement', *German History* 32 (2014): 288. Manjapra's own work relates to encounters between Indian and German intellectuals in the early twentieth century.

[49] Manjapra, 'Transnational Approaches to Global History', 275.

[50] Manjapra, 'Transnational Approaches to Global History', 288.

[51] See Carl Nightingale in this volume.

suitable resolution to the particular conundrum of urbanization that they faced in Salsette. When Masani and the *Bombay Chronicle* excoriated the provincial Government of Bombay for thwarting the Bell Committee and in particular the County Council model, on the other hand, they were speaking as critics of a colonial government that was seeking to retain control of urban development and governance through its Development Department even though local self-government was a subject transferred to Indian control after 1919.

The account presented here of this particular entanglement thus seeks to unyoke the transnational conversation about the city taking place here between England, India and Germany from the colonial power relationship between England and India. Through this, it is possible to see that the transfer of knowledge and practices about cities often took unexpected routes. The transfer of Town Planning ideas was not a straightforward movement from England to India as has been assumed. Rather, it was a more interesting movement from England via Germany to India and then back again to England, as suggested in Mirams' speech discussed above, where he indicates to members of the British Town Planning Institute that they could learn from the Indian Town Planning legislation. At the same time, by showing how the discussion about the County Council model was eventually assimilated into a quasi-nationalist critique of the provincial colonial state, this chapter offers a perspective on the linkages between the urban scale of Salsette and the regional and national scales.

Chapter 9

Whose 'Urban Internationale'? Intermunicipalism in Europe, c. 1924–36: The Value of a Decentred, Interpretive Approach to Transnational Urban History

Stefan Couperus and Shane Ewen

Introduction

The transnational historical turn has, since the mid-1990s, shed light on the increasingly common problems faced by municipal governments across Western Europe during the early twentieth century, as well as their responses to these issues.[1] Whereas the majority of responses have been varied and subject to specifically local circumstances, an international effort also emerged to develop a co-ordinated strategy for managing urban and municipal networks.[2] The Union Internationale des Villes/International Union of Local Authorities (UIV), formed at the Ghent International Exposition in 1913, marked the formalization of what Patrizia Dogliani identifies as an intermunicipalist approach, 'the idea that municipalities and local authorities worldwide should pool their knowledge and experience of technical and social advances in local government.'[3] Pierre-

---

[1]   For recent surveys of this literature see William Whyte, 'Introduction', in Helen Meller, ed., *Ghent Planning Congress 1913. Premier Congrès International et Exposition Comparée des Villes* (London: Routledge, 2014), v–xvii; Mariana Luna Pont, 'International Municipalism between the Wars: Local Governments as Modernizing Actors', in *Regional Integration and Modernity: Cross-Atlantic Perspectives*, eds Natalie J. Doyle and Lorenza Sebesta (London: Lexington Books, 2014), 21–42.

[2]   Elsewhere, we have labelled this process transnational municipalism, which owes a great deal to work in political geography, as well as urban studies. See, for example, Harriett Bulkeley, 'Reconfiguring Environmental Governance: Towards a Politics of Scales and Networks', *Political Geography* 24 (2005): 875–902; Shane Ewen, 'Le long XXeme siècle, ou les villes à l'âge des réseaux municipaux transnationaux', *Revue Urbanisme: Villes, Sociétés, Cultures* 383 (2012): 46–9.

[3]   Patrizia Dogliani, 'European Municipalism in the First Half of the Twentieth Century: The Socialist Network', *Contemporary European History* 11 (2002): 585.

Yves Saunier identifies the UIV as the best example of the emerging 'Urban Internationale' during the inter-war period, in which appropriate tools, methods and people came together to study the modern city.[4] This, in turn, has further opened up scrutiny of the diachronic nature of transnational networks across a range of geographical, politico-economic and cultural vistas.[5] However, whereas much recent scholarship has unearthed the institutional matrix and ideological values that have shaped this intermunicipalist ethos, less attention – with the exception of the planning history literature[6] – has been paid to the varied roles played by individuals – administrators, officials, mayors and academics – in building, steering and driving this institutional apparatus.[7] This omission overlooks an implicit understanding that networks are not agents in their own right, but are instead the product of human endeavour; that is, they constitute 'loci of transnational and intercultural communication and negotiation by individual human beings, not just collective actors'.[8]

In this chapter, we are interested in the changing dynamics of the UIV during the inter-war period and how these were the products of diachronic individual-

---

[4]   Pierre-Yves Saunier, 'Sketches from the Urban Internationale, 1910–50: Voluntary Associations, International Institutions and US Philanthropic Foundations', *International Journal of Urban and Regional Research* 25 (2001): 380–403.

[5]   For a flavour of this scholarship, see *The Palgrave Dictionary of Trans-national History: From the Mid-19th Century to the Present Day*, eds Akira Iriye and Pierre-Yves Saunier (New York: Palgrave Macmillan, 2009).

[6]   Recent examples include, Stephen V. Ward, 'What did the Germans ever do for us? A Century of British Learning About and Imagining Modern Planning', *Planning Perspectives* 25 (2010): 117–40; Natasha Vall, 'Social Engineering and Participation in Anglo-Swedish Housing 1945–1976: Ralph Erskine's Vernacular Plan', *Planning Perspectives* 28 (2013): 223–45.

[7]   This person-centred focus has begun to emerge, though it remains strongly wedded to the institutional matrix. See, for example, our own work in this instance: Shane Ewen and Michael Hebbert, 'European Cities in a Networked World during the Long 20th Century', *Environment and Planning C: Government and Policy* 25 (2007): 327–40; Stefan Couperus, 'Backstage Politics. Municipal Directors and Technocratic Ambitions in Amsterdam, 1916–1930', *In Control of the City: Local Elites and the Dynamics of Urban Politics, 1800–1960*, eds Stefan Couperus et al. (Leuven, Paris and Dudley, MA: Peeters, 2007), 175–90; Shane Ewen, 'Transnational Municipalism in a Europe of Second Cities: Rebuilding Birmingham with Municipal Networks', *Another Global City: Historical Explorations into the Transnational Municipal Moment, 1850–2000*, eds Pierre-Yves Saunier and Shane Ewen (New York: Palgrave Macmillan, 2008), 101–18; Stefan Couperus, 'In Between "Vague Theory" and "Sound Practical Lines": Transnational Municipalism in Interwar Europe', *Internationalism Reconfigured: Transnational Ideas and Movements Between the World Wars*, ed. Daniel Laqua (London: I.B. Taurus, 2011), 65–87.

[8]   Wolfram Kaiser, 'Bringing History Back in to the Study of Transnational Networks in European Integration', *Journal of Public Policy* 29 (2009): 235–6.

Figure 9.1   Florentinus Marinus ('Floor') Wibaut
Source: The Municipal Review 3 (1932): 197.

institutional interactions. We explore these by decentring the formal network, shifting the focus from the macro-institutional level and onto the role played by key individuals, in this case the Dutch socialist-alderman, Florentinus Marinus ('Floor') Wibaut (Figure 9.1), and the British civil servant-academic, George Montagu Harris (Figure 9.2). Wibaut (1859–1936) sat on the UIV Secretariat and was its President from 1925–36, whereupon he was succeeded by Harris (1868–1951), the honorary secretary to the British Standing Committee of the UIV and a former Chairman of Council of the International Garden Cities and Town Planning Association; Harris subsequently served as President until 1948. Both men are representative of their respective national traditions of local government: whereas Wibaut combined an ideological commitment to universal brotherhood with a working interest in housing and town planning, Harris was

Figure 9.2   George Montagu Harris
Source: Local Government Administration 3 (1937): 133.

dedicated to the practical contribution that local government could make in the comparison of administrative techniques, as well as the application of local government administration to planning practice. Both provide an alternative route into examining the role that cities and their representative bodies played in the forging of a networked urban world. Moreover, both men were well-known and respected advocates of transnational municipalism during the early twentieth century and their reputations transcended far beyond their national environments. However, whilst their professional and academic works are commonly cited in studies of international town planning and local government reform during this period, urban historians have paid little attention to how their own professional journeys influenced their subsequent understanding of the city and its municipal administration during the inter-war period. Urban historians have tended to scrutinize the wider structural explanations of urban governance at the expense of considering the tangible influence that key individuals can play in shaping or steering administrative reform and practice.

By taking a bottom-up approach to understanding network composition and behaviour, we posit that it is the beliefs and actions of individual actors and their relations with one another that make and remake the institutional apparatus of transnational networks. R.A.W. Rhodes, the expert in policy networks and intergovernmental relations, espouses a constructivist approach towards network analysis, insisting that '[t]he "facts" about networks are not "given" but constructed by individuals in the stories they hand down to one another'.[9] It is only through 'thick descriptions' of individual behaviour that one can unearth the multiple symbols behind these and, ultimately, their belief systems.[10] This lends itself to historical research because it can be achieved by studying the written texts – private documents, minutes, memorandums, published writings and lectures – of network members in order to identify their beliefs and motivations. Written documents are never simply the empirical record of decision-makers; they reveal social and cultural attitudes towards institutional change, as well as the administrative and bureaucratic practices of large organizations and their membership. Individuals – as chairmen, vice-chairmen, secretaries, clerks, executive and council members and so on – are instigators of collective decision-making and practice within institutions such as the UIV. The archival record, thus, sheds significant light upon the everyday life of the individual within the network and offers an alternative to the traditional empirical approaches in both urban and administrative history.

Consequently, the sources that inform the decentred analysis in this chapter stem from a wide range of backgrounds. They include published works by both protagonists, which are combined with personal papers that disclose the ways in which these publications came about. The published records are thoroughly contextualized to ensure that they reflect the social interactions and beliefs that informed their production. They also include unpublished notes, minutes, memorandums and correspondence, which form part of larger institutional collections in the fields of local government administration and town planning. Through close readings of our protagonists' fragmentary records, we have pieced together their transnational journeys as members of the UIV and, moreover,

---

⁹   Roderick Arthur William Rhodes, 'Putting People Back into Networks', *Australian Journal of Political Science* 37 (2002): 400–401.

¹⁰   Roderick Arthur William Rhodes, *Everyday Life in British Government* (Oxford: Oxford University Press, 2011), 298–9; Roderick Arthur William Rhodes, 'Everyday Life in a Ministry: Public Administration as Anthropology', *The American Review of Public Administration* 35 (2005): 3–25; C. Geertz, *The Interpretation of Cultures* (New York: Basic Books, 1973).

examined in detail the significant career moves and ideological influences that shaped their subsequent forays into and around the transnational municipal network. It is thus by combining published works, personal papers, institutional records and well-scrutinized biographies at a specific instance that it becomes possible to inscribe human agency, action and belief into the institutionalization of transnational municipalism.

A decentred approach to networks, according to Rhodes, Mark Bevir, David Richards and others, helps to explain policy change over time. In so doing, it questions the positivist assumption that we can easily learn the beliefs, interests and actions of individuals by studying the way that a network functions. Rather, networks should be seen as the creations of individuals working under their own beliefs and subjective experiences. It is, therefore, vital to tell the human stories behind networks in order to better understand how they originate, as well as how they are governed and how they govern urban society. Such an interpretative approach towards human action in a particular contingent, historical context enables comparative research in beliefs, attitudes and behaviour that cross traditional national and cultural borders.[11] Thus, we need to know more about how transnational networks function in their national and urban settings, but equally how the representatives of national associations influenced the actions and behaviours of these networks.

Florentinus Marinus ('Floor') Wibaut: the Mediating Internationalist

Florentinus Marinus ('Floor') Wibaut (1859–1936) ranked among the few wealthy proponents of socialism able to contribute financially to the 1894 foundation of the Dutch Socialist Party.[12] Having amassed a fortune in the lumber industry in the southern province of Zeeland, Wibaut increasingly engaged in high-society gatherings dedicated to the social question. From his late twenties onwards, he moved away from his Catholic background and into progressive liberal circles. His first meeting with the Amsterdam based journalist P.L. Tak in 1883 led to an intensive master-apprentice relationship which, ultimately, put Wibaut in the direction of the Dutch milieu of self-proclaimed Marxists.[13]

---

[11] Mark Bevir and David Richards, 'Decentring Policy Networks: Lessons and Prospects', *Public Administration* 87 (2009): 132–41; Mark Bevir, 'Public Administration as Storytelling', *Public Administration* 89 (2011): 183–95.

[12] For a biographical account of Wibaut's professional and personal life see: Gilles W.B. Borrie, *F.M. Wibaut, mens en magistraat: ontstaan en ontwikkeling der socialistische gemeentepolitiek* (The Hague: Staatsuitgeverij, 1987).

[13] For an account of Tak's life and his encounters with Wibaut see: Gilles W.B. Borrie, *Pieter Lodewijk Tak (1848–1907): journalist en politicus, een gentleman in een rode broek* (Amsterdam: Aksant, 2006).

In 1891, Wibaut, to many then still an unknown public figure, published his translation of Fabian Essays in Dutch. The preface gave an account of Wibaut's 'avowal of socialism'.[14] Many scholars have pinpointed this confession to mark the starting point of his career as the most remarkable (socialist) politician in Dutch local government in modern times.[15] However, his learned interest in Fabianism during the 1890s revealed two ambivalent outlooks that would become central to Wibaut's somewhat paradoxical intellectual and political beliefs.

Firstly, Wibaut indulged in many theoretical elaborations on Marxism whilst simultaneously promoting a strand of pragmatic, policy-based municipal socialism.[16] Secondly, his texts, speeches and political actions during the inter-war period navigated between – sometimes utopian – ideals of internationalism and the feasible yields of internationalist endeavours at the level of municipal administration.[17] As such, Wibaut initially was able to mediate between the various competing blood groups manifesting themselves within the Dutch and international socialist movement. He befriended (and corresponded intensively with) many convinced Marxists, both domestically as well as at the many Socialist International meetings he attended, but also expressed his empathy for those in favour of social reform through parliamentary democracy.

At the age of 45, Wibaut moved to Amsterdam to fully commit himself to the socialist movement and party. After a period as an elected councillor for Amsterdam, Wibaut accepted the position of alderman in 1914, which he kept, with some brief intervals, until 1931. His aldermanship, as an administrative position within the prevailing polity, produced a permanent rift between him and his Marxist relations, who continued to reject any form of participation in parliamentary democracy at any level of government. The start of his career as an alderman, during which he was mainly responsible for wartime distribution politics, municipal housing and finances, largely coincided with his engagement in what Saunier has coined the 'Urban Internationale'. In addition, notions of pacifism and feminism, finding expression in some joint publications with his wife, increasingly enlaced his public and private writings.

Attempts at synthesizing his governmental activities at the municipal level in Amsterdam with an ever-expanding agenda within a variety of

---

[14]   Florentinus M. Wibaut, *Socialisme: ('Fabian essays in socialism')* (Amsterdam: Van Looy Gerlings, 1891).

[15]   For the most recent reference see: Herman de Liagre Böhl, *Wibaut de machtige. Een biografie* (Amsterdam: Bert Bakker, 2013).

[16]   Florentinus M. Wibaut, *Gemeentebeheer: (Financieel beheer. Bedrijfsbeheer)* (Amsterdam: Ontwikkeling, 1926).

[17]   The most illustrative publication in this respect is a Dutch text from 1929 in which he tries to reconcile internationalist ideals with the daily routines of municipal administration. See: Florentinus M. Wibaut, 'Internationale gemeentepolitiek', *Haagsch Maandblad* 11 (1929): 484–95.

international networks, amounted to a narrowed-down focus on trans-border intermunicipalism. Starting from the early 1900s, Wibaut joined with the Belgian socialist senator Emile Vinck, who was the instigator behind the resolution adopted by the Socialist International in 1900 encompassing the propagation of a 'socialisme municipale'. Vinck was an ardent proponent of a well-organized structure for socialist local politicians in Belgium, resulting in a central information office and educational programme that was soon adopted by the Dutch Socialist Party as well.

As Patrizia Dogliani has rightly concluded, this socialist nexus of internationally oriented advocates of municipal socialism – also comprising individuals other than Wibaut and Vinck – produced the *Union International des Villes et Pouvoirs Locaux* (UIV), founded at the world exhibition in Ghent in 1913.[18] After its renaissance at the Amsterdam congress of 1924, Wibaut served as the UIV's president, together with Vinck, the general secretary in Brussels, constituting the organizational force behind the thriving inter-war organization. Urban housing conditions, another internationally shared socialist preoccupation, prompted Wibaut's involvement in the European housing and town planning movement. This began with his attendance at the tenth *Congrès International des Habitations à Bon Marché* in The Hague in 1913 at which he presented a paper on the overpopulation of residential premises as a key urban problem.[19] In the same year as the 1924 UIV conference, Wibaut chaired the second conference of the International Garden Cities and Town Planning Association (later Federation, IF). In 1928, in collaboration with the Dutch lobbyist Dirk Hudig and the German housing advocate Hans Kampffmeyer, Wibaut left the IF due to his conviction that scholarly town planning debates within the organization eclipsed the more pressing issues of social housing.[20]

One general thread runs through Wibaut's appearances at the many social gatherings, events and meetings integral to the maturation of transnational organizations such as the UIV and the IF: he always sought to mediate between antipodes. One example was his effort to ease the relationship between German and French delegates at the UIV congress of 1924 in Amsterdam. That particular congress, according to Wibaut, had to offer a feasible way to transcend the post-

---

[18]   Dogliani, 'European Municipalism', 573–96.

[19]   Florentinus M. Wibaut, 'Surpopulation des habitations. Le système de la loi néerlandaise en matière d'habitations surpeuplées', in *Xme Congrés international des habitations à bon marché, La Haye-Schéveningue, septembre 1913, rapports. Pt. 3* (Rotterdam: Nijgh en Van Ditmar, 1913).

[20]   National Institute for Architecture Rotterdam, Collection NIROV, inv.nr. a22, various correspondences involving the IF and the International Housing Association. See also: Florentinus M. Wibaut, *Private und gemeinnützige Wohnbautätigkeit: die sozialpolitische Bedeutung der Wohnungswirtschaft in Gegenwart u. Zukunft* (Frankfurt am Main: Verlag des Intern.Verbandes für Wohnungswesen, 1931).

Versailles geopolitical deadlock, having former enemies discussing possible solutions to universal problems of urban life through municipal intervention. In a similar vein, and within the organizational fabric of the UIV, Wibaut tried to personify the irreconcilable two-track direction the UIV was taking during its formative years, that is, the holistically inspired aspiration of widespread and universal municipal socialism instigated by the Brussels-based headquarters on one hand, and on the other the pragmatic exchange of administrative knowledge, experience and data which increasingly predominated the UIV's agenda from mid-1920s onward, due largely to George Montagu Harris' scholarly input.

Even Wibaut's split with the IF, leading towards the creation of the Frankfurt-based International Housing Organisation in 1928, did not prevent him from keeping on (very friendly) speaking terms with the London based secretary of the IF. In a personal memo, Wibaut wrote: 'Since the creation of the International Housing Organisation, I have tried every thinkable option to achieve the most efficient promotion of this highly significant field of public life. However, the cause is best and only served by full co-operation [between the IF and the IHA, sc]'.[21] A domestic equivalent was his continuous effort to restore bonds with his former Marxist friends who joined the Dutch communist party after 1909. In short, Wibaut was very prone to maintain and create (international) friendships, in part underpinned by his pacifist beliefs, but was not very good at admitting that public and international life also implied rejecting people and ideas.[22]

Whereas Wibaut's – and Vinck's – (geo)political ambitions increasingly shifted from the UIV to the Labour and Socialist International (founded in 1923), his passion for practical municipal policy-making accompanied the propagation of administrative techniques, comparisons, surveys and policy schemes at the subsequent meetings of the UIV. It was Montagu Harris' contribution to the 1925 Paris congress in particular that made Wibaut decide that the agenda of municipal socialism no longer fitted the UIV. In his memoirs, Wibaut remembered Montagu Harris' report as 'remarkable [...] in its comprehensiveness, in its depth' and 'much more elaborate, systematic and neutral' than, what he called, 'the propaganda for a single system, which is so common'.[23] At the same time, Wibaut exerted all his energy into lobbying – unsuccessfully – to have the UIV represented in the new economic organizations and committees of the League

---

[21]   International Institute for Social History Amsterdam (IISH), Wibaut Papers, inv.nr. 107, notes on the international concern of housing [undated].

[22]   A perfect illustration of Wibaut's long-pending trust in people is his contact with the American Christian-socialist Charles Bouck White in 1924, who claimed to lead a World League of Cities. After weeks of correspondence and talking, Wibaut indisputably distanced himself from White, who, as it turned out, wanted a global messianic movement of cities as an almost violent counterforce to the League of Nations.

[23]   Florentinus M. Wibaut, *Levensbouw: memoires* (Amsterdam: Em. Querido's uitgevers-maatschappij, 1936), 283.

of Nations in 1927.²⁴ To Wibaut, a peaceful social order on a global scale was still epitomized by cities, which had to be managed and maintained by their public administrative institutions. As such, it was the municipality and its agencies that would promote global order locally. Transnational organizations were the vehicles to arrive at best practices for all cities.

Keeping in mind this rock-solid belief in the potential of border-crossing encounters, one could argue that Wibaut's non-organizational works (for example papers, presentations, speeches, reports) on municipal administration were just his two cents to substantiate a transnationally moulded corpus of municipal texts which, in time, would culminate in a single, universal set of municipal best practices, which, in turn, would buoy a global social equilibrium. To him, cities, rather than nations, were promoters of global peace and stability *par excellence*.

From the late 1920s onward, this sub-narrative of pacifist transnationalism transformed into the master narrative of his intellectual work. At first glance, his paper at the International Congress of Scientific Management in Rome in 1927 might seem a technical case study about the enhancement of efficiency in municipal service delivery in Amsterdam.²⁵ However, the paper, among others, adds up to a series of techno-administrative contributions about local government and finance, which as a whole can be seen as the building block of the great global synthesis Wibaut was working on during the last five years of his life.

With his retirement from town hall politics and administration in 1931 he seemed to lose part of his tributary to transnational municipalism. Indeed, he attended and chaired the London congress of the UIV in 1932, but others had already largely determined the substantial agenda.²⁶ During the early 1930s, Wibaut showed a growing interest in the crystallizing notions about social and economic planning which traversed academia and socialist parties throughout Europe. The so-called International Industrial Relations Institute (IIRI), founded in 1925 by a group of feminist reformers, industrialists, trade union

²⁴ On this see: *Vth international congress of local authorities: London, May 1932 = Vme congrès international des villes et pouvoir locaux: Londres, mai 1932 = V. Internationaler Kongress der Städte und Lokalverwaltungen: London, Mai 1932* (Brussels: International union of local authorities, 1932); Couperus, 'In Between "Vague Theory" and "Sound Practical Lines"', 67–90.

²⁵ Florentinus M. Wibaut, 'Organization for securing efficiency in the municipal service of Amsterdam', *3rd International Congress of Scientific Management Rome* (1927), 3–7.

²⁶ *Vth international congress of local authorities: London, May 1932 = Vme congrès international des villes et pouvoir locaux: Londres, mai 1932 = V. Internationaler Kongress der Städte und Lokalverwaltungen : London, Mai 1932* (Brussels: International union of local authorities, 1932).

representatives and visual designers from the US, the Netherlands and Austria, attracted Wibaut's interest.[27]

The Amsterdam conference on World Social and Economic Planning in 1931 clearly appealed to his earlier beliefs in creating a new world order. The last sentence of the preface to the conference's proceedings, a quote from the Scottish author William Archer, could have been written by Wibaut himself: 'The human intellect, organizing, order-bringing, must enlarge itself so as to embrace, in one great conspectus, the problems, not of a parish, or of a nation, but of the pendant globe'.[28] In short, planning, and the management of the concomitant political economy, was embraced by Wibaut as the new tool to arrive at a new global order. The old ones, efficient municipal administration, social housing and local welfare arrangements, seemed to have lost their potential to some degree. Wibaut engaged in the so-called 'interim committee' that would dedicate itself to the foundation of a 'World Social Economic Center'.[29] Besides much correspondence and travelling, not much resulted from the committee.

By 1933, an aging Wibaut had to withdraw from his internationalist activities due to deteriorating health. In 1934, he published *A World Production Order* (published in English in 1935), in which he unfolded an all-encompassing economic system that would superimpose, partly due to inevitable structural societal changes, the existing capitalist reality of production and trade. Again, this alternative global order bore the clear traces of an idealist internationalism imbued with notions of pacifism, Marxism, feminism and scientific management. The main acting institution that would conduct the planning and regulation of this system was a so-called 'World Economic Council' (WEC). Within this WEC representatives of national Economic Councils (such as the Dutch *Economische Raad*, the German *Reichswirtschaftsrat*, and the British Economic Advisory Council), the International Labour Office and the economic agencies of the League of Nations would discuss the particularities of finely tuned planning schemes. The guiding principle of the WEC had to be 'efficiency' – the social version Wibaut had conceived of for local government in Amsterdam – which, eventually, would lead to a worldwide standard for wages and the international distribution of goods.[30]

---

[27] IISH, Wibaut papers, inv.nr. 353, letter from Mary van Kleeck to Wibaut, 17 December 1931.

[28] Mary Fleddérus, ed., *World Social Economic Planning: the Necessity for Planned Adjustment of Productive Capacity and Standards of Living: Material Contributed to the World Social Economic Congress, Amsterdam, August 1931* (The Hague and New York: International Industrial Relations Institute, 1932), 20.

[29] IISH, Wibaut papers, inv.nr. 353, 6 memorandums of the Interim Committee, 1931.

[30] Florentinus M. Wibaut, *Ordening der Wereldproductie* (Haarlem: Tjeenk Willink & Zoon, 1934); Florentinus M. Wibaut, *A World Production Order* (London: George Allen & Unwin, 1935).

Wibaut was one of many internationalists, who, during the inter-war period, were submerged in an avalanche of letters, meetings, proceedings, journeys, dinners and soirees produced and attended by many 'friends' (as Wibaut would call them) participating in a number of trans- and international organizations. Consequently, Wibaut had to navigate between a number of political, intellectual, ideological and social beacons, dispersed over the European continent and the Anglo-Saxon world. As his international career developed, Wibaut, counter-intuitively, was forced to ignore some beacons along the road. Being a mediator in the first instance, he always sought to compromise between people and ideas. Inspired by his daily experience in Amsterdam as a councillor and alderman, and intensified by the political and techno-administrative agenda of the UIV, Wibaut viewed municipal administration as the basic cell of a new global order. By the end of his life, he substituted municipal administration for socio-economic planning, trying to find yet another, though in his case final, synthesizing compromise for what ultimately was his lifetime ambition: to bring about a tangible global order which would deprive no individual from health and wealth.

The eulogy delivered by his close friend Vinck probably best illustrates Wibaut's ambivalence:

> For us, of the International Union of Towns, he was the man of science, the expert in the municipal sphere. It was to his accomplishments in that sphere that he devoted the best efforts of his intelligence and his soul. The local authority was to him a religion [...] From the foundation of our Union he has always fought for the defence of the international idea and he brought about its triumph. The struggle was not always easy, for even in matters of science it is sometimes difficult to isolate the international idea.[31]

George Montagu Harris: the Academic-Administrator as International Networker

George Montagu Harris' election as president of the UIV in June 1936, to succeed Wibaut who passed away two months earlier, came at a time when he was enjoying the fruits of his tireless efforts, over four decades, in researching and administering local government, building international networks in planning and related activities and advocating a comparative approach to the study of local government. The second edition of his *magnum opus, Local Government in Many Lands: A Comparative Study,* was published in 1933; in March 1935 he was appointed to a Research Lectureship in Public Administration by the

---

[31]   *Local Government Administration* 2 (1936).

University of Oxford's Social Studies Research Committee where he undertook a book-length comparative study of British municipal government, published as *Municipal Self-Government in Britain: A Study of the Practice of Local Government in Ten of the Larger British Cities*, in 1939. He was also elected onto the aldermanic bench of Oxford City Council at the end of 1936, and, by March 1941, was serving on 20 committees across the public, educational and voluntary sectors in and around the city, including the National Council of Social Service, the Barnett House Survey Committee and the Nuffield College Social Reconstruction Survey Committee.[32] Despite being 68 years of age himself upon his election to the UIV Presidency, Harris showed no signs of slowing down in his work; indeed, his enthusiasm for research, committee meetings and conferences remained unparalleled as Europe slid into war again.

Like many of his peers, Harris epitomized the uneven transition from an insular and elitist closed-shop to a professional pluralist civil service in the century following the 1850s.[33] The son of a Torquay vicar and grandson of the first principal of Upper Canada College, Toronto, Harris was educated, first, at Newton College, a public school in Devonshire, and, second, to Masters level at New College, Oxford. He was initially called to the Bar at Middle Temple in 1893 before forging a highly successful career in public administration, successfully straddling the artificial divide between public service and academic approaches to local government administration. In this way, he was one of Harold Edward Dale's gentlemanly civil servants, an 'expert in a difficult art' of public administration, and, for the large part of his career, an adherent to Dale's 'learning by doing' philosophy.[34] Yet he bucked against Dale's dislike for the scholarly civil servant, being actively involved in the Institute of Public Administration from its formation in 1922, a regular contributor to its learned journal, *Public Administration*, editor of two short-lived professional journals, *Local Government Abroad* (1927–30) and *Local Government Administration*

---

[32] George M. Harris, *Local Government in Many Lands: A Comparative Study*, 2nd edition (London: P.S. King & Son, 1934); George M. Harris, *Municipal Self-Government in Britain: A Study of the Practice of Local Government in Ten of the Larger British Cities* (London: P.S. King & Son, 1939); University of Oxford University Archives (UOUA), UR6/MS/3A, file 1, Minutes of the Social Studies Research Committee, 8 October 1935; Oxfordshire History Centre, C/TC/1/A1/27–36, City of Oxford Year Books, 1937–45; Nuffield College Library (NCL), Nuffield College Social Reconstruction Survey, NCSRS/ A2/196, correspondence, George M. Harris to G.D.H. Cole, 16 March 1941.

[33] Geoffrey K. Fry, 'More Than "Counting Manhole Covers": The Evolution of the British Tradition of Public Administration', *Public Administration* 77 (1999): 527–40; John A. Chandler, *Explaining Local Government: Local Government in Britain since 1800* (Manchester: Manchester University Press, 2007), 111.

[34] Harold E. Dale, *The Higher Civil Service of Great Britain* (Oxford: Oxford University Press, 1941), 212–23.

(1935–37), and an internationally renowned expert in the nascent discipline, not least in pioneering comparative methodology for the study of local government systems.

Harris' administrative career began in 1901 as Secretary of the short-lived New Reform Club,[35] an avowedly Liberal organization, but he soon moved on to the Secretaryship of the County Councils Association (CCA) from 1902–19, whereupon he was inculcated into parliamentary procedure through his regular appearances in ministerial delegations and as a witness to enquiries into subjects ranging from public health to traffic management to educational endowments.[36] Christine Bellamy argues that the CCA, from its origins in 1890, was oriented towards working through the central government's cumbersome bureaucracy in the pursuit of its goals. As the representative local authority association for the new county councils, the CCA's leadership built close ties with the traditional land-owning interests in parliament. It preferred to influence local government policy from within, effectively embedding itself into the administrative structures and financial arrangements of central government.[37] As such, Harris' embedding into these institutional relationships influenced his repeated advocacy of institutional approaches towards local government reform, involving national associations of local authorities like the CCA and its urban countertype, the Association of Municipal Corporations (AMC), which was framed within a formal supervisory framework of central government control.

It was during his tenure at the CCA that Harris developed two significant interests that shaped his subsequent career. First, he edited, from 1908, the CCA's Official Circular, which included a record of the official proceedings, as well as notes and brief articles on matters of interest to CCA members, the majority of which he wrote himself. This included international subjects, such as the First International Road Congress, held in Paris in 1908, at which Harris attended and subsequently co-authored an account of the proceedings for an English readership. This interest in collecting, translating, editing and publishing news and notices on local government topics across the world subsequently shaped his research methods and later editorial responsibilities. It also chimed with Emile Vinck's vision of the UIV as a clearing house of technical information from which municipalities around the world could benefit. Indeed, it is likely that Vinck and Harris' relationship began with their participation at international events like the 1908 Paris Congress, the first Congress on the Administrative

---

[35] Harris was also a member of the long-established Reform Club from 1895.

[36] University of Birmingham Cadbury Research Library (CRL), County Councils Association, CCA/A/1/5 Unsigned minutes, Executive Council Meeting, 8 May 1902, 40.

[37] Christine Bellamy, *Administering Central-Local Relations 1871–1919: The Local Government Board in its Fiscal and Cultural Context* (Manchester: Manchester University Press, 1988), 60–63.

Sciences in Brussels in 1910 (Harris was the Secretary to the British Committee) and the follow-up Congress in Madrid in 1915.[38]

Second, Harris developed an interest in housing reform and planning at a time that county councils had become statutorily engaged with rural housing provision. The CCA had, from 1908, a Housing and Small Holdings Committee, which took particular interest in the Housing, Town Planning, &c. Act, 1909, the first national legislation to introduce a system of town planning within local government.[39] Harris was already a member of the Garden Cities Association (renamed, in 1909, the Garden Cities and Town Planning Association (GCA)), and had authored a short pamphlet on Ebenezer Howard's model in 1906. He subsequently joined the GCA's Council and Executive Committee, wrote for its periodical, *The Garden City* (later renamed *Garden Cities and Town Planning*), on the housing of the working classes, and lectured widely on its work, including local branches of the National League of Young Liberals.[40]

Having developed a nascent interest in studying overseas local government problems during his formative years at the CCA, Harris subsequently built an international reputation for his knowledge and expertise of administrative practice during his tenure as Head of the Foreign Branch of the Intelligence Division in the Ministry of Health, a position he held from 1919 until his retirement from the civil service in 1933. He developed a large network of overseas contacts in order to pursue comparative research; practically, this involved collating and assessing data on foreign and commonwealth local government collected on behalf of the Royal Commission on Local Government in 1924–25. The Commission had been formed in response to long-standing CCA pressure to curb the ambitions of county boroughs to extend their jurisdictional powers into rural areas. However, faced with a mass of data, in a variety of languages, the Commission omitted it from its report, 'owing both to want of knowledge and to want of time.'[41]

To capitalize on the rich database at his disposal, Harris wrote a book-length study of the structure of local government across a large swathe of the world. Initially published in French for the UIV, neither the Ministry of Health

---

[38] CRL CCA/B/2/1, Official Circular, Volumes 1–12, boxes 1–3; George M. Harris and H.T. Wakelam, *The First International Road Congress, Paris, 1908* (London: Wyman & Sons, 1908). Harris's report on the Brussels Congress is published in George M. Harris, *Problems of Local Government* (London: P.S. King & Son, 1910).

[39] CRL CCA/A/2/2, Signed Minutes of the Executive Council of the CCA, 28 May 1908.

[40] George M. Harris, *The Garden City Movement* (London: Garden City Association, 1906); *The Garden City* 2 (February 1907): 275, 280–81.

[41] English National Archives (NA) HLG/8/62, Royal Commission on Local Government Paper No. 222: M.(ontagu) H.(arris), 'Note on the publication of information received as to local govt in the British Empire and in foreign countries', 30 January 1926, 3.

nor Foreign Office were interested in sanctioning an official publication, so P.S. King & Son issued an English version with an additional chapter on local government in Britain.[42] The book had a dual influence over Harris' later work. Firstly, although it was organized into separate chapters on individual countries, it pointed the way forward in approaching the academic study of public administration through a comparative empirical methodology. In so doing, the book built upon earlier comparisons of municipal government, his summary chapter identifying three key areas in which local authorities everywhere were subject to increasing constraints: in their level of financial control over their budgets, their legal relations with central government and their increasing reliance on unelected officials. Central control was welcomed where it intended to improve local service delivery; whereas centralization as an end in itself was a more worrying matter entirely. In the revised second edition, he further warned against emerging tendencies to centralize public service delivery, with the eradication of local democracy in totalitarian regimes serving as a lesson for democratic local government in Britain, the United States and elsewhere.[43]

Secondly, Harris exposed the difficulties of talking about local government in any holistic way, distinguishing instead between 'local government' and 'local self-government'. Since the former historically referred to '... the power of the local authority, whatever it may be, to act independently of any external control', this was an increasingly redundant definition in an interdependent world. The latter concept, on the other hand, required a broader understanding to render it useful, notably 'the participation of the community as a whole in the public administration', itself a growing concern with increasingly apathetic local electorates.[44] Driven by his growing concerns at diminishing voter turnout in English local elections, Harris later argued that, in order to encourage better citizen engagement with local democracy, local authorities, along with other bodies like the Workers' Educational Association, should take the initiative in educating adults in citizenship and also employ officers to publicize their activities.[45]

In a later book, Harris sharpened this dual definition by distinguishing between 'local state government' – 'the government of all parts of a country by means of local agents appointed, and responsible only to, the central government' – and 'local self-government' – that is, 'government by local bodies, freely elected, which, while subject to the supremacy of the national government, are endowed in some respects with power, discretion and responsibility, which

---

[42]   George M. Harris, *Local Government in Many Lands: A Comparative Study* (London: P.S. King & Son, 1925).

[43]   Harris, *Local Government in Many Lands*, 375–93.

[44]   Harris, *Local Government in Many Lands*, 2.

[45]   NCL, NCSRS/B6/12 Box 53, George M. Harris, 'Local Government Publicity', 21 May 1942.

they can exercise without control over their decisions by the higher authority.'[46] For Harris, 'local state government' was coterminous with local administration in that power tended to reside in either the centrally appointed agents – the French prefects and German burgomasters, for instance – and not with the elected representatives of local ratepayers, as was the case in England and Wales where 'local self-government' was commonplace:

> To an Englishman ... He is imbued with the idea that genuine self-government means the participation of the whole community by means of representative councils, which are themselves vested with the legislative, executive and administrative authority to the exclusion of any other local body or person. The existence, therefore, of an executive which is independent of the representative council, the handing over of the actual government of a town for a number of years to a burgomaster or a small number of commissioners, even though these are locally elected, is to him the negation of self-government.[47]

Harris' involvement with the UIV, therefore, came about through his academic scholarship as much as his governmental responsibilities and professional and personal connections. His continued participation in other national and international town planning networks – he was one of the founders and honorary secretary of the International Garden Cities and Town Planning Association in 1913 and the president of the Town Planning Institute in 1927–28 – broadened and deepened his expertise in local government matters from his roots in county council administration, and allowed him to share his blossoming enthusiasm for international models and comparative study.[48] It was this international exposure – as an administrator, author and networker – and his connections to leading governmental elites within the Ministry of Health that gave him pre-eminence as one of the leading local government officials in Britain from the mid-1920s.

British participation in the UIV's activities was, at best, lukewarm for the first decade or more of its existence, which made Harris' involvement all the more significant. Notwithstanding sporadic interest from individual municipal officers, there was no sustained co-ordinated institutional interest in participation. The UIV's proposal to establish a central statistical office in Brussels was dismissed within central government circles as 'entirely mischievous', the work of a small group of self-serving socialists seeking to undermine the work

---

[46]   George M. Harris, *Comparative Local Government* (London: Hutchinson's University Library, 1948), 9.

[47]   Harris, *Local Government in Many Lands*, 376.

[48]   His election as President was, according to his predecessor, designed to 'keep them in touch with what was being done in other parts of the world': *Journal of the Town Planning Institute* 13 (July 1927): 272.

of existing international bodies like the League of Nations and the International Congress on Administrative Sciences.[49] Despite Vinck's repeated efforts to secure ministerial support for the venture, civil servants – notably the Ministry of Health's principal assistant secretary, Ioan Gwilym Gibbon (Harris' superior officer) – were deliberately stand-offish. Gibbon warned Vinck that 'the one chance of obtaining active support from the British municipalities is to convince them that the "Union" is going to be of practical help to them in dealing with their own problems ... [T]he mere collection of facts is not sufficient; their significance must be appreciated, and a proper value attached to them.'[50]

Harris' involvement – which formally began with his participation at the second UIV congress in Amsterdam in 1924[51] – can, therefore, be read as the overlapping of two agendas. Firstly, it was the natural extension of Harris' personal and academic interest in intermunicipalism. Secondly, he was hand-picked by Gibbon, himself an advocate of marrying scholarship with administrative expertise, to monitor Vinck's motives and movements. Careful to cultivate a neutral political identity so as not to ostracize his peers, Harris was a popular choice to act as the link between the reformist-minded internationalists on the UIV and the more conservative elements of the English civil service. Indeed, his contributions at meetings drew repeated praise for their practical benefits to other British participants. For example, at the Paris Congress in 1925, he acted as *de facto* translator for the vast majority of French papers, and allegedly provided the only sustained intellectual discussion on the papers.[52] Meanwhile, his growing friendship with Vinck gave him intimate access to the UIV's Secretariat, which he used to convince Gibbon of Vinck's practical motives. Harris and Gibbon subsequently convinced the English local authority associations to join the UIV on a trial period; the individual had evidently laid the groundwork for institutional proliferation in the urban network, though it helped that he himself was a product of this environment.[53]

Official sanction inevitably brought greater local authority participation in the UIV's activities, aided in no small part by its adoption, following Harris' involvement, of the English title 'International Union of Local Authorities' alongside its French title. An English Standing Committee of the Union was constituted in March 1927 with Harris as its general secretary and editor of its quarterly journal, *Local Government Abroad*, which carried news and reports

[49]   NA HLG/52/1000, Anonymous note on the work of the IULA, 17 January 1921.

[50]   NA HLG/52/1000, Correspondence between Emile Vinck and I.G. Gibbon, 15 May 1924–28 December 1924. Quote from letter, 6 June 1924.

[51]   NCL NCSRS/B8/17 Box 59 comprises a folder of UIV material collected over the years by Harris. The earliest document pertains to the Amsterdam congress.

[52]   NA HLG/52/1000, Report by English representatives on 'Union Internationale des Villes et Communes Congress at Paris', 28 September to 4 October 1925, 3.

[53]   NA HLG/52/1000, note by G.M. Harris, 11 February 1926.

on international municipal activities. In 1928 he was elected as one of England's three representatives on the UIV Permanent Bureau. Harris' involvement is noticeable for signalling a changed direction in the Union's work, away from its initial utopian objectives of pacifism and universal brotherhood and towards more practical matters of local administration. Harris himself noted the English delegation's 'considerable influence' in framing new policy at the Düsseldorf council meeting in October 1926, which approved of addressing practical subjects at its congresses – the Seville and Barcelona congress in 1929 duly discussed local government finances, municipal trading and land expropriation – and the collation of useful information for local authorities' practical use; the AMC approved of this too.[54] All documentation would also be available in English upon request; Harris himself translated and published abridged articles from the UIV's official periodical, *L'administration locale*, for his journal's readership, further indicating his influence over its changed direction.

As the chief English representative on the UIV, Harris played a pivotal role in seeking official sanction and organizing the programme for the 1932 Congress in London.[55] Working in tandem with officials in the London County Council, with input from a special committee of the AMC, Harris devised a programme around two themes that were pertinent to contemporary English local government: the practical working of local authorities, and the recruitment and training of paid officials. During the preparations, the comparative dimension was continuously flagged up as a point of interest, Harris being particularly interested in the contrasts between the English committee, German burgomaster, French prefecture and North American city manager systems.[56] The stress on administrative practice and comparative study obviously resonated with the US government, which sent its first official delegation of local authority representatives to the congress, as well as numerous large British municipalities; Birmingham, Liverpool, Manchester, York and Cardiff were each invited to serve on the Congress committee.[57]

The Congress was, by and large, a success: despite not attracting the number of overseas delegates as anticipated, owing to the world depression, 44 countries

---

54   NA HLG/52/1000, Harris to Gibbon, 11 October 1926; Minutes of Standing Committee for England and Wales, 10 March 1927, 11 May 1927; NA HLG/52/1001, Minutes of Standing Committee for England and Wales, 27 January 1928; CRL AMC/A/2/10, Association of Municipal Corporations, Minutes of Council, Report of Sub-Committee on the Union Internationale des Villes et Communes, 1 February 1927.

55   NA HLG/52/1001, Vinck to Harris, 4 June 1928; CRL AMC/A/2/10, Minutes of Council, 17 October 1929, 163.

56   NA HLG/52/1001, Minutes of Standing Committee, 28 February 1929, 2; *The Municipal Review* (*TMR*) 1 (December 1930): 523.

57   NA HLG/52/1001, Minutes of Standing Committee, 4 July 1929, 2. Leeds and Sheffield were later added, along with Edinburgh and Glasgow.

were represented in an official capacity, including some from the British Commonwealth, and a good number from South and North America, who had shown little interest in the UIV's activities hitherto.[58] Most significantly, the Congress cemented Britain and, in particular, Harris as integral members of the intermunicipalist framework, so much so that Harris was earmarked as Wibaut's likely successor as President. Following his retirement from the Ministry of Health in 1933, he embarked on a year-long tour of local government, studying municipal systems in North America, India, Jamaica and Japan, and lecturing on comparative local government to universities, state leagues of municipalities and research institutes.[59] His subsequent book, published by the Union, comprised a series of observations on municipal systems in these countries, and reiterated his belief in the comparative method.[60] The book builds on his prior administrative experience by offering a window onto the historically specific contexts within which local authority associations evolved. Whilst his case studies (beginning with the Florida League of Municipalities and ending with the Local Self-Government Institute of Bombay) lack comparative or theoretical depth, they point towards a growing convergence of urban and municipal experiences, particularly across the vista of existing and former empires, as recently recognized by historians.[61] Indeed, Harris cites the paucity of systematic 'municipal research' in Britain relative to the United States as proof that such studies highlight important lessons for metropolitan policy-makers and challenge the assumptions of 'those who still think (perhaps rightly) that our [British] system of local government is the best in the world'.[62]

Harris never wavered in his conviction that there was a practical value in international networking. Having succeeded Wibaut to the UIV presidential chair, his first official responsibility was to preside over the 1936 Congress in Berlin where he met privately with the German Chancellor, Adolf Hitler.[63] Although the Ministry of Health refused to send any official delegates, Harris justified his attendance in robust fashion in a letter to one of the Ministry's senior officials: 'it would be absurd for a body of the character of the International Union to stand aloof from Germany on account of the present form of

[58] For a summary of the Congress papers and reports, see *TMR* 3 (May 1932): 195–207 and 3 (June 1932): 255–61.
[59] *TMR* 5 (July 1934): 313.
[60] George M. Harris, *Westward to the East: The Record of a World Tour in Search of Local Government* (Brussels and London: International Union of Local Authorities, 1935).
[61] Andrew Brown-May, 'In the Precincts of the Global City: The Transnational Network of Municipal Affairs in Melbourne, Australia', in Saunier and Ewen, eds, *Another Global City*, 19–34; John Griffiths, 'Were There Municipal Networks in the British World c.1890–1939?', *Journal of Imperial and Commonwealth History* 37 (2009): 575–97.
[62] Harris, *Westward to the East*, 143–5.
[63] *Local Government Administration* 2 (September 1936): 133–4.

government, especially as it is definitely precluded from paying attention to any of the politics of any of the countries to which it may visit or with which it may be connected.'[64] The absence of local democracy in Germany made no difference to Harris in this sense; German local government had effectively become 'a purely bureaucratic institution' under the direct control of the central government, which inevitably rendered it even more important to study as a comparator to other Western models.[65]

Conclusion

As this chapter has shown, a decentred take on individual agency, on personal beliefs, orientations and actions, allows for an interpretative approach of the constructivist and agency-driven nature of transnational municipalism during the inter-war period. Stepping away from macro-institutional inquiries into the networks and events of transnational municipalism, and instead highlighting the way in which historical protagonists – in this case Wibaut and Harris – actually operated within a variety of networks and organizations, provides us with insights into how transnational institutions were vested with acts, ideas and ideals stemming from personal beliefs and motivations.

We argue that a decentred interpretation helps to explain institutional practice and change. Human action renders visible institutional practice. Institutions reflect social realities and human personalities; they are constructed categories, perceived (temporary) structures that, simultaneously, enable possibilities and limitations of human action within a particular setting in time and space. As Rhodes and Bevir, amongst others, have demonstrated, it is this decentring of human agency that reveals the ways in which individuals influence institutional practice.

In addition to this, Rhodes and Bevir have established the value of providing thick descriptions of the lives and careers of political actors. The same can be said for Wibaut and Harris. Firstly, their stories make a significant historiographical contribution to our wider understanding of inter-war transnational municipalism, not least because they have both been overlooked actors on the international stage. Secondly, they provide a human link between the local and the international spheres of government: both men represented local government interests through their work for, in Wibaut's case, the Amsterdam municipality, and, in Harris' case, as secretary for the County Councils Association; they subsequently manifested these local interests on the international stage. Thirdly, the fact that both men juggled a plethora of

---

64 NA HLG/52/1001, G.M. Harris to H.S. Hunter, 22 June 1936.
65 Harris, *Comparative Local Government*, 14–15.

interests, their lives are – to the historical eye at least – fragmented across a range of archival sources, many of which require 'reading against the grain' in order to identify their own voices and piece together their career path. Thick description offers a way of linking together these multiple roles in order to flesh out their individual roles and establish their cultural beliefs and attitudes. Finally, Wibaut and Harris' contributions to the organization and management of the UIV were shaped by their work elsewhere: Harris' commitment to the UIV's practical work, for example, was the product of his work with the local authority associations and the garden cities movement, where he also developed his enthusiasm for comparative research as the best method for identifying solutions to urban problems.

Photographs visibly demonstrate the changing roles and influences of individuals in the international networks that they participated in. The official photograph of delegates at the 1924 UIV Congress in Amsterdam (Figure 9.3)

Un groupe de délégués au Deuxième Congrès International des Villes.
AMSTERDAM 1924.

Figure 9.3   UIV Congress in Amsterdam, 1924

Source: IIème Congrès International des Villes organisé par l'Union Internationale des Villes sous le Patronage de la Municipalité d'Amsterdam: Amsterdam, 30 juin et 1er juillet 1924. Documents Préliminaires, Rapports, Délibérations, Voeux, Annexes (Brussels: Union Internationale des Villes, 1924).

Figure 9.4   Members of the UIV Permanent Bureau meet at the offices of the Union of Dutch Communes in The Hague, 1935

Source: Local Government Administration 1 (June 1935): 63.

places Wibaut, as UIV President, centre-stage, flanked by Emile Vinck, the UIV Secretary-General and Director, and Henri Sellier who, as the mayor of Suresnes (1919–41) and General Secretary of the Union of French Towns, was an influential figure on the UIV's Permanent Bureau.[66] Harris, attending his first UIV meeting, is placed on the second row, second from left, physically removed and somewhat aloof from the main focus of the photograph. Eleven years later, in June 1935, in the photograph of members of the UIV Permanent Bureau for a meeting at the offices of the Union of Dutch Communes in The Hague (Figure 9.4), Harris has moved to the front row (second from right) and is flanked by Wibaut and Dr Kurt Jesserich, President of the German Association of Municipalities and Director of the Institute of Communal Science at the University of Berlin, cigarette in hand. This photograph captures a more relaxed and informal mood for the Bureau and Harris, in particular, looks at ease in his role as one of the UIV's three vice-presidents (with Sellier and Jesserich), with a bundle of committee papers under his left arm and his right-hand tucked in his pocket.

A striking similarity between Wibaut and Harris is their coexisting belief in, on the one hand, the practical functionality of transnational endeavours and collaboration, and, on the other hand, an overarching, deeply rooted intellectual outlook. However, this coexistence of incentives of feasible, physical output and theoretical, metaphysical input also points at a major difference between the two. Harris, being one of the leading experts in public administration studies in Britain, elegantly interlinked his scholarly skills and findings to the comparative setup of the UIV's substantial agenda from the mid-1920s onwards. Wibaut, in contrast, openly appreciated the comparison between policy schemes, organizational models, municipal finance and administrative routines as a means to arrive at best practices, but in the same breath espoused ideals of universalism and brotherhood, which were so key during his formative years as a publicist and administrator.

The beliefs and motivations of Wibaut amounted to a blend of municipal socialism, socialist internationalism and pacifism which all materialized during the last decades of the nineteenth century. As such, the institutional genesis of the UIV in 1913 was the culmination of an ongoing differentiation within the expanding universe of – mostly ideology laden – internationalist movements, of which the 'Urban Internationale', and thus the UIV, was one outcome. After its rejuvenation in 1924, Wibaut's generation within the UIV was confronted with the beliefs of Harris' generation, which expressed a firm belief in the non-political methods of social science and boasted its practical experience in public service, not as politicians but rather as scholars and administrators.

---

[66]   On Sellier, see Stéphane Frioux, 'Henri Sellier, Un maire au service de la circulation des savoirs sur et pour la ville, 1919–1939', *Histoire Urbaine* 37 (2013): 107–23.

Chapter 10

The (Trans)National Question: Nazi Spatial and Urban Planning

Janet Ward

This chapter applies transnational insights regarding urban and regional space to what appears at first sight to be a diametrically opposed context: Nazi German exterminatory policies of supranational expansion across central and Eastern Europe.[1] The *space+race* planning activities of Nazi Germany are of particular importance for understanding why transnationalism, while apparently functioning in German cities today much as it does in other European metropolitan environments, has nonetheless emerged out of a rather different earlier set of contexts than can be found in (say) Milan, Madrid or London. Anthropologist Ruth Mandel, for example, has demonstrated the legacy of Nazi-era citizenship ideologies for Turkish-German urban identities in Berlin today.[2]

---

[1] Scholars are increasingly advocating a renewal of the historiography of the Holocaust and the Second World War by means of a highly differentiated *spatial* understanding of the Third Reich. See for example, Götz Aly and Susanne Heim, *Vorkenker der Vernichtung: Auschwitz und die deutschen Pläne für eine neue europäische Ordnung* (Hamburg, 1991); Niels Gutschow, *Ordnungswahn: Architekten Planen Im 'Eingedeutschten Osten' 1939–1945* (Gütersloh: Bertelsmann Fachzeitschriften, 2001); Uwe Mai, *'Rasse und Raum': Agrarpolitik, Sozial- und Raumplanung im NS-Staat* (Paderborn: Ferdinand Schoeningh, 2002); Tim Cole, *Holocaust City: The Making of the Jewish Ghetto* (New York: Routledge, 2002); David Blackbourn, *The Conquest of Nature: Water, Landscape and the Making of Modern Germany* (London, UK: Random House, 2006); Ariane Leendertz, *Ordnung schaffen. Deutsche Raumplanung im 20. Jahrhundert* (Göttingen: Wallstein Verlag, 2008); and Geoff Ely, *Nazism as Fascism: Violence, Ideology, and the Ground of Consent in Germany 1930–1945* (New York: Routledge, 2013). A recent example of this growing historiographical awareness can also be found in Winson Chu, Jesse Kaufman, and Michael Meng, 'A Sonderweg through Eastern Europe? The Varieties of German Rule in Poland during the Two World Wars', *German History* 31 (2013): 318–44.

[2] Ruth Mandel, *Cosmopolitan Anxieties: Turkish Challenges to Citizenship and Belonging in Germany* (Durham, NC: Duke University Press, 2008). For an exploration of German urban-national heritage in the transnational age, see Jeffry M. Diefendorf and Janet Ward, eds, *Transnationalism and the German City* (New York and Basingstoke, UK: Palgrave Macmillan, 2014).

Moreover, the Nazis' encounters with and adaptations of transnational urban and regional processes in the Eastern territories of the Second World War can help offset some of the still-prevailing assumptions that transnationalism somehow carries its own progressive politics within itself. Perhaps we have wished to believe this too readily since, as Saskia Sassen has remarked, '[t]he national as container of social process and power is cracked'.[3] For Sassen, the ideal, creative urban drive blends localized, participatory practice with transnational range and relevance – her focus is on economic processes that interlink cities into a network more dynamic than that of nationality. With reference to the global city, the existence of which proves that the national is but a 'cracked container' from here on out, Sassen points to a transnationally informed, urban *civitas*: the 'possibilities for a politics of membership that is simultaneously localized and transnational'.[4]

None of this, however, speaks to the rather less impressive proximity of transnational processes with the tyrannies of self and empire. At best, urban cosmopolitanism today often emerges from a selfish elitism behind the purportedly non-parochial veneer: transnational spaces are 'always situated, always imbued with partiality', and often serve prejudice, passion and hatred.[5] Worse for transnationalism is how Arjun Appadurai has seen that transnational processes in our contemporary era of post-9/11 racial intolerance have inadvertently spawned a new wave of 'geographies of anger'. But of course, such 'geographies of anger' are not new, and emerged first from imperial practices. Nazi Germany's impulse toward making Eastern Europe into its compensatory post-First World War empire – its *Drang nach Osten* – re-oriented Western modernity's imperial legacy from overseas toward a far closer, and even harsher, inner continental land-grab, and may indeed be designated one of the most intricately planned 'geographies of [transnational] anger'.[6] The recent transnational reorientation of scholars as part of the 'spatial' (place- or milieu-based) turn in the study of German history and culture reveals a focus not just on the rise of nineteenth-century nationalism and imperial expansion amidst transnational, Grail-like quests for a Germanic-Aryan past:[7] attention is now

---

[3]   Saskia Sassen, 'The Repositioning of Citizenship: Emergent Subjects and Spaces for Politics', *Berkeley Journal of Sociology* 36 (2002): 4–25, 18.

[4]   Sassen, 'The Repositioning of Citizenship', 4.

[5]   David Ley, 'Transnational Spaces and Everyday Lives', *Transactions of the Institute of British Geographers* 29 (2004): 151–64, 162.

[6]   Arjun Appadurai, 'Fear of Small Numbers: An Essay on the Geography of Anger', in Gary Bridge and Sophie Watson, eds, *The Blackwell City Reader*, 2nd ed. (Malden, MA and Oxford, UK: Blackwell, 2010), 138–43, 140.

[7]   Jennifer Jenkins, 'Transnationalism and German History', H-Net (23 January 2006): http://geschichte-transnational.clio-online.net/transnat.asp?type=diskussionen&id=875 &view=pdf&pn=forum. Date accessed 10 January 2015.

also being directed toward the National Socialist sense of territory, planning and space, leading increasingly to a reassessment of its role in that regime's genocidal ideology. In the case of Nazism, 'a relational history of identity spaces cannot stop at national boundaries'. Rather, scholars of the Third Reich like Claus-Christian W. Szejnmann and Maiken Umbach are now finding many 'local', 'regional', and 'supranational' arenas at work.[8]

As David Harvey has noted, 'the most fanatical localism and nationalism' were the successful products of intensely unifying visual-spatial displays under Nazism.[9] Yet Nazi policies and actions, no matter how monolithic in staged rituals or in official discourses, tended to become much more diverse when applied in practice to the newly (and partly re-)acquired territories of Eastern Europe. Over 1.8 million ethnic Germans, mostly from the Soviet Union, were brokered back into these Eastern territories in a series of population transfers that expelled Slavs and exterminated Jews. Not surprisingly, the planning processes of both urban racial-spatial destruction and urban racial-spatial reconstruction for the Third Reich proved to be a massively complex undertaking.

We can refer to diaspora-theorist Robin Cohen's various horticultural typologies of migratory diasporas so as to better recognize some applications of the Nazis' transnational encounters, planned and otherwise, as they moved eastwards across the 'inland empire' of their newly (re-)Germanized Europe.[10] Cohen's taxonomy of gardening terms helps demonstrate how the Nazis deployed several distinct types of spatial diasporas – hence not solely the most infamous technique of ethnic cleansing's 'weeding' via expulsion and mass murder. They engaged in 'sowing', with their eastbound out-migrations of Aryan Reich Germans, plans that were in turn fuelled by 'transplanting' people in their slave labour/service diaspora. In this regard, we can pay particular attention to the way in which outermost Eastern border areas of the Third Reich were to be demographically enhanced (that is, Germanized), and new, purified small city-settlements were to be devised and maintained. The Organisation Todt's systematic infrastructural enhancements of Eastern Europe can also be understood as the replantings, or as Cohen suggests 'layerings', of an expanding Nazi business/trade diaspora.

Further, instances of what Cohen intriguingly refers to as an open, uncontrolled 'cross-pollination' certainly occurred in Nazi urban contexts, even if only sporadically: the Jewish and then Polish uprisings in Warsaw, for example,

---

[8]   Claus-Christian W. Szejnmann and Maiken Umbach, eds, *Heimat, Region, and Empire: Spatial Identities under National Socialism* (New York and Basingtoke, UK: Palgrave 2012), 14.

[9]   David Harvey, *The Condition of Postmodernity: An Enquiry into the Origins of Cultural Change* (Cambridge, MA: Blackwell, 1989), 277.

[10]   Robin Cohen, *Global Diasporas: An Introduction* (New York: Routledge, 1997, 2nd ed. 2008).

certainly impacted the Nazis' implementation of severe urban planning changes for the Polish capital. Moreover, the Jews' ghetto uprising in Warsaw caused the Nazis to speed up the Final Solution: liquidations of ghettos immediately increased across the Eastern territories. At the same time, the Warsaw ghetto uprising inspired other Jewish uprisings in ghettos and camps across Eastern Europe. Unexpected 'cross-pollination' occurred in the post-war years, too: 'Central Place' geographer Walter Christaller's Nazi plans for occupied Poland were adopted in, of all places, the new state of Israel. Israeli planners in the 1950s, following the US's lead in uncritically adopting post-war CPT as a yardstick of post-war quantitative geography, reapplied the very same Central Place Theory that had been intended for a Jew-free Eastern Europe, when they set up a hierarchical system of villages (*moshavim*) and cities up against the border with Lebanon (for example, Kiryat Shmona), or near the southern end of the West Bank (for example, the town of Kiryat Gat in the Lachish region).[11]

Human border fortification was found immediately necessary for the National Socialist borders of empire. As both David Blackbourn and Geoff Ely have pointed out, it was no coincidence that Reinhard Heydrich gave a speech in September 1941 (four months before he hosted the Wannsee Conference) highlighting the use of German-Aryan populations who were being placed in the European East as human 'walls' or ramparts to protect the empire: 'We slowly lay down one German wall after another so that, working eastwards, German people of German blood can carry out German settlement'.[12] Reichsminister for the Occupied Eastern Territories Alfred Rosenberg advocated this same 'strategic border-fortification' point when he lectured a month later on urban planning for the Nazi European East, asserting that the long-term '*fertility* of the soil' of the borderlands was at stake here, and so the hard task of embedding the best (and not the absolute dregs)

---

[11]   See Walter Christaller, 'Die zentralen Orte in den Ostgebieten und ihre Kultur- und Marktbereiche'. Part 1 of a series entitled *Struktur und Gestaltung der zentralen Orte des deutschen Ostens*, for the Reichsarbeitsgemeinschaft für Raumforschung (Leipzig: K.F. Koehler Verlag, 1941), 2–22. See also Arnon Golan, 'Israeli Historical Geography and the Holocaust: Reconsidering the Research Agenda', *Journal of Historical Geography* 28.4 (2002): 554–65; and Joshua Davidovich, 'How a Nazi Planner Shaped Early Israel', *The Times of Israel* (October 11, 2013) and T.J. Barnes and C. Minca, 'Nazi Spatial Theory: The Dark Geographies of Carl Schmitt and Walter Christaller', *Annals of the Association of American Geographers* 103.3 (2013): 669–87.

[12]   Quoted by Geoff Eley, 'Commentary: Empire, Ideology, and the East: Thoughts on Nazism's Spatial Imaginary', in Szejnmann and Umbach, eds, *Heimat, Region, and Empire*, 252–75, 264; and David Blackbourn, *The Conquest of Nature: Water, Landscape and the Making of Modern Germany* (London, UK: Random House, 2006), 273.

of Germanic colonizing populations right next to the Slavic edge would be key to the Third Reich's ultimate success.[13]

The Nazi land grab disguised itself as a purifying, civilizing mission for Europe. A veritable *Ostrausch* reigned for planners and other professionals alike.[14] Nazi planners of the Reich Office for Spatial Order (Reichsstelle für Raumordnung [RfR], founded in 1935), and after 1939 those involved in drawing up the 'Generalplan Ost' of Heinrich Himmler's SS main planning office (RKF[DV]: Reichskommissariat für die Festigung deutschen Volkstums, led by Konrad Meyer), conceived of the radical Germanizing colonization of Europe's East.[15] New arteries, townships and regions were intended as sites that would be conveniently ready for Christaller's transnationally applicable Central Place planning typologies, because they would be ethnically cleansed of their existing populations. One RfR diagram featured an 'eye of the space planner' that could reach across panoptically in order to transform all levels of social and economic life: 'People, Nature, Economy, Energy, Transportation' (Figure 10.1). Indeed, RfR offices were strategically positioned all across the Occupied Eastern Territories.

The Nazi occupation of Europe reveals a defensive, fortifying, reactive obsession that impacted both the external borders of the 'Großgermanisches Reich deutscher Nation' as well as its internal urban core. This was a defensive obsession amidst multiple dispersions, demolitions, liquidations and negations of urban and spatial form. Some of these urban dispersions were the transnational by-products of invasion, some were the enablers of genocide and others were consequences of the air war: in the end, they became interrelated. Heydrich and Rosenberg portrayed ethnic German settlers (*Volksdeutsche*) becoming a human racial rampart along the empire's eastern borders and then ethnically cleansed the populations of Europe according to the Final Solution's goals; while the Organisation Todt built infrastructural linkages securing points across Germany's new East, as well as literal, concrete defense structures along perimeter lines like the Atlantikwall; and Albert Speer led a bunker-building program for Germany's cities targeted in the Allied air war. And yet none of it ultimately held.

In 1941, Heinrich Dörr, a contributor to the planning journal *Raumforschung und Raumordnung*, enthused from the war front that total war meant the total subsuming and redesign, if necessary by destruction, of the urban environment in order to remake both the national city as well as the transnationally occupied

---

[13] Minutes of executive planning meeting, 30 October 1941, Reichsministerium für die besetzten Ostgebiete: Bundesarchiv Militärarchiv Freiburg, RW19 1620.

[14] Eley, in Szejnmann and Umbach, eds, *Heimat, Region, and Empire*, 262; and Blackbourn, *The Conquest of Nature*, 250, 252.

[15] See Ariane Leendertz, *Ordnung schaffen. Deutsche Raumplanung im 20. Jahrhundert* (Göttingen: Wallstein Verlag, 2008), 98–216.

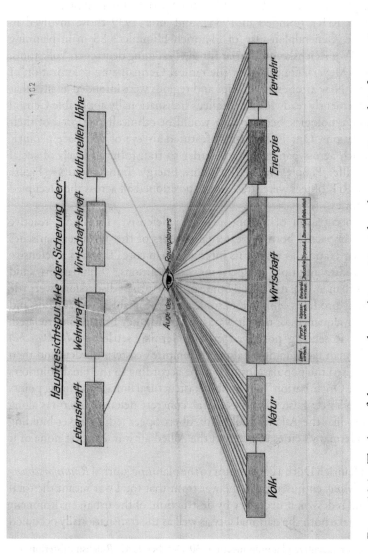

Figure 10.1 The 'eye of the space planner' is positioned as the panoptic conduit for securing Nazi 'vitality, military force, economic strength, and cultural superiority' by overseeing 'people, nature, economy, energy, and transportation'

Source: Bundesarchiv Berlin Lichterfelde, R 113 / 98 Reichsstelle für Raumordnung (1943/1944).

city in accordance with Nazified society. Be prepared as Nazis, Dörr beckoned, to 'tackle and solve' the question of urban formation ('Stadtgestaltung'). No longer reliant on Oswald Spengler's distaste for cities, Dörr asserts: 'Today we are the *co-creators of a National Socialist spatial planning*' ('Heute sind wir *Mitschaffende einer nationalsozialistischen Raumplanung*') that will lay the foundation stones of the Thousand Year Reich. Total war means total spatial synchronization: Dörr sees cities of any country controlled by Nazi Germany as sites that are to be violently remade, adhering not to urban planning principles alone but those of a 'German spatial order' in service of the state.[16] From Dörr's point of view, a clear and efficient consequence of the air war by the Allies was but a means toward constructing the new cities of the Reich that would be racially and spatially purified, decentralized and ultimately better defendable. Planning for the new East (or the reconstructed bombed-out cities of the Old Reich) would therefore avoid over-concentration in massive, high-density cities: Garden-City tenets were thus to be corroded into a new gear.[17]

This attempted urban re-formation was also a racial de-formation. The transformation of the Nazi *Lebensraum* across Eastern Europe was wholly contingent upon the displacement of Jews into their own 'death-space'. Concurrent with the air war's unavoidable impact and its creation of *tabula rasa* possibilities, there occurred within Nazi spatial and racial planning a disruption of the traditional equation between Western civilization and the human-cum-urban ideal form. As Primo Levi and Giorgio Agamben made experientially and conceptually clear, and historians Debórah Dwork and Robert Jan Van Pelt, Paul Jaskot and Tim Cole have explored in depth, the mechanisms of the Holocaust built alternative city-anatomies for urban modernity – of ghettos, slave labour camps, concentration camps and death camps.[18] Urban form itself was thereby changed.

This obsessive form of metropolitan-racial transformation can be seen in the series of maps issued by Albert Speer's GBI office (Generalbauinspektion

---

16   Heinrich Dörr, 'Bomben brechen die 'Haufen' Stadt: Stadtplanerische Betrachtung des Luftkrieges', *Raumforschung und Raumordnung* (1941): 269–73, 270, 271, 272. Emphasis original.

17   See Jeffry M. Diefendorf, 'Wartime Destruction and the Postwar Cityscape', in Charles E. Closmann, ed., *War and the Environment: Military Destruction in the Modern Age* (College Station, TX: Texas A&M University Press, 2009), 171–92.

18   Primo Levi, *The Drowned and the Saved*, trans. Raymond Rosenthal (New York: Vintage International, 1989); Giorgio Agamben, *Homo Sacer: Sovereign Power and Bare Life*, trans. Daniel Heller-Roazen (Stanford: Stanford University Press, 1998); Debórah Dwork and Robert Jan Van Pelt, *Auschwitz. 1270 to the Present* (New York: W.W. Norton, 1996); Paul B. Jaskot, *Architecture of Oppression: The SS, Forced Labor and the Nazi Monumental Building Economy* (New York and London, UK: Routledge, 2000); and Tim Cole, *Holocaust City: The Making of the Jewish Ghetto* (New York: Routledge, 2002).

zur Neugestaltung der Reichshauptstadt). These maps from 1941 display the
new 'Jew-Free Areas' ('Judenreine Gebiete') that Speer's GBI office helped to
forge. They served as confidence-boosting predictor-models for the coming
Berlin-as-Germania.[19] Expulsions and ghettoization and encampment of Jews
necessarily emptied some urban spaces and filled or created others. One of the
clearest examples of the urban-human abuse of city and human form is Sajmiste,
an international trade fair site in Belgrade, which the Nazis swiftly displaced
and degraded into a very different form of transnational Babel. The exhibition
grounds, completed in 1937, were turned into not just a concentration camp but
also a death camp for 8,000 Serbian Jews, replete with mobile gas vans travelling
right through the city.[20]

   In his article, Dörr categorizes Nazi space planning as being governed by
the Führer's 'Rücksiedlungstempo' across Europe.[21] The Holocaust's and the
Allied air war's impact on Nazi planners' urban visions fused together toward a
radically altered anthropomorphization of the modern European city, negating
and emptying out the original, naïve confidence of the Vitruvian measuring
(living, controlling) man. The forced shrinking of cities and populations was
the Nazis' own perverse method of destroying unwanted or feared demographic
strengths. The Jewish ghetto of Warsaw was completely levelled by the Nazis
after the Jews' surprise rebellion. Himmler's order to raze the Warsaw ghetto in
the spring of 1943 was intended to ensure that it would, as he stated, 'disappear
from the scene' entirely and assist thereby in the process of literally shrinking
Warsaw.[22] After the ghetto fighters' uprising, the Nazis sealed off the section
they had levelled, and vindictively wrote as the title for their official photo
album of the battle (the infamous 'Stroop Report'): 'There is no more Jewish
Sector in Warsaw!' ('Es gibt keinen jüdischen Wohnbezirk in Warschau mehr!')

   The spatial planning policy of forced removal against Jews also extended to
Warsaw itself and to Warsaw's Poles. The entire city, to be renamed simply 'Die
neue Deutsche Stadt', was to be physically re-centered with a Gauforum by the
Vistula river, and vast sections of the old city were to be demolished and not

---

[19]   Johann Friedrich Geist and Klaus Kürvers, 'Tatort Berlin, Pariser Platz: Die
Zestörung und "Entjudung" Berlins', in Jörn Düwel, Werner Durth, Niels Gutschow and
Jochen Schneider, eds, *1945. Krieg – Zerstörung – Aufbau. Architektur und Stadtplanung
1940–1960* (Berlin: Henschel Verlag, 1995), 95–7. See also Werner Durth and Günter
Behnisch, eds, *Berlin Pariser Platz. Neubau der Akademie der Künste* (Berlin: jovis Verlag,
2005), 73.

[20]   Christopher R. Browning, 'Sajmiste as a European Site of Holocaust Remembrance',
paper presented at the conference: 'If Not Now, When ...? The Future of the Site of the Old
Fairgrounds (Sajmiste) in Belgrade', Belgrade, Serbia, 2012.

[21]   Dörr, 'Bomben', 269.

[22]   Cited in Niels Gutschow and Barbara Klain, *Vernichtung und Utopie. Stadtplanung
Warschau 1939–1945* (Hamburg: Junius Verlag, 1994), 119–20.

replenished with any new citizens at all. Friedrich Gollert, in his role as head of spatial planning for Warsaw under the Nazi governorship of the Warsaw district, wrote that apart from removing Poles from the city by moving their businesses and factories elsewhere, 'a final solution of the Warsaw problem is necessary' that would effectively remove the threat of any remaining urban concentration of Poles, since only then will 'a new German center come into being instead of the former Polish citadel'. The title of the Nazi destruction and re-conception of Warsaw renames the city as 'Warsaw – the Demolition of the Polish City. The Construction of the German City'.[23] The ensuing demographic voids and gaps after the deportation and mass murder of over 300,000 Jews, as well as the planned removal of 650,000 Poles, were to be only partially refilled with Aryan German colonizers.[24]

From late 1939 on, this plan for 'Warsaw – the New German City' (better known as of 1942 as the Pabst Plan) aimed to shrink the Polish capital to 10 fully reconstituted, decentralized zones (or 'cells') each with 30,000 to 40,000 purified inhabitants. But the Poles' own uprising in their capital against the Nazis in the fall of 1944 resulted not just in the capture of the resistance fighters from the Polish Home Army, but the vindictive killing of some 150,000–200,000 of Warsaw's non-combatant inhabitants, plus the removal of those remaining. Himmler's euphemistic vision, for the Nazis' carefully plotted revenge demolition of Warsaw underway in October 1944, right up until the Red Army's arrival in the deserted and desolate city in January 1945 stopped them in the act, was 'pacification'. 'This city', announced Himmler, following Hitler's wish, 'is to disappear completely from the surface of the earth ...'[25] By the time the Soviets marched in, over half the citizens of the city were dead. More than 85 per cent of Warsaw's structures were gone, including 94 per cent of all the historic buildings: either levelled during the Warsaw uprising (25 per cent), or revenge-demolished by the Nazis (35 per cent), or already destroyed as a result of the Jewish Ghetto uprising of April and May in 1943, as well as the Nazis' air attacks of September 1939.[26]

---

[23] 'Warschau – der Abbau der Polen Stadt. Der Aufbau der deutschen Stadt. Das Aussiedeln der Juden'. Section 1 of the map shows where Hitler's Gauforum was to go; sections 2, 3, and 4 were to be rebuilt, with section 4 containing the party HQ; while sections 5 through 8 of the city were to be torn down altogether.

[24] Friedrich Gollert, 'Grundsätzliche Bemerkungen über die Gestaltung Warschaus während des Krieges und nach dem Kriege' (prob. 1944), in Niels Gutschow and Barbara Klain, eds, *Vernichtung und Utopie. Stadtplanung Warschau 1939–1945* (Hamburg: Junius Verlag, 1994), 129–30.

[25] Cited in Gutschow and Klain, *Vernichtung und Utopie*, 134.

[26] On the post-war reconstruction of Jewish sites in Warsaw, see Michael Meng, *Shattered Spaces: Encountering Jewish Ruins in Postwar Germany and Poland* (Cambridge, MA: Harvard University Press, 2011), 67–84, 175–80, 231–3.

The destruction and remaking of the Third Reich's cities and continental space during the Second World War and the Holocaust are far from separate. Final Solution techniques from the Eastern Territories were even applied to post-air-war clear up. W.G. Sebald has charted one of the war's most grotesque instances of Nazi transnational substitution between the hollowed-out spaces of urban form caused by the decimation of European Jews during the Holocaust and the German civilian bodies massacred during the air war. Such Holocaust-to-air-war interchange is overtly articulated when Sebald mentions in his air war essay how it was precisely SS guards, trained at the Treblinka death camp in the art of burning masses of gassed Jewish bodies, who were brought in to apply their transnationally acquired, very specific skills to getting rid of a massive pile of German corpses in Dresden after the incendiary bombing of February 1945.[27]

Trying to offset the potential spread of disease in the immediate wake of the bombings, Dresden officials invited the Treblinka experts to cremate the bodies – between 6,800 and 9,000 of them, according to varying estimates. This was done on a funeral pyre at the Altmarkt. The men from from the *Ostraum*'s second most efficient death camp after Auschwitz burned 500 at a time over a two-week period, covering the corpses in gasoline after first layering them on top of a metal platform made out of ruined iron girders, with broken window frames serving as the lattice supports for the multiple layers of people placed on top, and some straw to assist in the process. 'That's how I did it before in the East', explained a helpful SS officer to eye-witness Max Seydewitz, Saxony's future minister president in the German Democratic Republic, in his diary of the city. 'When one burns, they all burn'.[28] While the 9,000 square feet of ashes of these German civilians were respectfully spread in a mass grave in a local cemetery, the Heidefriedhof, Holocaust victims by contrast, after being gassed and cremated at the Nazi death camps, became as Primo Levi mourned a 'a handful of ashes in some near-by field'.[29]

The grotesquely transnational intersection here between the Treblinka guards' special expertise in the death camp obliteration of civilian corpses and their useful assistance in the 'natural history of destruction' in Dresden is still being censored out of the arena of public memory. For example, in an art project by the group 'kunstplan' that was sponsored by the city Dresden in 2001 to visually mark the wounds of the air attack across the city, there is no reference

---

[27]   W.G. Sebald, *On the Natural History of Destruction*, trans. Anthea Bell (New York: The Modern Library, 2004), 98.

[28]   Max Seydewitz, *Die unbesiegbare Stadt. Zerstörung und Wiederaufbau von Dresden* (Berlin: Kongress-Verlag, 1956), 166.

[29]   Primo Levi, *Survival in Auschwitz* (New York: Collier, 1993), 89; see also Levi, *The Drowned and the Saved*, 125.

to the Treblinka link at this particular new 'site of memory', the Altmarkt.[30] At the Altmarkt itself the memorial plaque makes no mention of the Treblinka guards whatsoever – a blindspot in collective memory offering, perhaps, a foreboding regarding Dresden's suitability as the birthplace, in the autumn of 2014, of the anti-immigrant Pegida movement ('Patriotische Europäer gegen die Islamisierung des Abendlands').

As the post-bombing response in Dresden shows, the German *Altreich* was not unaffected by the transnational consequences of war. The Nazis' desired infallibility of the re-planning of the occupied East, their technics of fortification design, and their insistent injection of ideology into urban and empire defense, can best be charted according to the motifs of the protecting German home: *Heimat*, or more literally, a fortified *domus*.[31] Articulations of the *domus* in the Nazi ideology of civil defense are frequent in the myriad engineering and design journals, books and public training manuals that arose after 1933 as Germany began building ideology into structural realities across the country.[32] Civilian defense preparations, however, had already commenced in earnest in most European cities in the 1920s in the wake of the trauma of the First World War. Berlin received its first bunker in 1935, a year after the government had categorized all of Germany's cities and towns into first, second and third tiers of risk for air attack. Ninety-four German cities designated in the first-ranked zone received public funds for building their air defense structures. The 'Führer's

---

30   56 memorial depots were installed across the city on the 56th anniversary of the Dresden bombings in 2001, and since then one additional depot has been added each year. See Kunstplan, *Gravuren des Krieges. Scars of War. Dresden 1945: Stadtführer. City Guide* (Altenburg: DZA, 2006), 9–10. The text of the memorial plaque of 2005 reads: 'Nach den Luftangriffen vom 13. Bis 14. February 1945 auf Dresden wurden an dieser Stelle die Leichen von 6865 Menschen verbrannt'. The omission is also continued by Oliver Reinhard in his essay in Reinhard, Matthias Neutzner, and Wolfgang Hesse, eds, *Das rote Leuchten. Dresden und der Bombenkrieg* (Dresden: edition Sächsische Zeitung, 2007), 100–101. Both publications are sponsored by the organization '13. Februar 1945' ('Remember 13 February 1945') chaired by Neutzner. The organization was vocal in 2003 in its opposition to the US-led war in Iraq.

31   Martin Heidegger, 'Building, Dwelling, Thinking', in Heidegger, *Poetry, Language, Thought*, trans. Albert Hofstadter (New York: Harper Colophon Books, 1971). See Jean-François Lyotard's essay on Heidegger, 'Domus and the Megalopolis', in Lyotard, *The Inhuman*, trans. Geoffrey Bennington and Rachel Bowlby (Cambridge, UK: Polity Press, 1991), 191–204; and Neil Leach, 'The Dark Side of the Domus: The Redomestication of Central and Eastern Europe', in Leach, ed., *Architecture and Revolution: Contemporary Perspectives on Central and Eastern Europe* (New York: Routledge, 1999), 150–62.

32   See the journals *Die Sirene*; *Baulicher Luftschutz*, an insert of *Gasschutz und Luftschutz*; and more generally *Technik und Kultur* and *Deutsche Technik*; as well as for example, Präsidium des Reichsluftschutzbundes, ed., *Luftschutz – anschaulich gemacht* (Berlin: Dienststellen des Reichsluftschutzbundes, 1940).

Emergency Program' ('Führer-Sofortprogramm') of October 1940 announced a massive bunker-building program for Berlin and 60 other German urban areas, necessitating multiple engineering conferences and overnight training for city councils.[33] Everyone was to become part of the *domus* – a Germanic *domus* that would shield and protect against influence or invasion from without. A proselytizing article in the opening issue of the journal *Baulicher Luftschutz* in 1942 emphasizes the need for a 'community' of bunker-protected civilians, a veritable '"castle" of air defense' ('"Burg" des Luftschutzes') guaranteeing safety for all.[34] Civilians' air defense training became an additional component of the 1.4 million-strong labour force compulsorily drafted for the Organisation Todt that built the empire's defense structures in the first place.

Conceptually, the *domus*-ideology of defense adopts aspects from Heidegger's philosophy of 'dwelling'. The Heideggerian dwelling offers absolute shelter and protection for the members-only German *Volk* by dint of its natural 'situatedness' (its architectural *Dasein*) in its environment. The *domus* is forged, then, in its relation to the German 'blood and soil'. Nazi defense structures – whether in citadelized cities with their below- and above-ground bunkers and flak towers; or human and cement versions along the ramparts of the empire's edges, desperately trying to impose German identity and keep out the perils of enemy non-Germanness – constituted a new version of Heidegger's iconic temple or rural shepherd's hut, to be sure. Yet their function was to shield that ideal vision of dwelling. Digging bunkers into and out of the earth was intended, just like the Nazis' post-Expressionist take on the 'Dissolution of the Cities', to protect not just the physical lives of citizens but the utopia of ideological-racial territoriality that they were busy forging across the 'inland empire'.[35]

Put simply, the intended mastery of the *domus* did not work. Internal memos from both Albert Speer and Fritz Todt's offices reveal how the structures that were intended to defend proved rather like Franz Kafka's interminable building, un-building and rebuilding story, 'Der Bau'. The program of building and completing them was an impossible task.[36] There were not enough urban bunkers to go around, so the fact that bunker walls were 1–3 metres thick and

---

[33]   Hitler's memorandum of 10 October 1940; Bundesarchiv Militärarchiv Freiburg, RL 4/340.

[34]   A. Weiß, 'Der bauliche Luftschutz im Nationalistischen Bund Deutscher Technik', *Baulicher Luftschutz* 1.1 (1942): 7.

[35]   Bruno Taut, *Die Auflösung der Städte* (Hagen: Volkwang-Verlag, 1920).

[36]   Speer wrote a report on Berlin's bunkers on 19 November 1941 in response to General Field Marshal E. Milch; Bundesarchiv Militärarchiv Freiburg, RL 4/340. An ongoing lack of resources, according to Fritz Todt complaining just before his death in February 1942, included insufficient fuel for transporting materials or coal for heating cement, despite the free enforced labour of (mostly Soviet) POWs. Fritz Todt's letter to Milch on 22 October 1941, Bundesarchiv Militärarchiv Freiburg, RL 4/340.

up to tens of thousands of civilians could fit into them did not amount to much. We find a similar series of errors in the design and construction of the Atlantic Wall: cement deliveries to the Atlantic Wall became increasingly difficult during the war; ultimately, the bunker monoliths along the fortification line did not suffice, and all the Allies had to do – and did do – was to aim elsewhere. In late 1941, Speer ambitiously recorded 237 existing bunkers in the German capital for just under 60,000 people in total; 53 additional bunkers under construction for an additional 21,000; and plans for 100 future bunkers for 94,000 more. But even Speer admitted construction delays and 'difficult work conditions'. And a massive 70 per cent of the 600,000 German air-war fatalities were caused by carbon monoxide and phosphorous poisoning, or simply heat asphyxiation.[37] Kurt Vonnegut wrote of the disposal methods for corpses found in makeshift cellars and bunkers after the bombing of Dresden; the dead looked like people who had fallen asleep while sitting in a bus.[38] Nuremberg Race Laws co-author Dr Wilhelm Stuckart admitted in 1943 to Hermann Göring that an overall loss of confidence was leading people to nickname the shelters 'air raid traps' (*Luftschutzfallen* instead of *Luftschutzbauten*). Immediately following the firebombing of Hamburg in July 1943, Goebbels' Propaganda Ministry reported on the psychological damage being done to Berliners' morale by the horror stories of those who had survived Hamburg and were now fleeing to the capital. In December 1943, Speer, by now armaments minister, shifted emphasis away from failed defensibility toward the rebuilding of the country's broken cities, and founded the 'Arbeitsstab Wiederaufbauplanung bombenzerstörter Städte'.[39]

To conclude, the Nazis' dissolution-and-defense-based urban planning functioned not just within its immediate physical environments: it was situated within broader and also deeper sets of echoes and strata (city, intrastate, and interstate – shelters above and below ground, and with fortification lines that were wholly part of the Nazi racial, spatial and technological imaginary). Their planned expansion across a cleansed and fortified pan-German Europe ultimately led to an urban and territorial collapse. Citadels in cities and on perimeters (both human and non-human) proved unworkable in practice. The hyper-protective yet fallible *domus* of the Nazi urban centre and the conquering border zones of the Third Reich, nervously fortified by means of race and bunker alike,

---

[37] Stockholm Peace Research Institute (SIPRI), *Incendiary Weapons* (Cambridge, MA: MIT Press, 1975). Cited by Kenneth Hewitt, 'Place Annihilation: Area Bombing and the Fate of Urban Places', *Annals of the Association of American Geographers* 73 (1983): 274.

[38] Kurt Vonnegut, *Slaughterhouse 5* (New York: Delacorte, 1969), 157.

[39] Letter of 7 July 1943 from Dr Wilhelm Stuckart to Hermann Göring; Bundesarchiv Militärarchiv Freiburg, RL 4/340; and, memo from Goebbels from the NSDAP Reichspropaganda office, 30 July 1943; Bundesarchiv Berlin-Lichterfelde, NS 18/1325. On the reconstruction task force planned for after the war, see Diefendorf, 'Wartime Destruction and the Postwar Cityscape', in Closmann, ed., *War and the Environment*, 180–81.

merged architectural and planning megalomanias with genocidal colonization and air and ground defense. A contamination-narrative emerges, wholly at odds with the purportedly purified and purifying signals sent by the planning efforts emanating from both Speer's Germania and the Generalplan Ost. Despite the 'interlocking ideological levers' that brought race and territory, blood and soil, genocidal killers and engineers/city councils/planners/architects ever closer together, the combined effect ended up replenishing neither *Blut* nor *Boden*.[40]

---

[40] Ben Kiernan, *Blood and Soil: A World History of Genocide and Extermination from Sparta to Darfur* (New Haven, CT: Yale University Press, 2007), 454; Kiernan is citing Dr Erhard Wetzel, 'Stellungnahme und Gedanken zum Generalplan Ost des Reichsführers SS' (Berlin, 27 April 1942), repr. *Vierteljahrshefte für Zeitgeschichte* 6 (1958).

REFLECTIONS

Chapter 11

Cities of Fear: The Globalization of Insecurity in the Age of the Gated Community

Harold L. Platt

Introduction: The Gated Community in Historical Perspective

Over a century ago, Ebenezer Howard gave the Trans-Atlantic world its modern version of utopia, the Garden City. The gated community is simply a hybrid form of this suburban ideal, according to the author of *Privatopia*, Evan McKenzie. Moreover, the real estate developers of early models such as Letchworth, England, and Radburn, New Jersey, set a precedent by retaining private control over their public space. And for over 50 years, William H. Whyte has given us the archetype of their inhabitants, the 'organization man'. His post-war study of the new town of Park Forest, Illinois, discovered that these white-collar professionals were members of a new class of nomads. Surprised by the high turnover of residents in this Levittown-like suburb of Chicago, Whyte found that their jobs required them to move from city to city across the country. Finally, urban theorist Reyner Banham declared in 1968, 'Beverly Hills, too, is a ghetto'. In this suburb of Los Angeles, the price of admission keeps undesirable 'others' out without any need for walls. From this perspective, then, neither transnational urbanism nor well-protected preserves of the social elite are new.[1]

---

[1] Evan McKenzie, *Privatopia* (New Haven: Yale University Press, 1994); William Hollingsworth Whyte, *The Organization Man* (New York: Simon and Schuster, 1956); Gregory C. Randall, *America's Original GI Town – Park Forest, Illinois* (Baltimore: Johns Hopkins University Press, 2000); and Anthony Vidler, 'Introduction', in Reyner Banham, *Los Angeles: The Architecture of Four Ecologies* (Berkeley: University of California Press, 2001 [1971]), xxi. Also see Robert Fishman, *Urban Utopias in the Twentieth Century* (New York: Basic, 1977); Lynn Hollen Lees, 'Urban Public Space and Imagined Communities in the 1980s and 1990s', *Journal of Urban History* 20 (1994): 443–65; Robert Fishman, 'Global Suburbs', *First Biennial Conference of the Urban History Association* (Pittsburgh, September 2002); and Sarah Blandy, 'Gated Communities in England: Historical Perspectives and Current Developments', *GeoJournal* 66 (2006): 15–26.

Nonetheless, an international conference of housing experts proclaimed in 2003 that the gated community was indeed a new, 'radical urban form'. Their survey of these places was marked by an endless variety of physical design, social demographics, institutional structures and cultural meaning. The virtually limitless diversity of their shapes on the ground makes them fertile subjects of study to gain a better understanding of the interactions between the global, national and local in the production of urban space. Although gated communities adopted many hybrid forms, their residents shared in common a premium on personal/family security over other values in deciding where to live.[2]

From Los Angeles to San Salvador and São Paulo, fear of violent crime was the primary engine driving the construction of this new way of life behind the walls. What made this age-old condition of urban life into a transnational phenomenon was the oil embargo of 1973–74. Bringing the post-war economic 'miracle' to an end, the energy crisis set into motion a global restructuring of capitalism that changed the urban condition. A growing gap of inequality between the rich and the poor was reflected in rising crime rates and skyrocketing fear of crime on the mean streets of the 'urban jungle'. A vicious cycle of urban decline began as the privileged classes fled to the safety of gated communities, leaving the poor behind in lawless wastelands. In the post-oil embargo world of globalization, the Garden City ideal morphed into a generic, First World 'radical urban form' of fortified space, while other neighbourhoods became Fourth World 'ghettos of exclusion'.[3]

After 1973, the lowering of trade barriers spurred the proliferation of multinational corporations, transforming Whyte's organization men (and women) into globetrotters. Helping to usher in the Age of Information, they were outsourced to the countries offering their employers the most favourable terms of trade. These elite, albeit swelling corps of technocrats climbed up the rungs of the corporate ladder by moving around the world from one foreign subsidiary to the next. Indispensible to bringing about the interconnectivity of global markets, these nomads could demand oases of safety as they trekked with their families in tow from one strange land to the next. However, the worldwide recession following the oil embargo undermined the ability of local

---

[2]   Rowland Atkinson and Sarah Blandy, 'Introduction', *Gated Communities*, eds Rowland Atkinson and Sarah Blandy (London and New York: Routledge, 2006), vii. They define gated communities as 'walled or fenced housing developments, to which public access is restricted, characterized by legal agreements which tie residents to a common code of conduct and (usually) collective responsibility for management'. See ibid., vii–viii.

[3]   United Nations Human Settlements Programme, *Enhancing Urban Safety and Security* (London and Sterling, VA.: Earthscan Publications, 2007); and United Nations Human Settlements Programme, *The Challenge of Slums 2003* (London and Sterling, VA: Earthscan Publications, 2003). Also see Jon Bannister and Nick Fyfe, 'Introduction: Fear and the City', *Urban Studies* 38 (2001): 807–13.

governments to provide a safe environment for these elite visitors, let alone their own citizens. Economic restructuring forced deep cuts in Town Hall budgets, including paying their police departments and maintaining public space. Long-term settlement patterns of suburbanization, often accelerated by the urban crisis of the 1960s, further reduced their capacities to fulfil the most basic duty of the social contract between the government and its people. Simultaneously, more and more desperate people moved into the informal economy in order to survive, including the criminal underworld.[4]

In addition to new levels of violence, two other new conditions of urban life added momentum to the psychological panic of residents and businesses in search of defensible space. On the one hand, the developers of gated communities used scare tactics in their marketing campaigns to stampede potential homebuyers to their properties. On the other hand, the example of the cosmopolitan organization man acted as a social magnet of prestige and exclusivity for local elites. In the United Kingdom, for example, a 2001 census listed 1,000 gated communities in spite of very low violent crime rates.[5]

The spread of gated communities also raised new forms of urban social conditions, tensions built into the spatial segregation of insiders from outsiders. Were the residents within the walls locking out dangerous criminals, or were they locking themselves in to comfortable, albeit solitary confinement cells? Did the physical safety behind the gates breed the psychological insecurity of paranoia that inflates outsiders into diabolical monsters? Were new residents joining a democratic institution of self-government, the homeowners association, or surrendering basic rights of citizenship to an authoritarian regime when they signed its code of conduct? And a final paradox worth exploring is the

---

[4]   William I. Robinson, 'Globalization and the Sociology of Immanuel Wallerstein: A Critical Appraisal', *International Sociology* 26 (2011): 723–45; and John Bellamy Foster, Robert W. McChesney and R. Jamil Jonna, 'The Global Reserve Army of Labor and the New Imperialism', *Monthly Review* 63 (2011): 1–31. Also see William I. Robinson, *Transnational Conflicts* (London and New York: Verso, 2003); Barbara Weinstein, 'Presidential Address: Developing Inequality', *American Historical Review* 113 (February 2008): 1–18; and Immanuel Maurice Wallerstein, *World-Systems Analysis* (Durham: Duke University Press, 2004).

[5]   William J.V. Neill, 'Marketing the Urban Experience: Reflections on the Place of Fear in Promotional Strategies of Belfast, Detroit, and Berlin', *Urban Studies* 38 (2001): 815–28. Also see Oscar Newman, *Defensible Space* (New York, 1972); Rowland Atkinson and John Flint, 'Fortress UK? Gated Communities, the Spatial Revolt of the Elites and Time-Space Trajectories of Segregation', *Housing Studies* 19 (2004): 875–92; McKenzie, *Privatopia*, chap. 1; Edward James Blakely and Mary Gail Snyder, *Fortress America* (Washington, DC: Brookings Institution Press, 1997); and Thomas W. Sanchez, Robert E. Lang and Dawn M Dhavale, 'Security Versus Status?: A First Look at the Census's Gated Communities', *Journal of Planning Education and Research* 24 (2005): 281–91.

contradiction contained in public policies that encourage the privatization of public space.

City of Walls – Alphaville Revisited

While the residents of the Watts section of Los Angeles were witnessing a living hell of arson, anarchy and armies in the streets during the hot summer of 1965, the followers of French *Nouvelle Vague*/New Wave were safe inside cool movie theatres watching an imaginary dystopia. Filmmaker Jean-Luc Godard encapsulated all of the anxieties of the middle classes that had been accumulating since the start of the Cold War in a science-fiction parable, *Alphaville*. Viewers' suspicions were confirmed that the race of technological modernization was on a path leading to a frightening future of a robot-like existence. An inter-galactic policeman, Lemmy Caution, is sent on a mission to assassinate the totalitarian ruler of this cyborg world, a sentient computer named Alpha 60. In spite of being set in a distant time, all of *Alphaville*'s visual and historical reference points are set in the present, including the detective's obligatory trench coat. Godard used locations in the streets and interiors of Paris to frame his cautionary tale of runaway technology. Entering a gated city of walls in a Ford Galaxie, the secret agent from the 'Outlands' has to pass through several security checkpoints on a long highway from the periphery to the centre.

In the end, the all-seeing machine – the enemy of nature, especially human nature – is slain by the emotional power of poetry. Three years after the film's release, the swelling malaise of post-war society would burst and spread into massive urban protests throughout Europe and the Americas. In many respects, the demonstrators, who marched on some of those very same streets as Lemmy Caution, were on the same mission.[6] This makes the real Alphaville, a suburb of São Paulo, Brazil, the logical place to start this investigation of the interactions between transnationalism and urbanism in the post-1973 era of economic restructuring. This first, full-scale city of walls was built in a country where the gaps of class and racial/ethnic inequality have long remained among the largest in the world. At the centre of its modernization project, the industrial city of São Paul also became one of the most dangerous places in the world outside of war zones.[7]

---

[6]   Colin Jones, *Paris* (1st American ed.; New York: Viking, 2005); 448–56; Steven L. Goldman, 'Images of Technology in Popular Films: Discussion and Filmography', *Science, Technology, and Human Values* 14 (1989): 275–301. Also see Matthew Gandy, 'Urban Visions', *Journal of Urban History* 26 (2000): 368–79; and Theodor G. Wyeld and Andrew Allan, 'The Virtual City: Perspectives on the Dystopic Cybercity', *Journal of Architecture* 11 (2006): 613–20.

[7]   Peter B. Evans, *Dependent Development* (Princeton: Princeton University Press, 1979); Robert M. Levine, *The History of Brazil* (Westport, CT: Greenwood Press, 1999),

This exploding metropolis had long been divided between a high security centre of tower blocks and a lawless *periferia*/periphery of self-built shantytowns called *favelas*. But in 1974, the opening of Alphaville broke this pattern, creating a radical form of urban space and inaugurating a new way of city life behind the gates. Its groundbreaking coincided with the global energy crisis and subsequent recession. This was also the nadir of the country's oppression and suffering under the brutal regime of a military dictatorship.

Perhaps the ultimate expression of the ascendancy of technocratic, neo-liberal approaches to urban planning, Alphaville is void of public space. It is a fortress city with layer upon layer of security, and walls within walls of exclusive access to its various residential enclaves, commercial offices and recreational venues. In 2011, its police force had over 1,000 armed men, who guard the walls containing over 2,300 businesses and 35,000 residents in 14 separate villages. Many residents work here in addition to 150,000 commuters from the 'Outlands'. They have to pass through a series of checkpoints on limited access toll roads into the citadel. Since opening, its tremendous success has been demonstrated not only in these numbers but also in the way that its builder, Alphaville Urbanismo, has been able to stamp out duplicates and complete gated communities throughout the country and the world.[8] Yet, this whole scenario takes place within a physical space surrounded by a six-metre-high security fence, and a psychological environment permeated with fear. 'Everything is conditioned by the possibility of violence', urban scholar Christopher Lindner reminds us by retelling how, '[t]he narrator of Teixeira Coelho's brilliant comic novella *Niemeyer, Um*

chap. 6; Andres Paulo, John Rodriguez-Pose and John Tomaney, 'Industrial Crisis in the Centre of the Periphery: Stabilization, Economic Restructuring and Policy Responses in the São Paulo Metropolitan Region', *Urban Studies* 36 (1999): 479–98; Jose F. Graziano da Silva, 'Capitalist 'Modernization' and Employment in Brazilian Agriculture, 1960–1975: The Case of the State of São Paulo', *Latin American Perspectives* 11 (1984): 117–36; and Verena Stolcke, *Coffee Planters, Workers, and Wives* (New York: St Martin's Press, 1988). Also see Teresa Pires do Rio Caldeira, *City of Walls* (Berkeley: University of California Press, 2000); Mike Davis and Daniel Bertrand Monk, eds, *Evil Paradises* (New York: New Press: Distributed by W.W. Norton, 2007); Weinstein, 'Presidential Address'; and Lucio Kowarick and Milton A. Campananrio, 'Industrialized Underdevelopment: From Economic Miracle to Economic Crisis', *Social Struggles and the City*, ed. Lucio Kowarick (New York: Monthly Review Press, 1994), 45–59.

[8] Alphaville, São Paulo, Wikipedia: http://en.wikipedia.org/wiki/Alphaville,_S%C3%A3o_Paulo (accessed 24 January 2010); and Christopher Lindner, 'Architecture and the Economics of Violence: São Paulo as a Case Study', *Globalization, Violence, and the Visual Culture of Cities*, ed. Richard J. Williams (London and New York: Routledge, 2010), 17–31. Also see Charles Mueller, 'Environmental Problems Inherent to a Development Style: Degradation and Poverty in Brazil', *Environment and Urbanization* 7 (October 1995): 67–84; and Lucio Kowarick and Clara Ant, 'One Hundred Years of Overcrowding: Slum Tenements in the City', *Social Struggles and the City*, 60–76.

Romance (2001) has a neurotic dread of the city he inhabits, returning time and again to his *expectativa de ser assassinado a qualquer instante*, or his "belief that he will be killed at any minute".[9]

After the Second World War, the policing of social boundaries had hardened into a new spatial form, a 'city of walls'. On the one hand, according to sociologist Teresa Pires do Rio Caldeira, the upper classes began retreating inside 'fortified enclaves' within the central zone. 'These are privatized, enclosed, and monitored spaces', she explains, 'for residence, consumption, leisure, and work. Their central justification is the fear of violent crime ... . Thus, the fortified enclaves constitute the core of a new way of organizing segregation, social discrimination, and economic restructuring in São Paulo'.[10] On the other hand, the lower classes were forced farther and farther out, forming an area that today sprawls over 8,000 square kilometres. The lure of a job in one of the factories and a better life in the city had set off a human tidal wave. Most of the newcomers were like ex-president Luiz Inácio Lula da Silva's family, non-whites from the country's impoverished, drought-stricken northeast.

Avoiding racial words, the upper classes tagged them with the euphemism, *norestinos*/northerners. 'They are characterized', according to Caldeira, 'as ignorant, lazy, dirty, promiscuous, immoral. In a word, they are criminals'. Deep-seated fears of racial pollution among the affluent classes produced strong impulses of exclusion to keep evil from 'infesting' their neighbourhoods. The *norestinos* became the latest category of social pariah subject to repressive levels of police control and spatial segregation.[11]

In the period leading up to the military takeover in 1964, São Paulo became a tale of two cities: a fortified, well-equipped centre for the elites, and a lawless, hazardous periphery for the masses. The official plan was to have no plan for the outlands. 'In actual fact', according to scholars Lúcio Kowarick and Nabil G. Bonduki, 'it was the *deliberate strategy* of the local authorities to turn a blind eye to the opening up of the new estates and then to forget they existed'.[12]

Moreover, the blurring of the city's bi-focal space into a more complicated landscape of more or less 'networked' and 'consolidated' neighbourhoods reinforced the crisis of fear set off by the crime wave. According to Caldeira,

9   Linder, 'Architecture and the Economics of Violence', 18.
10 Caldeira, *City of Walls*, 31.
11 Caldeira, *City of Walls*.
12 Lucio Kowarick and Nabil G. Bonduki, 'Urban Space and Political Space: From Populism to Redemocratization', *Social Struggles and the City*, 127, 121–47; and Suzana Pasternak, 'Squatter Settlements as a Kind of Perverse Outcome: History of Popular Housing Policies in São Paulo', *Proceeding of the 13th Meeting of the International Planning History Society* (Chicago: IPHS, 2008): 1182–201. Also see R. Batley, 'Urban Renewal and Expulsion in São Paulo', in Alan Gilbert, Jorge Enrique Hardoy and Ronaldo Ramírez, eds, *Urbanization in Contemporary Latin America* (Chichester, New York: J. Wiley, 1982), 231–62.

'a context of uncertainty, in which people feel threatened socially and see transformations occurring, seems to stimulate the policing of social boundaries...
. In other words, proximity leads to the refinement of separations in order to sustain a perception of difference'. Alphaville offered the elite not only a relatively safe haven from crime, but also a new status symbol of difference.[13]

Alphaville represents the post-1960s trend of everyday life towards social fragmentation into disconnected private worlds. This mini-city of walls within walls reflects the postmodern condition of polycentric enclaves of metropolitan space and segregated geographies of social inequality. Pulling out the lens on the Brazilian megalopolis, cultural historian Lúcia Sá observes, 'perhaps this provisional portrait, made up of incomplete parts, mirrored, incommunicable and multiplying each other to infinity, in the end might be the only viable realism for the São Paulo of our time'.[14]

The commodification of residential space into private neighbourhoods like Alphaville also illustrates the ways in which the post-1960s crosscurrents of the global and the local became new, hybrid forms of urban space and culture. The marketing of gated communities or 'common interest developments' worldwide reveals the production of a full line of consumer packages: some were advertised by playing on fears of the 'other', but many others appealed in positive terms of individual desires for social prestige, improved amenities, better administration and the good life within a retirement, golf or arts community.[15]

Equally pivotal in the planning history of São Paulo, Alphaville represents a historic break in the city centre's path of growth in a southwestern direction. From the coming of the electric trolley at the turn of the century to the mid-1970s, the expansion of a dense core of commercial and residential tower blocks defined a line in time and space that divided the high-security centre from the lawless *periferia*. This moving line also demarked the west side as a good place to live from the east side, which became a neglected area of factories, warehouses and remnants of working-class tenements. Alphaville would be built 23 kilometres northwest of the 1900s *Centro Novo*/New Center. It was constructed on farmland in the suburban municipality of Barueri. The developers co-

---

[13]   Caldeira, *City of Walls*, 74, chap. 2.

[14]   Lúcia Sá, *Life in the Megalopolis* (New York: Routledge, 2007), 32. Also see Derek Parkman Pardue, 'Blackness and Periphery: A Retelling of Marginality in Hip-Hop Culture of São Paulo, Brazil' (PhD diss., University of Illinois, 2004); Justin A. Read, 'Obverse Colonization: São Paulo, Global Urbanization and the Poetics of the Latin American City', *Journal of Latin American Cultural Studies* 15 (2006): 281–300; Fishman, 'Global Suburbs'; and William Sites, 'Global City, American City: Theories of Globalization and Approaches to Urban History', *Journal of Urban History* 29 (2003): 222–46.

[15]   See note 1, above. Also see Mike Davis, *The City of Quartz* (New York: Vintage, 1990); John M. Findlay, *Magiclands* (Berkeley: University of California Press, 1992); and Michael Sorkin, ed., *Variations on a Theme Park* (New York: Noonday, 1992).

ordinated their plans with the opening of a superhighway nearby to ensure their elite clientele a convenient and secure passageway through the outlands to the relative safety of downtown.[16]

The periphery too became more complicated, a polymorph of disconnected, layered and overlapping places linked more or less into larger flows of information, power and money. Alphaville's design as a self-contained mini-city with American-style suburban housing represented a symbolic as well as a physical break from a half-century of rapid growth. Building it began a process of metropolitan de-concentration that would erect high-security zones of First World urban space within the periphery's ghettos of exclusion.

The interconnectivity of modern technologies both on intra-urban and extra-local levels made these new, hybrid patterns of economic development and residential settlement possible. The official planners' expansion of the 'networked city' of modern infrastructure from the central zone into the illegal *favelas* also made pivotal changes in the quality of everyday life for their residents, especially water and sewer hook-ups. While these do-it-yourself homeowners/*construção* could see solid gains in their health and environment, others were forced to erect shelters in remote areas, where conditions of deprivation and misery were worse than ever.[17]

The prime engine driving the transformation of São Paulo into a sprawling megacity without limits was an exploding population. During the 1970s alone, it skyrocketed in the metropolitan region by 4.5 million people to a total of 12.5 million. Taking a little longer view, this demographic tidal wave of urbanization swept over an area of land that was 900 per cent larger in 1990 than 30 years earlier.[18]

Bursting political and environmental boundaries at the edge, São Paulo's swelling numbers simultaneously added to congestion in the centre. Gridlocked streets, overcrowded sidewalks, crime and fear of crime soared to unbearable levels of claustrophobia. It rivalled New York and Hong Kong in sheer density of space. 'But there is something more impressive – or terrifying – about São Paulo for the first-time visitor', historian Christopher Linder notes, 'because unlike those other high-rise cities, this one appears to have no end. The buildings rise up in seemingly endless waves, apparently unbounded ... there is barely space to

16   Read, 'Obverse Colonization', 281–300; and Caldeira, *City of Walls*.

17   Ricardo Silva Toledo, 'The Connectivity of Infrastructure Networks and the Urban Space of São Paulo in the 1990s', *International Journal of Urban and Regional Research* 24 (2000): 139–64; and Eduardo Cesar Marques and Renata Mirandola Bichir, 'Public Politics, Political Cleavages and Urban Space: State Infrastructure Policies in Sao Paulo, Brazil, 1975–2000', *International Journal of Urban and Regional Research* 27 (2003): 811–27.

18   Caldeira, *City of Walls*, 216; and Kowarick, and Campananrio, 'Industrialized Underdevelopment', 45–59. Also see Kowarick and Ant, 'One Hundred Years of Over-crowding'.

breathe'. In large part, Alphaville and its instant success was a response by local elites to these pressures and anxieties in spite of reassurances by the national military that it could keep the social peace.[19]

From a postmodernist perspective, this exploding city can be seen as a 'no place', an urban space without an identity. 'Unlike Mexico City and other Latin American cities', according to the linguist Justin A. Read, 'São Paulo is not marked by history, but by a fundamental modernity erasing the past ... Indeed one's ground-level perspective in São Paulo is largely marked by a *lack of vision*, left amidst a seemingly endless sea of 20- to 30-story concrete buildings that block out both sunrise and sunset'. Ever since the trolley line traversed the Anhangabaù Valley from the old centre to the *Centro Novo* in the 1900s, the city had been growing too fast to gain an identity of place.[20]

Like its moving line of downtown development to the southwest, São Paulo's other districts were also undergoing constant change in land uses and residential patterns. Portuguese-Brazilians, African-Brazilians, Italians, Japanese and mixed-race groups had created their own communities in distinct neighbourhoods. But the swelling and migrating high-security zone of the upper classes in the city centre expelled the lower classes to the lawless outlands. In such a landscape of kaleidoscope-like change, its inhabitants experienced the city in so many different ways as to preclude the crystallization of a single, fixed image of the place where they were living. On the contrary, the city and its meaning remain in a perpetual state of contestation.[21]

Casting the 1970s within a much longer historical context of Latin American colonization puts Read in Immanuel Wallerstein's camp of continuity in the development of globalization. Read disagrees with Manuel Castell's observation that the restructuring of capitalism after 1973 gave birth to a process of 'simultaneous economic development and underdevelopment, social inclusion and social exclusion'. Rather than describing the emergence of a new type of 'global city', Read argues that these conditions have been present in São Paulo ever since the early twentieth century, when it became an exploding city. From his point of view, the cities of the First World such as Berlin, New York and Tokyo are simply catching up with the São Paulo's of the Third World. Calling this process 'obverse colonization', Read posits that 'structural disequilibrium is the historical constant of São Paulo's urban growth. In essence, São Paulo has been generating its own 'Fourth World' for most of its modern history, long before the structural alterations of globalization. What has changed is that the

---

[19]   Lindner, 'Architecture and the Economics of Violence', 120, 122.

[20]   Read, 'Obverse Colonization', 290.

[21]   Sá, *Life in the Megalopolis*; and Simon Romero, 'At War with São Paulo's Establishment, Black Paint in Hand', *New York Times* (29 January 2012), 5; and the conclusions, below.

'First World' global city has merely lagged behind São Paulo in terms of poverty growth and concentration.'[22]

City of Gates – Los Angeles

In Los Angles, we will be able to observe the transnational process of 'obverse colonization' of the Third World's cities of walls and ghettos of exclusion in the urban centres of the First World. At the same time, we will also have to travel to San Salvador, where LA's first generation of Salvadorian-Americans affiliated with local street gangs was expelled. Thrown out of their homeland, these heavily tattooed members of the La Mars Salvatrucha supergang, or *Maras* (MS), were treated as dangerous, foreign criminals that deserved merciless repression and long-term residence inside the walls of overstuffed prisons. Similar patches of the ganglands of LA have emerged in Guatemala City, Managua and Panama City.[23]

Coming full circle to link these ghettos of exclusion of the Third World back to the First, the incarcerated exiles of the MS have morphed into globetrotting organization men, engaged in drug, weapons and human trafficking in Los Angeles and other cities throughout the Americas. New patterns of Pan-Americanism, in turn, inspired new forms of urban popular culture equal to Alphaville in giving expression to the postmodern, hybrid landscapes of the local and the global. The spread of ghetto rap and graffiti around the world was deeply rooted in local identities of place at the same time that their creation takes place within a self-conscious framework of an international youth culture.[24]

[22]   Manuel Castells, *End of Millennium* (Malden, MA: Blackwell Publishers, 1998), 87; and Read, 'Obverse Colonization', 297. Also see Davis, *City of Quartz*, chap. 4.

[23]   Elana Zilberg, 'Fools Banished from the Kingdom: Remapping Geographies of Gang Violence between the Americas (Los Angeles and San Salvador)', *American Quarterly* 56 (2004): 759–79; Oliver Jutersonke, Robert Muggah and Dennis Rodgers, 'Gangs, Urban Violence, and Security Interventions in Central America', *Security Dialogue* 40, nos 4–5 (2009): 373–97 Alma Guillermoprieto, 'In the New Gangland of El Salvador', *New York Review of Books* (10 November 2011): 45–8; and Guatemala, and Human Rights Commission/USA, *Gangs in Guatemala*, 2013. Available from http://www.ghrcusa.org/wpcontent/uploads/2011/12/GangFactSheet.pdf (accessed 8 July 2013). Also see Elana Zilberg, *Space of Detention: The Making of a Transnational Gang Crisis between Los Angeles and San Salvador* (Durham and London: Duke University Press, 2011).

[24]   See Sá, *Life in the Megalopolis*; Will Hermes, *Love Goes to Buildings on Fire* (New York: Farber and Farber, 2011); David Toop, *Rap Attack 2* (London and New York: Serpent's Tail, 1994); George Yudice, 'The Funkification of Rio', *Microphone Fiends*, eds Andrew Ross and Tricia Rose (London, New York: Verso, 1994), 193–220; Hilbourne A. Watson, 'Globalization as Capitalism in the Age of Electronics: Issues of Popular Power, Culture, Revolution, and Globalization from Below', *Latin American Perspectives* 29 (2002): 32–43; and Murray Forman and Mark Anthony Neal, eds, *That's the Joint!* (New York: Routledge, 2004).

Whether culture production in the ghettos or master-planned communities in the suburbs, the urban crisis of the 1960s set into motion a different set of forces, which would give shape to urban space and society for the next quarter century. Historian Robert Fishman agrees that it opened a 'new chapter in the 250-year long history of bourgeois suburbs of privilege that first took shape outside London in the mid-eighteenth century'.[25]

Economists give greater emphasis to the global restructuring and integration of markets ranging from natural resources to financial services and manufacturing industries. Los Angeles, for example, enjoyed a long-term building boom as the American headquarters of a steady surge in the movement of people, capital and trade around the 'Pacific Rim'. Simultaneously, it was also erecting Fourth World ghettos of exclusion. To interrogate the process of 'obverse colonization' in the cities of the First World, we need to get on its freeways and travel from the downtown center to the edge of the periphery. There, we will find another global prototype of the gated community: the research park.[26]

After 1965, the steady flow of non-Anglos into this region transformed it into a multi-racial/ethnic patchwork, a post-suburban 'mongrel city'. Its white Anglos were in flight from the centre to the periphery, but newcomers from Latin America and Asia more than compensated for their loss. By 1980, the sheer numbers of immigrants shrank the white population within the county to about half. Yet, new, fortified enclaves of white-only privilege were rising at the outer edges of settlement. And other suburbs in between were taking steps to resegregate their neighbourhoods and schools.[27] At the same time, the Latinization of the city was creating a different kind of 'magical land', according

---

²⁵   Fishman, 'Global Suburbs', 2–3.

²⁶   Edward W. Soja, 'Los Angeles, 1965–1992: From Crisis-Generated Restructuring to Restructuring-Generated Crisis', *The City*, eds Allen John Scott and Edward W. Soja (Berkeley: University of California Press, 1996), 426–62; and Edward W. Soja, *Thirdspace* (Cambridge, MA: Blackwell, 1996). Also see Davis, *The City of Quartz*; Robert M. Fogleson, *The Fragmented Metropolis* (Cambridge: Harvard University Press, 1967); Greg Hise, *Magnetic Los Angeles* (Baltimore and London: Johns Hopkins University Press, 1997); William B. Fulton, *The Reluctant Metropolis* (Baltimore: Johns Hopkins University Press, 2001 [1997]); and Raphael Sonenshein, *The City at Stake* (Princeton: Princeton University Press, 1993).

²⁷   See Leonie Sandercock, *Cosmopolis II* (New York: Continuum, 2003). Also see Carol A. O'Connor, 'Sorting out the Suburbs: Patterns of Land Use, Class, and Culture', *American Quarterly* 37 (1985): 382–94; Allen John Scott and Edward W. Soja, 'Introduction to Los Angeles: City and Region', *The City*, 1–21; Davis, *The City of Quartz*, chap. 1; Charles M. Lamb, *Housing Segregation in Suburban America since 1960* (New York: Cambridge University Press, 2005), chaps 5–6; Gerald Frug, 'The Legal Technology of Exclusion in Metropolitan America', *The New Suburban History*, eds Kevin Michael Kruse and Thomas J. Sugrue (Chicago: University of Chicago Press, 2006), 205–19.

to urban commentator Mike Davis. Bursting the barrio walls of East LA, Latinos rebuilt residential neighbourhoods and reinvented urban space. 'In the most fundamental sense', he notes, 'the Latinos are struggling to reconfigure the "cold" frozen geometries of the old spatial order to accommodate a "hotter", more exuberant urbanism. Across the vast Pan-American range of cultural nuance, the social reproduction of *latinidad*, however defined, presupposes a rich proliferation of public space'.[28]

After 1965, this almost exclusively Mexican-origins community became far more diverse, as refugees of wars in El Salvador, Guatemala and Nicaragua were joined by a brain-drain of middle-class professionals and organization men from South America. Cuban refugees too formed new communities around parish churches, social clubs, restaurants and nightlife spots. The polyglot nature of the region's demographic landscape was further complicated by a surge of immigrants from Asia. Little Saigons, Seouls, Bangkoks and New Chinatowns sprang up around the central business district (CBD). And in the suburbs, some became majority, ethnic minority.[29]

In spite of the Watts uprising, Los Angeles continued to attract not only people from all over the world, but also investment capital in new industries, commerce and real estate. Money poured in from Japan, Canada, South Korea and Hong Kong in a global restructuring of markets and a communications revolution that shrank the Pacific Ocean into the 'Pacific Rim', an integrated economic zone. For instance, California was such an important part of the Sony Corporation's customer base that the Japanese consumer products giant treated the state as a part of its internal market area.

In short, Los Angeles became a thousand and one different places at once. It became a crazy quilt of hybrid spaces, a crossroads of neighbourhood decline and reinvention, deindustrialization and reindustrialization, desegregation and retrenchment of white racism. This regional scale place became a many centred, urbanized suburbia. It was experienced on so many overlapping layers of daily life that attempts to tell its story is like trying to excavate what was going on in the biblical Tower of Babel. Consider what was happening every day inside

---

[28] Mike Davis, *Magical Urbanism* (New York: Verso, 2000), 65. Also see Davis, *City of Quartz*, chap. 6; Raymond A. Rocco, 'Latino Los Angeles: Reframing Boundaries/Borders', *The City*, 365–89; Ricardo Romo, *East Los Angeles* (Austin: University of Texas Press, 1983); Alexander Von Hoffman, *House by House, Block by Block* (New York: Oxford University Press, 2003), chap. 6; and Eric Avila, *Popular Culture in the Age of White Flight* (Berkeley: University of California Press, 2004).

[29] Rocco, 'Latino Los Angeles'; Ronald T. Takaki, *A Different Mirror* (Boston: Little, Brown & Co., 1993); Walter T.K. Nugent, *Into the West* (New York: A.A. Knopf, 1999); Zilberg, 'Fools Banished from the Kingdom'; and Michael Nevin Willard, 'Nuestra Los Angeles', *American Quarterly* 56 (2004): 807–43.

the ubiquitous, small convenient stores in the South Central area. Narratives of their Korean owners and their African-American customers are worlds apart.

Here, pieces of this fractured tale will be examined to draw impressionist sketches of the morphing of Los Angeles into an 'ecology of fear': high-security zones for the rich and lawless badlands for the poor. These illustrations will consist of fragments of urban space undergoing change in the downtown and the outer periphery. This approach will help expose the ways in which global markets and national policies produced unequal, security outcomes on the local level for the rich and the poor.[30] In the downtown area, this bi-focal perspective draws attention to the construction of a São Paulo-like, high-security zone of tower blocks, surrounded by communities-in-formation of newcomers. They tended to cluster around the CBD because it was generating lots of jobs in two growth sectors of the local economy: services and manufacturing.[31]

The city centre was reindustrialized by fashion-oriented and mass media industries that demanded close communications between their sales and production departments. They set up factories that in-sourced Third World methods of production. Undocumented women immigrants found employment in sweatshops making clothing and jewellery; their male counterparts made furniture and toys. Others toiled in back lot, culture factories turning Hollywood's scripts into animated feature films, TV programs and commercials.

In post-oil embargo Los Angeles, global finance and local politics combined to produce a 'Renaissance' of the downtown area. The main source of investment capital underwriting this frenzy of commercial development was Japan. Multinational companies in other countries also established beachheads

---

[30]   Edward T. Chang and Russell Leong, eds, *Los Angeles-- Struggles toward Multiethnic Community* (Seattle: University of Washington Press, 1994); Edward T. Chang and Jeannette Diaz-Veizades, *Ethnic Peace in the American City* (New York: New York University Press, 1999); Gerald Horne, *Fire This Time* (Charlottesville: University Press of Virginia, 1995); and John Lie, 'The Black-Asian Conflict?', *Not Just Black and White*, eds Nancy Foner and George M. Fredrickson (New York: Russell Sage Foundation, 2004), 301–14. Also see Paul Ong and Evelyn Blumenberg, 'Income and Racial Inequality in Los Angeles', *The City*, 311–35; L. Pulido, S. Sidawi and R.O. Vos, 'An Archaeology of Environmental Racism in Los Angeles', *Urban Geography* 17 (1996): 419–39; Laura Pulido, 'Rethinking Environmental Racism: White Privilege and Urban Development in Southern California', *Annals of the Association of American Geographers* 90 (2000): 12–40; Lawrence Bobo, et al., eds, *Prismatic Metropolis* (New York: Russell Sage Foundation, 2000); Gilbert Valdez Estrada, 'How the East Was Lost: Mexican Fragmentation, Displacement, and the East Lost Angeles Freeway System, 1947–1972' (Master's Thesis, California State University Long Beach, 2002); and Greg Hise, 'Border City: Race and Social Distance in Los Angeles', *American Quarterly* 56 (2004): 545–58.

[31]   Nugent, *Into the West*, chaps 9–10. Also see Robinson, *Transnational Conflicts*; W.A.V. Clark, *The California Cauldron* (New York: Guilford Press, 1998); and W.A.V. Clark, *Immigrants and the American Dream* (New York: Guilford Press, 2003).

in the emerging US capital of the Pacific Rim. They set up their subsidiary headquarters in the metropolitan region in addition to taking stakes in speculative office buildings and shopping mall projects. While the skyline of the CBD underwent a major transformation, its so-called 'Renaissance' accounted for less than a quarter of the total space added. Like the outflowing and infilling patterns of its social geography, Los Angeles was undergoing a recentring of its economic landscape.[32]

Moving north into the San Fernando Valley, a final impression of Los Angeles traces westward migration along a highway corridor of high technology industries in the northern tier of the outer perimeter. Mapping their trail across the San Fernando Valley from Burbank to Simi Valley in Ventura County sketches an evolutionary, economic process of the 'creative destruction' of capitalism. Like Justin Read's depiction of downtown São Paulo, time-lapse photography is needed to illustrate this moving line of suburban development. Simi Valley was built around a new generation of knowledge factories, college campus-like, 'research parks'. In this case of double vision, postmodernist 'technoburbs' of white-only, gated communities contrast against throwback, colonies of foreign-born workers in Third World sweatshops, where they assembled electronic circuit boards. As historian Mary Pugh O'Mara uncovered, '[t]he story of the city of knowledge is thus one of *disguise* on a number of levels – where polluting industrial activities were billed as "clean" by economic development advocates, where race and class homogeneity was largely unspoken but crucial criterion of research park design, whose public face was the white-collar scientist and whose hidden workforce was often working class and nonwhite'.[33]

To find the prototype of this radical new form of urban space, we must cut across Ventura County to the far end of settlement. Simi Valley was different; it was built to house a military-industrial-university complex. Its centrepiece, a cluster of postindustrial 'research parks' were designed to disguise these knowledge factories as institutions of higher learning. Their white-collar workers lived nearby in communities that excluded low-income housing. In O'Mara's estimation, the resulting segregation was more a by-product of class bias than racial/ethnic prejudice. 'This is a story of suburbanization', she proposes, 'that has less to do with white flight and more to do with the deliberate creation of enclaves for a rarified upper stratum of the white-collar class: the professor, the scientist, the engineer'. In 1970, Simi Valley's population of 56,000 would

[32]   Davis, *City of Quartz*, chaps 3–4; and Fulton, *Reluctant Metropolis*.

[33]   Margaret Pugh O'Mara, 'Uncovering the City in the Suburb: Cold War Politics, Scientific Elites, and High-Tech Spaces', *The New Suburban History*, 78–9, 57–79; and Allen J. Scott, 'High-Technology Industrial Development in the San Fernando Valley and Ventura County: Observations on Economic Growth and the Evolution of Urban Form', *The City*, 276–311. Also see Kristen Hill Maher, 'Borders and Social Distinction in the Global Suburb', *American Quarterly* 56 (2004): 781–806.

be 98.7 per cent white Anglos, a purity maintained with less than 2 per cent African-American for the next 20 years.[34] As the metropolitan region entered the 1980s, all of the contradictory forces fracturing and fusing its landscape was creating a multidimensional mosaic of hybrid places segregated into the security haves and have-nots. On the one hand, the elite, pro-growth coalition of private developers and political leaders continued to push the construction of large-scale, gated communities. On the other hand, working- and middle-class Angelenos continued to form new identities of place and movements of insurgent citizenship in defense of their rights to community self-determination.

Mobilized by neighbours, these grassroots organizations covered a broad spectrum ranging from a conservative homeowners association to racial/ethnic- and gender-bending acts of radical culture production. In Compton, for instance, a local group of African-American teenagers calling themselves 'Niggers With Attitude' (NWA), are given credit for inventing 'gangsta rap'. While they claimed to be only reporting their experience of everyday life in suburban hell, the mass media condemned their lyrics as a danger to the social peace that should be censored. The shock of disbelief in mainstream America of what was coming 'straight out of Compton' reflects in bold relief just how far its world of gated communities was moving apart from this Fourth World ghetto of exclusion.[35]

City of Nomads – San Salvador

The globalization of urban security and insecurity has produced its own unique, hybrid urban spaces. A good example is San Salvador, where thousands of LA's young gang members were dumped in the 1990s. They became the antipodes of Whyte's organization men; they were nowhere men, trapped in a transnational space-time trajectory without a place to call home, except prison. Almost all of them had come to Southern California as small children with their parents during the civil war, making them undocumented, permanent residents, not illegal immigrants. They grew up in the Mexican-American/Mexican 'city-

---

[34] O'Mara, 'Uncovering the City in the Suburb', 134. Also see Scott, 'High-Technology Industrial Development'; Soja, 'Los Angeles, 1965–1992'; and US Census Bureau, Gibson, and Jung, 'Historical Census Statistics on Population'.

[35] Davis, *City of Quartz*, chap. 3; Josh Sides, 'Straight into Compton: American Dreams, Urban Nightmares, and the Metamorphosis of a Black Suburb', *American Quarterly* 56 (2004): 583–604; and note 25, above. Also see Brian Cross, *It's Not About a Salary – Rap, Race, and Resistance in Los Angeles* (London and New York: Verso, 1993); and Murray Forman, *The 'Hood' Comes First: Race, Space, and Place in Rap and Hip-Hop* (Middletown, Conn: Wesleyan University Press, 2002).

within city' just to the east of CBD in the Pico-Union district. And they joined their neighbourhood street gangs, which were also often mongrel groups of teens from multiple racial/ethnic backgrounds.

They all began as young people in search of place-based identities and self-defense in a hostile environment of social disorder and police brutality. Some gangs like the *Maras* recruited its members exclusively from its own racial/ethnic group. In either case, these gangland 'homeboys' aged between 15 and 25 years old were at greatest risk of violent death in Los Angeles.[36] In 1996, their futures became even more precarious when the US Congress changed their status from local residents to global nomads in the aptly named, Immigration Reform and Personal Responsibility Act. Under its provisions, the national government set up office in the state's prisons to deport their non-citizen inmates back to the country of their origin. Even those convicted of a nonviolent offense could be summarily expelled. Treated like pariahs in El Salvador, they were tattoo-covered strangers in a strange land. Nonetheless, their membership in an LA street gang followed them, transporting their place-based identities into their new neighbourhoods in San Salvador. One story recorded by ethnographer Elana Zilberg is about a 'homie' who had identified with his 'hood', rather than his ethnicity. His membership in the Mexican-American 18th Street Gang proved fatal. Exiles from its archrivals, the Salvadorian MS, murdered him. In another narrative, membership in the Westside Los Crazies saved the life of a dislocated youth from the Pico Park neighbourhood. Since the local gangs could not identify his barrio, they could not identify him as a friend or an enemy to be added to the death lists. Denied passports and treated as foreigners, many of these gang-affiliated young men end up back in prison. As one 29-year-old serving a 50-year sentence for murder put it, 'I feel at ease here. This is my home.'[37]

Conclusions: Transnational Urbanism and Geographies of Insecurity

The flow of people and goods – legal and illegal – back and forth between Los Angles and San Salvador represent what Zilberg calls a 'politics of simultaneity'. 'In the north-south relations under consideration here', she explains, 'deported Salvadoran immigrant gang youth oscillate between "home" and "abroad", where both home and abroad are themselves unstable locations. At the same

---

[36] Zilberg, 'Fools Banished from the Kingdom'; and Guillermoprieto, 'In the New Gangland'.

[37] Alex Ramírz, as quoted in Alma Guillermoprieto, 'In the New Gangland', 48, 45–8; and Zilberg, 'Fools Banished from the Kingdom'. Also see Michael T. Klare, 'Policing the Empire', *Policing America*, eds Anthony M. Platt and Lynn Cooper (Englewood Cliffs, NJ: Prentice Hall, 1974), 56–65; and Jutersonke, Muggah and Rodgers, 'Gangs, Urban Violence, and Security Interventions'.

time, Salvadoran gang youth who have never been to the United States construct their identities around imagined urban geographies of cities like Los Angeles'.

The economic restructuring of the MS and other local street gangs into multinational business syndicates completes the causal links between the ultimate ghetto of exclusion, an overcrowded prison and the gated communities of the privileged elites living in Simi Valley and Alphaville. Repressive national policies in the US and El Salvador backfired; the prisons became incubators of these criminal organizations. During the 1970–80s, an insatiable consumer appetite for cocaine transformed the drug trade into a worldwide, multi-billion dollar operation that funded subsidiary illegal enterprises in weapons and human trafficking across international borders.[38]

Fuelling a dramatic rise in gun violence, the blood of the dead and wounded in the ensuing drug wars over market territories also reinforced the search for defensible space, fortified enclaves of safety from this new urban crisis of law and order. The growing gap of inequality between the rich and the poor became reflected in the fragmentation of society into radical new forms of gating urban space ranging from private islands of the white-collar elites like Simi Valley to the public housing projects of the lowest-income families. In between, working- and middle-class homeowners have been closing off streets into their neighbourhoods to keep criminals out, while the police have been developing strategies to lock in racial/ethnic groups suspected of criminal activity. In Los Angles, for example, the security forces have set up roadblocks around the Pico-Union neighbourhood, with signs declaring 'Narcotics Enforcement Area – Open to Residents Only – No Outlet'. This breakdown of civic society in Los Angeles and other urban centres around the world into fortified enclaves is what gives Mike Davis reason to call them 'Carceral Cities'.[39]

In historical perspective, then, the transnational geography of insecurity after 1973 can be pictured in postmodern terms as centres and peripheries that keep reversing position. The ancient dichotomy between metropolis and colony has become more complicated by obverse processes of the production of urban space in the First World by influences coming out of the Third World. The global restructuring of capitalism following the oil embargo widened the gap of inequality, raised fear of urban crime and triggered a search for defensible space by rich and poor alike. From this point of view, the urban condition can be seen as a transnational city of flows. Whether at home or moving through the space-time corridors of no-place, security has become a commodity. Whyte's organization

---

[38]   Zilberg, 'Fools Banished from the Kingdom', 774; and Jutersonke, Muggah, and Rodgers, 'Gangs, Urban Violence, and Security Interventions'.

[39]   Davis, *City of Quartz*, 279, 253, chap. 3.

man can afford to live in a gated community of safety, while Zilberg's dislocated immigrant must struggle to survive in a gangland of violent death.[40]

A revisit to Alphaville today would reveal the new frontiers of private security for the insiders as well as the radical spaces of public resistance appropriated by the outsiders. On the one hand, the elite of São Paulo own the world's largest fleet of private helicopters because travelling at street level – even in an armoured car – is no longer considered safe to thwart the kidnappers. On the other hand, a new form of graffiti has begun showing up on bridge overpasses, transit stations, office blocks and other highly visible public spaces in the city centre. The black-only roller-painters call it *'pichação'*, from the verb meaning to cover in tar. Organized in small raiding parties from the periphery, they see themselves as foot soldiers in a class war. 'We take our risks', one *pichação* gang leader stated, 'to remind society that this city is a visual aggression to begin with, and hostile to anyone who is not rich.'[41]

[40]   Maria Kaika, *City of Flows* (New York: Routledge, 2005).
[41]   Djan Ivson Silva, as quoted in Romero, 'At War with São Paulo's Establishment', 5.

Chapter 12

Reflections: Putting the 'Trans' into Transnational Urban History

Richard Rodger

The dynamics of the urban, whether historical or contemporary, are perennially fascinating, and contested. Variations of the term 'urban' – 'urbanism' and 'urbanization' – all have inflexions of meanings that complicate comparative analysis, and are the more problematical at a transnational level given linguistic subtleties as revealed, for example, in *L'aventure des mots de la ville*.[1] The words ville, ciudad, polis, stadt and citta appeared on each of the book jackets in the Historical Urban Studies series and were a deliberate acknowledgement of the cultural and temporal variations to the meanings of town and city.[2]

It is possible to formulate the essence of the city in various ways that are not dependent on Max Weber's emphasis on the physical attributes of market, fort, temple, circus and palace. An urban focus can be identified with power and public administration; with science, technology and medicine; class and status; with ideas and ideals; and people and places. Not much is left out of such an urban agenda. No wonder that urban historians are sometimes overwhelmed by the scope of their subject matter, more than a little reticent to discuss their work in terms of 'grand processes'[3] for fear of appearing to be arrogant, and of course, fearful that they are easy targets for their critics. More confidently, Sam Bass Warner captured the range and diversity of the urban in his presidential address to the Urban History Association in 1991 entitled 'When urban history is at the center of the curriculum'.[4] He began: 'How well urban history might serve as the focus of an entire liberal arts curriculum'. It was, admitted Warner, 'a fantasy university'. But as he developed the imaginary curriculum, he dreamed that

---

[1]   Christian Topalov et al., *L'aventure des mots de la ville: à travers le temps, les langues, les societies* (Paris: Robert Laffont, 2010).

[2]   See https://www.ashgate.com/urbanstudiesseries for a list of titles in the Historical Urban Studies series.

[3]   The term was coined by S.G. Checkland, 'An Urban History Horoscope', in Derek Fraser and Anthony Sutcliffe, eds, *The Pursuit of Urban History* (London: Edward Arnold, 1983), 449–66.

[4]   Sam Bass Warner Jr, '*When Urban History is at the Center of the Curriculum*', *Journal of Urban History*, 18 (1991): 3–9.

'science professors will connect their science problems to the environments, the health and the technology of the metropolis; the writers, painters and musicians will connect their craft studies to urban literature, painting and music; and social scientists will focus on the analysis of urban society, culture and politics'. Where issue should be taken with Warner's 'fantasy' is in the passive or container role accorded to the city. The city is itself an active variable.

Despite the intimidating complexity, urban historians have long sought – indeed have regarded it as axiomatic from the outset – that high-quality historical scholarship embeds transnationalism within a comparative approach. Practical demonstration of this was already evident in the 1970s when H.J. Dyos as editor of the *Urban History Yearbook* framed the disciplinary scope and geographical reach of the journal by involving distinguished scholars from across the continents as members of the Editorial Board.[5] Intuitively and intellectually, urban historians as social science historians were wary of the individual case, and thus of antiquarianism, particularism and localism. If the urban history agenda was to investigate general processes or laws, then the focus had necessarily to be wider than the individual event, or town.

Nonetheless, the sheer complexity of the urban dimension has encouraged many scholars to focus on an individual place in an effort to reveal the fundamentals of urbanism through a case study approach. Core research on a specific town or city remains the most common form of town or city-based historical study, despite Dyos' warning in 1975 that 'the day of individually posed, idiosyncratic study of a town that has no particular analytical purpose or significance is probably on the wane'.[6] The practical reasons for this continuing emphasis on the local are easy to discern: research is manageable and affordable, and subjecting a single place to deeply quarried archival research provides an empirical rigour that reveals underlying processes testable elsewhere, sometimes on a comparative basis. This is a quite different activity to that of the inquisitive local historian, or antiquarian, where particularities of place are often valued for their own sake, and generally are not located in a wider urban historiography. This is not to disparage the acquisitive nature of local historians or to regard them as the Sunday drivers of historical research with different rights or archival access.[7] Far from it: local or antiquarian historians are essential generators of much detailed information and nuanced local circumstances. They thereby feed in to

5 These included François Bedarida, Geoffrey Blainey, Alberto Caracciolo, Graeme Davison, Herman Diederiks, Robert Fairbanks, Clyde and Sally Griffen, Narayani Gupta, Ingrid Hammarstrom, Zane Miller, Antoni Maczak, Lutz Niethammer, Gil Stelter and Kaoru Ugawa. Cincia Sicca, Alan Mayne,and G.M. van der Waal.

6 H.J. Dyos, 'Editorial', *Urban History Yearbook*, 1975, 3, See also Harry S.J. Jansen, 'Wrestling with the Angel: Problems of Definition in Urban Historiography', *Urban History* 23 (1996): 277–99.

7 Richard Rodger, 'Historiens du dimanche', *Urban History* 23 (1996): 86–9.

town and city 'biographies' by academic historians who then seek to illuminate the functioning of place as a totality, that is to say, where all the urban variables are functioning simultaneously and where their varied interrelationships are part of the drama that captures the particularity of a place – its DNA. Held constant in an effort to constrain one dimension of the town (its space). other features can be subjected to greater scrutiny. Done well, urban biography is enlightening and performs an important role in public education by making a place they inhabit and use known to its resident population. It deepens awareness and enhances understanding.

Historical studies of towns and cities often concentrate on a specific aspect – housing, schooling, planning, manufacturing, transporting, suburbanizing or worshipping. Such topics are the subject of study; the urban is the object, and scholars are said to be 'merely passing through' a city which is in fact incidental to them.[8] Comparative and transnational studies are not immune to the same criticism. As a result the drama of the urban, the powerful forces of interrelationships, often remain in the shadows of such works by those with different disciplinary backgrounds – education, sociology, architecture and so on – as distinct from those who concentrate holistically and historically upon the town or city as an entity. Even so, the cumulative effect of such studies enables historians to peel away layers of the urban tissue to reveal the articulation of the corporate parts. It is by these processes that the city as palimpsest is revealed, with its layers of historical development better understood. In the quest for analytical frameworks that have relevance across time and space it is useful to note that the idea of the city as a natural system is in tension with the man-made city and that social theorists used the body with its heart, lungs, arteries and circulation as a basis to explain the growth and decay of urban systems. Cities were the creations of intelligent and civilized humans that, despite their self-regulation and exceptional sophistication, were accompanied by examples of man's inhumanity to man and accordingly have formed the basis of many social-scientific analyses over the years. Studies of exclusion, of social injustice and environmental discrimination, as represented in urban living conditions and life expectancy, capture the polarity between the health of nations and the wealth of nations.[9]

Urban network theory and its different variants have long since pointed to the linkages in the system and the need to consider the 'other'. Core and periphery, like the terms primate cities and megalopolis, each imply a hierarchical relationship in which it is impossible, and ahistorical, to regard developments

---

8   H.J. Dyos, 'Editorial', *Urban History Yearbook* (1974): 5–6.

9   See, for example, the various transnational studies in Geneviève Massard-Guilbaud and Richard Rodger, eds, *Environmental and Social Justice in the City: Historical Perspectives* (Cambridge: The White Horse Press, 2011).

in one city without considering conditions in another. Generic terms such as 'creative cities', 'industrial cities', or as a recent *Atlas* categorized them, 'rational', 'green', 'intelligent' and 'celebrity' cities are in competition with one another as members of the same family of cities.[10] 'Derby' games link cities in competition, and competitions for Olympic, pan-American and Commonwealth games, not to forget the World Cups of various sports, oblige comparisons of the relative merits of each city across a range of criteria. Even the term 'city' is itself associated with status and privilege. City boosterism by public authorities seeks to place the home town or city above and beyond that of a perceived competitor and in so doing provides both an implicitly and explicitly comparative frame of reference; 'twinned' cities' attempts much the same by searching for similar structural and scale identifiers, and implicitly rejecting others. In these senses the *trans* refers to beyond, rather than to across, and is an important or subtle reminder of the linguistic root of transnationalism. Or, rather than looking for happy families of cities coalescing in their common features, should the transnational be re-focussed on disjunctures? Would superficially dysfunctional places be more revealing – both in typologies such as New Towns and imperial settlements, or in zany pairings (Paris Texas v. Paris France; Melbourne Australia with Melbourne Derbyshire) or simply in randomly generated places? And if so, what is the intellectual justification for doing so? Do innovative housing strategies overlap in disparate urban places, or diverge in ones where similarities might be expected?

By contrast with urban biographies, comparative historical analyses of two or more towns or cities have generally addressed a thematic dimension in order to analyse cultural and socio-political frameworks. Entire 'families' of cities have formed part of historical urban studies – Canadian prairie cities, American sun-belt cities, Braudel's Mediterranean cities, ports, metropolises and places synonymous with their core industry, such as the Ruhr and Clydeside conurbations. Many such typologies existed in an industrializing Europe where the key industries of cotton and iron-smelting provided powerful commonalities through their organizational arrangements and relationships. With this approach the city forms a living laboratory: one common element of the typology, its industrial specialism, is considered as fixed, while other variables associated with that typology are examined under the historical microscope in order to observe how they respond under different conditions. The common denominator, the socio-economic structures associated with the principal product, provides a comparative, potentially a transnational, basis for analysis and illuminates an understanding of the urbanizing process. This in turn prompts subordinate questions: how do different members of the city typology address the problems associated with rapid increases in the population? Does the

---

[10]   Paul Knox, ed. *Atlas of Cities* (Princeton: Princeton University, Press, 2014).

mix of institutional or financial or technical factors vary between the towns and cities in the typology? Understanding urban systems and processes, therefore, has been the driver in many such comparative studies.[11]

If the comparative methodology is illuminating in understanding the urban paradigm, then cross-border studies should be particularly helpful. The 'transnational' has thus entered the lexicon as a mode urban analysis. It should be remembered, of course, that the 'nation', and therefore the 'transnational', is a recent concept in historical, political and in intellectual terms. The nineteenth century is considered an era in which many new national entities were constructed, and post-war peace treaties and agreements in the twentieth century shaped many more, as did the retreat of European imperialism. So, strictly speaking, the transnational perspective is a temporally constrained one, and in scholarly terms is spatially constrained, being an essentially Eurocentric one. These constraints can be overcome both by accepting regionalism as providing bounded areas or spheres of influence – in a European context often marked by tolls and taxes extracted by princelings and chieftains – and incorporating a different scale of analysis. This is particularly important because until relatively recently the nature of trade and travel, marriages and markets took place in a world dominated by the local and preoccupied with subsistence agriculture. Indeed, all authors concerned with urbanization at any selected minimum threshold scale (2,000, 5,000, or 20,000 inhabitants) agree that society was overwhelmingly rural until the twentieth century.[12]

So maybe the term 'transnational' might be allied with 'transurban' to escape the reservation that the national scale is essentially a recent invention. Could transnational and transurban be redefined to consider jurisdictional areas within and between regions and localities so as to form a convincing historical basis for effective comparators between places and across a longer time frame than the 'modern' or 'contemporary' eras? A refocusing of the scale of analysis could yield productivity and add value to the terms. For example, studies of cities across a river boundary where the institutional and cultural framework is different but the topographical and climatic factors are very similar would make for potentially fertile comparisons. This might work in a variety of settings: the transnational scale between Brownsville (USA) across the Rio Grande with

---

[11] See especially Bernard Lepetit, *The Pre-industrial Urban System: France 1740–1840* (Cambridge: Cambridge University Press, 1994), particularly chapter 4, 'An Essay in Urban Typology'.

[12] In Europe only England, Belgium and the Netherlands recorded a majority of their populations in settlements of 5,000 or more people in 1910. Paul Bairoch, *Cities and Economic Development* (Chicago: University of Chicago Press, 1988), 221, reproduced in Andrew Lees and Lynn Hollen Lees, *Cities and the Making of Modern Europe 1750–1914* (Cambridge: Cambridge University Press, 2007), 133. The tipping point for European urbanisation was in 1950 when urban residents constituted 51 per cent.

Matamoros (Mexico), or Strasbourg under French and German, and then again French administrations; the transurban scale of different states or counties as between St Louis (Missouri) and St Louis (Illinois) or Newcastle and Gateshead (UK). To escape the essentially modern, though, as in the case of the border towns of Dumfries (Scotland) and Carlisle (England), the shared river basin, climate, agrarian hinterland and building materials contrast not simply in a translocal manner but in a transnational dimension because of the significantly different legal, educational, financial, and religious conditions under which they operated. These are urban test benches for the wider English-Scottish disparities in the built form. Others could be identified. And this is one of the great virtues of such transurban studies since they provide insights with much wider significance within and between nations.

Most important, and urgent, is the need to consider regions as a basis for comparative research. As clusters or conurbations which included the natural resources of their hinterlands, it was the regions of the genuinely transnational Sambre-Meuse, west Flanders, Pas-de-Calais, Saxony, Silesia, Rhine-Ruhr, northern Bohemia and in Eastern Europe, the Donbas, many of them straddling what eventually became national boundaries, that were critical to the pace and form of urban development. Multiple systems of weights and measures, currencies and languages emphasize the fractured and autonomous areas of these regions, and even within unified countries such as France. Such non-national dimensions are important legacies for urban historical analyses, and demand a greater degree of caution when focusing on comparative urbanism. Indeed, internal borders and jurisdictions, rather than formal national ones, provide real opportunities to understand how towns and cities adapted to regulatory frameworks.

Perhaps it is the concept of 'trans' that should be our historical focus. The 'trans' root – as in 'across' or 'beyond' – demands a comparative element: across what or beyond what is implicit? But this might be across or 'trans' at different scales of analysis – national, regional, urban and local – and it is the elaboration of and interplay between these combined with ideas and ideologies that provides the most convincing explanation of the uniqueness of place – its DNA. This still remains a sound historical method, with quantification thrown in for good measure to add empirical underpinnings. Methodologically innovative approaches have added new elements to the historians' craft, and it is highly likely that studies of emotion, folklore, customs, songs and speech patterns, just like sounds and smells, aided in many cases by digital technologies, will present new transnational opportunities and perspectives. This is because these are everyday experiences of everyday people, comparable because the digital medium eliminates some of the barriers of language, and shorn of the elitism associated with planning and regulation in the built environment which have featured widely in transnational studies to date. Digital databases are already making research across frontiers significantly easier, though not entirely without their own dangers since what is digitized is privileged as a source. New intellectual agendas can be anticipated, therefore, in which the urban imagination and memory play a significant role. Are towns and cities invariably represented in film, literature and drama as hothouses of modernity and the avant-garde? Are cities brutalizing for the poor? Is there potential for transnational studies of the ways urban street culture is reproduced? How and when did the term metropolis or suburb emerge in different countries? How do linguistic conventions change the way racism is represented across different cities? 'Painting the Town', a recent exhibition mounted by the National Gallery of Scotland covering two centuries in over 70 towns and cities, revealed many common themes from the glossy to the gritty, while leaving room to ponder whether these were reproduced transnationally. Recordings recapture not just the voices but also the values of the past; the feel of the city, its urban grain, can be caught by the testimony and fed in to transnational ideas of urbanity. The parameters of the 'trans' in transnational may, indeed should, become more pliable and ambitious.

The *trans*fer of knowledge, a central theme of urban historiography since towns and cities were seen as key agents of modernity, has understandably been embedded in comparative and transnational studies for some time. There have been long distance migrations, traders and pilgrims for many centuries and the spread of ideas across Europe and the Middle East often took place through them. Medical students made for Leiden and Paris in the seventeenth and eighteenth centuries and imported the latest ideas and practices to their own countries. Municipal delegations and international exhibitions were conduits of modern manufacturing and engineering information, and transnational studies have paid considerable attention to these topics.[13] Bounded limits were the means by which inclusivity was enforced, and these were not necessarily geographical, and only sometimes transnational. So internal borders and jurisdictions, rather than formal national ones, provide real opportunities to understand how cities forged and adapted regulatory frameworks. Professional standards and institutional procedures produce behavioural conformity. Nowhere was this better demonstrated than by medieval craft guilds whose production standards were normally defined by a jurisdiction limited to a specific radius from a fixed point in the town. Borough charters provided exclusion zones around towns and legitimated sanctions applied to interlopers. The Zollverein deconstructed the tariff and trade boundaries between autonomous German princedoms in the first half of the nineteenth century. Perhaps the ultimate exclusive transnational club, and one that might enable several key criteria to be identified, was the

---

[13] See, for example, Pierre-Yves Saunier, 'Introduction: Global City, Take 2: A View from Urban History', in Saunier and Shane Ewen, eds, *Another Global City: Historical Explorations into the Transnational Municipal Moment 1850–2000* (New York: Palgrave Macmillan, 2008), 1–18.

Hanseatic League, which, by 1400, included approximately 170 towns. Policed by a communally financed fleet and with an element of political leverage, the alliance shared risks and mutually supported one another when faced with powerful princes. Behaviour considered as *trans*gressive was therefore met by collective action across borders.

In short, the comparative framework is enshrined in rigorous historical research and analysis; and comparison inevitably embraces phenomena from different nations and regions. The internal versus the external, the domestic versus the international, are polarities that sound scholarship invariably embraces. The balance of historical explanation, however, depends on the extent to which the opposing domestic or foreign forces are, or were, dominant. So for centuries distance and the associated time and transport costs insulated local markets, knowledge, beliefs and public policy. The ability of external or transnational forces to induce change was inhibited. As external influences on the city gained momentum, so the previously long-run dominance of commercial and administrative influences that were essentially local and regional began to recede, though not to disappear. If this process might be considered to be a transnational force for homogenization, as reflected in the efforts made by French cultural agencies in the late-twentieth century to oppose the process of anglicization, then the converse is now valid. A Polish immigrant can listen to and watch Polish programmes from Sweden, send text messages to his or her relatives in Poland and essentially inhabit a dual world where the virtual vies with the practical tasks of making a living and raising a family. The transnational takes on a greater relevance in the contemporary world.

At the height of the international depression in the 1930s scholars sought to understand the dynamics of the national and international system.[14] Business cycle analysts identified the instability, but rather than accord primacy to domestic or foreign influences, they recognized powerful and iterative relationships between these scales which were also inherent in a capitalist system in which production and exchange responded to changes in the relative rates of return on capital and labour. Ebb and flow in the pace urbanization, it was argued in an overtly occidental view of the international economy, was inversely related on either side of the Atlantic. Though rather simplistic in its early formulation – alliteratively (and ahistorically), Oldham and Oklahoma, Dalmarnock (Glasgow) and the Dakotas were inversely linked in their growth and development – the central mechanisms explicitly recognized inter-dependencies between places across the globe. There was an inherently transnational dimension to the process of capital accumulation and its associated urbanization. With more than a tinge of

---

[14]   See for example, W.C. Mitchell, *Business Cycles and their Causes* (Berkeley: University of California Press, 1941) and A.K. Cairncross, 'The Glasgow Building Industry 1870–1914', *Review of Economic Studies* 2 (1934): 1–17.

Marxist theory, the city itself became a major variable in an international system that had been slow to recognize its significance.[15] Understanding the urban became a vital element in national policy, and remains so.

Braudel's conclusion that 'Toute ville est, se veut un monde à part'[16] ('Every town is and wishes to be a separate world') is a powerful statement of the independent, if somewhat indefinite, urban variable and the uniqueness of place. It is a reminder that it is possible to be part of an urban system yet stubbornly apart from it. The search for an urban identity and sense of place is elusive and, in an ultra-competitive world, cities seek an edge by scrutinizing and emulating the activities of others. This brings the comparative and transnational into play, though it is inappropriate to reduce urbanization 'to a mere by-product of capitalist relationships'.[17] In searching for a key driver across American cities, Monkonnen offered a penetrating insight into the urban process in which he claimed that, through their legal status and administrative powers, cities possessed a corporate status that enabled them to 'borrow and lend, build and destroy, expand and contract, appear and disappear'.[18] From this perspective, American urbanization is the history of how cities 'came to their corporate status, what they have done with this status, and how they have shaped themselves'. The critical factor was not the spatial entity of the city but the 'shape' of the organizational unit; the most significant shift was from a 'regulatory' to an 'active' city, or from a relatively simple organizational form with limited scope using powers on a reactive basis, to an organizationally complex, pro-active city.

Towns and cities are organisms: they are founded (born), annexed or overrun (married?) and decay (die). In humans, DNA (deoxyribonucleic acid) is a complex molecule that is unchangeable and captures the fundamental information to build and maintain the organism. Like humans, where the DNA is unique to each individual, so it is with cities, and even when twinned with other cities they are never identical. So though cities share common elements – exchange and circulation; rhythms and rites; legal and customary rights; power and authority; social hierarchy; associational organizations; and institutions – their identity is unique through the distinctive blend of these elements. Some are local, some regional and others have national and international characteristics, the composition of which varies from place to place just as the topography,

[15] Manuel Castells, *The City and the Grassroots: A Cross-Cultural Theory of Urban Social Movements* (Berkeley: University of California Press, 1988); David Harvey, *Social Justice and the City* (London: Edward Arnold, 1973).

[16] Fernand Braudel, *Capitalism and Material Life 1400–1800* (London: Weidenfeld and Nicolson, 1973), 382.

[17] Theodore Koditschek, *Class Formation and Urban Industrial Society: Bradford 1750–1850* (Cambridge: Cambridge University Press, 1990), 80–81, n.4.

[18] Eric H. Monkkonen, *America Becomes Urban: the Development of U.S. Cities and Towns 1780–1980* (Berkeley: University of California Press, 1988).

hydrology and geology provide a distinctive character to a site based on the mix of minerals and muds, and coastal and fluvial floods. The DNA of each city is unique. Let there be no mistake about that. But where transnational history may help is in decoding and explaining how the identity of our city has been influenced by factors beyond the immediate hinterland.

Bibliography

Chapter 1

Akkermans, Peter M.M.G and Schwartz, Glenn M. *The Archaeology of Syria: From Complex Hunter-Gatherers to Early Urban Societies, c.16,000–300 BC* (Cambridge: Cambridge University Press, 2003).

Bayly Christopher A. et al., 'AHR Conversation: On Transnational History', *American Historical Review* 111 (2006): 1440–64.

Beckett, John V. *City Status in the British Isles, 1830–2002* (Aldershot: Ashgate, 2005).

Bloch, Marc. 'Pour une histoire comparée des sociétés européennes', *Revue de synthèse historique* 46 (1928): 15–50.

Calvino, Italo. *Invisible Cities*, trans. William Weaver (Harcourt Brace, 1974).

Clark, Peter. ed. *Cities in World History* (Oxford: Oxford University Press, 2013).

Cohen Deborah and O'Connor, Maura. eds. *Comparison and History: Europe in Cross-National Perspective* (London: Routledge, 2004).

Davies, Gary. 'The Rise of Urban History in Britain, c. 1960–1978' (PhD diss., University of Leicester, 2014).

Dennis, Richard. *Cities in Modernity: Representations and Productions of Metropolitan Space, 1840–1930* (Cambridge: Cambridge University Press, 2008).

Detienne, Marcel. *Comparing the Incomparable*, trans. Janet Lloyd (Stanford: Stanford University Press, 2008).

Diefendorf Jeffry M. and Ward, Janet. eds. *Transnationalism and the German City* (New York: Palgrave Macmillan, 2014).

Dyos, Harold James. *The Urban History Yearbook*, 1974.

Fraser Derek and Sutcliffe, Anthony. eds. *The Pursuit of Urban History* (London: E. Arnold, 1983).

Fredrickson, George M. 'From Exceptionalism to Variability: Recent Developments in Cross-National Comparative History', *Journal of American History* 82 (1995): 587–604.

Frost Lionel and O'Hanlon, Seamus. 'Urban History and the Future of Australian Cities', *Australian Economic History Review* 49 (2009): 1–18.

Green, Nancy L. *Ready-to-Wear and Ready-to-Work: A Century of Industry and Immigrants in Paris and New York* (Durham: Duke University Press, 1997).

Grew, Raymond. 'The Case for Comparing Histories', *American Historical Review* 85 (1980): 763–8.

Howard, Michael C. *Transnationalism in Ancient and Medieval Societies: The Role of Cross-Border Trade and Travel* (Jefferson, NC: McFarland, 2012).

Huyssen, Andreas. ed. *Other Cities, Other Worlds* (New York: Palgrave Macmillan, 2008).

Kenny, Nicolas. *The Feel of the City: Experiences of Urban Transformation* (Toronto: University of Toronto Press, 2014).

Khagram Sanjeev and Levitt, Peggy. eds. *The Transnational Studies Reader: Intersections and Innovations* (New York: Routledge, 2008).

Kocka, Jürgen. 'Comparison and Beyond', *History and Theory* 42 (2003): 39–44.

Krätke, Stefan, Wildner, Kathrin and Lanz, Stephan. eds. *Transnationalism and Urbanism* (New York: Routledge, 2012).

Lemanski, Charlotte. 'Hybrid Gentrification in South Africa: Theorising across Southern and Northern Cities', *Urban Studies* 51 (2014): 2943–60.

Madgin, Rebecca. *Heritage, Culture and Conservation: Managing the Urban Renaissance* (Saarbrucken: VDM Verlag, 2009).

Mayne, Alan. *The Imagined Slum: Newspaper Representation in Three Cities, 1870–1914* (Leicester: Leicester University Press, 1993).

McFarlane, Colin. 'Comparative Urbanism' (Special Issue) *Urban Geography* 33 (2012): 765–915.

Miller, Jaroslav. *Urban Societies in East-Central Europe, 1500–1700* (Aldershot: Ashgate, 2008).

Mumford, Lewis. *The City in History: Its Origins, its Transformations, and its Prospects* (New York: Harcourt, Brace and World, 1961).

Nightingale, Carl H. *Segregation: A Global History of Divided Cities* (Chicago: University of Chicago Press, 2012).

O'Flanagan, Patrick. *Port Cities of Atlantic Iberia, c. 1500–1900* (Aldershot: Ashgate, 2008).

Platt, Harold L. *Shock Cities: The Environmental Transformation and Reform of Manchester and Chicago* (Chicago: University of Chicago Press, 2005).

Polasky, Janet. *Reforming Urban Labor: Routes to the City, Roots in the Country* (Ithaca: Cornell University Press, 2010).

Rao, Nikhil. *House, but No Garden: Apartment Living in Bombay's Suburbs, 1898–1964* (Minneapolis: University of Minnesota Press, 2013).

Robinson, Jennifer. 'Cities in a World of Cities: The Comparative Gesture', *International Journal of Urban and Regional Research* 35 (2013): 1–23.

Robinson, Jennifer. 'Introduction to a Virtual Issue on Comparative Urbanism'. *International Journal of Urban and Regional Research* (published online, April 2014).

Rodger, Richard. *European Urban History* (Leicester: Leicester University Press, 1993).

Rodger Richard and Sweet, Roey. 'The Changing Nature of Urban History', *History in Focus* (2008).

Rodgers, Daniel T. *Atlantic Crossings: Social Politics in a Progressive Age* (Cambridge: Harvard University Press, 1998).

Saasen, Saskia. *Globalization and its Discontents: Essays on the New Mobility of People and Money* (New York: New Press, 1998).

Samman, Khaldoun. 'The Limits of the Classical Comparative Method', *Review (Fernand Braudel Center)* 24 (2001): 533–73.

Sandoval-Strausz Andrew K. and Kwak, Nancy Haekyung, et al. 'Why Trans-nationalise Urban History?' See programme of Urban History Association, 2014: http://uha.udayton.edu/2014Conf/UHA%20Program%20FINAL%20Web.pdf.

Saunier, Pierre-Yves. 'Transatlantic Connections and Circulations in the 20th Century: The Urban Variable', *Informationen zur modernen Stadgeschichte* 1 (2007): 11–24.

Saunier, Pierre-Yves. *Transnational History* (Houndmills, Basingstoke, Hampshire: Palgrave Macmillan, 2013).

Saunier Pierre-Yves and Ewen, Shane eds. *Another Global City: Historical Explorations into the Transnational Municipal Moment, 1850–2000* (New York: Palgrave Macmillan, 2008).

Smith, Michael Peter. *Transnational Urbanism: Locating Globalization* (Malden: Blackwell Publishers, 2001).

Smith, Michael Peter. 'Transnational Urbanism Revisited', *Journal of Ethnic and Migration Studies* 31 (2005): 235–44.

Stanger-Ross, Jordan. *Urban Change and Ethnic Life in Postwar Toronto and Philadelphia* (Chicago: University of Chicago Press, 2009).

Tilly, Charles. 'What Good Is Urban History?', *Journal of Urban History* 22 (1996): 702–19.

Topalov, Christian. et al. *L'aventure des mots de la ville à travers le temps, les langues, les sociétés* (Paris: Robert Laffont, 2010).

Wade, Richard C. *The Urban Frontier: Pioneer Life in Early Pittsburgh, Cincinnati, Lexington, Louisville, and St. Louis* (Chicago: University of Chicago Press, 1964).

Walton John and Masotti, Louis H. eds. *The City in Comparative Perspective: Cross-National Research and New Directions in Theory* (New York: Sage, 1976).

Ward, Kevin. 'Towards a Comparative (Re)Turn in Urban Studies? Some Reflections', *Urban Geography* 29 (2008): 405–10.

Ward, Kevin. 'Towards a Relational Comparative Approach to the Study of Cities', *Progress in Human Geography* 34 (2010): 471–87.

Werner Michael and Zimmermann, Bénédicte. 'Penser l'histoire croisée: entre empirie et réflexivité', *Annales Histoire, Sciences Sociales* 58 (2003): 7–36.

Xiangming Chen and Ahmed Kanna. eds. *Rethinking Global Urbanism: Comparative Insights from Secondary Cities* (New York: Routledge, 2012).

Chapter 2

Bender, Thomas. 'Keynote Address' at Conference on the Atlantic in Global Perspective, University at Buffalo, State University of New York, Buffalo, NY, 2004.

Cañizares-Esguerra Jorge and Seeman, Erik. eds. *The Atlantic in Global Perspective, 1500–2000* (Upper Saddle River, NJ: Pearson Prentice Hall, 2007).

Couperus, Stefan, Smit Christianne and Wolffram, Dirk Jan. eds. *In Control of the City: Local Elites and the Dynamics of Urban Politics, 1800–1960* (Leuven, Paris and Dudley, MA: Peeters, 2007).

Ewen Shane and Hebbert, Michael. 'European Cities in a Networked World during the Long 20th Century', *Environment and Planning C: Government and Policy* 25 (2007): 327–40.

Fredrickson, George M. *White Supremacy: A Comparative Study in American and South African History* (Oxford: Oxford University Press, 1981).

Fredrickson, George M. *The Comparative Imagination: On the History of Racism, Nationalism, and Social Movements* (Berkeley: University of California Press, 1997).

Hodos, Jerome I. *Second Cities: Globalization and Local Politics in Manchester and Philadelphia* (Philadelphia: Temple University Press, 2011).

Keller, Lisa. *Triumph of Order: Democracy and Public Space in New York and London* (New York: Columbia University Press, 2009).

Klemek, Christopher. *The Transatlantic Collapse of Urban Renewal: Postwar Urbanism from New York to Berlin* (Chicago: University of Chicago Press, 2011).

Lake, Marilyn and Reynolds, Henry. *Drawing the Global Colour Line: White Men's Countries and the International Challenge of Racial Inequality* (Cambridge, UK: Cambridge University Press, 2008).

Laqua, Daniel. ed. *Internationalism Reconfigured: Transnational Ideas and Movements Between the World Wars* (London: I.B. Taurus, 2011).

Molho Anthony and Wood Gordon S. eds. *Imagined Histories: American Historians Interpret the Past* (Princeton: Princeton University Press, 1998).

Nightingale, Carl H. *Segregation: A Global History of Divided Cities* (Chicago: University of Chicago Press, 2012).

Organization of American Historians (OAH), 'The La Pietra Report: A Report to the Profession' (2000) at http://www.oah.org/about/reports/reports-statements/the-lapietra-report-a-report-to-the-profession/.

Rabinow, Paul. *French Modern: Norms and Forms of the Social Environment* (Cambridge, MA: MIT Press, 1989).

Rodgers, Daniel T. *Atlantic Crossings: Social Politics in a Progressive Age* (Cambridge: Harvard University Press, 1998).

Saunier Pierre-Yves and Ewen, Shane. eds. *Another Global City: Historical Explorations into the Transnational Municipal Moment, 1850–2000* (New York: Palgrave Macmillan, 2008).

Stanger Ross, Jordan. *Staying Italian: Urban Change and Ethnic Life in Postwar Toronto and Philadelphia* (Chicago: University of Chicago Press, 2009).

Wright, Gwendolyn. *The Politics of Design in French Colonial Urbanism* (Chicago: University of Chicago Press, 1991).

Chapter 3

Baldwin, Peter. *Domesticating the Street: The Reform of Public Space in Hartford, 1850–1930* (Columbus: Ohio State University Press, 1989).

Barber, Shelley. ed. *The Prendergrast Letters: Correspondence from Famine-era Ireland, 1840–1850* (Amherst: University of Massachusetts Press, 2006).

Barry, Andrew, Osborne, Thomas and Rose, Nikolas. eds. *Foucault and Political Reason: Liberalism, Neo-Liberalism and Rationalities of Government* (Chicago: University of Chicago Press, 1996).

Belchem, John. *Merseypride: Essays in Liverpool Exceptionalism* (Liverpool: Liverpool University Press, 2000).

Berman, Marshall. *All that is Solid Melts Into Air* (London: Verso, 1983.

Buckner, Phillip and Francis, R. Douglas. eds. *Canada and the British World: Culture, Migration and Identity* (Vancouver: University of British Columbia Press, 2006).

Bukowczyk John, J. et al. eds. *Permeable Border: The Great Lakes Basin as a Transnational Region, 1650–1900* (Pittsburgh: University of Pittsburgh Press, 2012).

Calhoun, Craig. ed. *Habermas and the Public Sphere* (Cambridge: MIT University Press, 1992).

Calhoun, Craig. *The Roots of Radicalism: Tradition, the Public Sphere and Early Nineteenth-Century Social Movements* (Chicago: University of Chicago Press, 2012).

Curtis, Bruce. *Ruling by Schooling Quebec: Conquest to Liberal Governmentality – A Historical Sociology* (Toronto: University of Toronto Press, 2012).

Davis, Mike. *Planet of Slums* (London: Verso, 2006).

Dawson, Michael and Dummitt, Christopher eds. *Contesting Clio's Craft: New Directions and Debates in Canadian History* (Vancouver: University of British Columbia Press, 2008).

Dennis, Richard. *English Industrial Cities of the Nineteenth Century: A Social Geography* (Cambridge: Cambridge University Press, 1986).

Ducharme, Michel. *Le concept de liberté au Canada à l'époque des Révolutions atlantiques (1776–1838)* (Montreal: McGill-Queen's University Press, 2009).

Ducharme Michel and Constant Jean-François. eds. *Liberalism and Hegemony: Debating the Canadian Liberal Revolution* (Toronto: University of Toronto Press, 2009).

Evans, Eric. *The Forging of the Modern State: Early Industrial Britain, 1783–1870* (Harlow: Longman Group, 1983).

Fecteau, Jean-Marie. *La liberté du pauvre: crime et pauvreté au XIXe siècle québécois* (Outremont: VLB, 2004).

Gallman, Matthew. *Receiving Erin's Children: Philadelphia, Liverpool and the Irish Famine Migration, 1845–1855* (Chapel Hill: University of North Carolina Press, 2000).

Greer, Allan and Radforth, Ian. *Colonial Leviathan: State Formation in Mid-Nineteenth-Century Canada* (Toronto: University of Toronto Press, 1992).

Greer, James. *The Patriots and the People: The Rebellion of 1837 in Rural Lower Canada* (Toronto: University of Toronto Press, 1993).

Hall, Catherine. *Civilising Subjects: Metropole and Colony in the English Imagination, 1830–1867* (Chicago: University of Chicago Press, 2002).

Hall, Catherine, McClelland, Keith and Rendall, Jane. eds. *Defining the Victorian Nation: Class, Race, Gender and the British Reform Act of 1867* (Cambridge: Cambridge University Press, 2005).

Hamlin, Christopher. *Public Health and Social Justice in the Age of Chadwick,* (Cambridge: Cambridge University Press, 1998).

Harvey, David. *Paris: Capital of Modernity* (New York: Routledge, 2003).

Havard, Gilles. *The Great Peace of Montreal of 1701*, trans. Aronoff and Scott (Montreal: McGill-Queen's University Press, 2001).

Hoare, Quintin. ed. *Antonio Gramsci: Selections from Political Writings (1921–1926)* (Charlottesville: University of Virginia Press, 1978).

Horner, Dan. 'Taking to the Streets: Crowds, Politics and Identity in Mid-Nineteenth-Century Montreal' (PhD diss., York University, 2010).

Horner, Dan. 'Shame upon you as men!': Contesting Authority in the Aftermath of Montreal's Gavazzi Riot'. *Histoire sociale/Social History* 44 (2011): 29–52.

Horner, Dan. 'The Public Has the Right to be Protected from A Deadly Scourge': Debating Quarantine, Migration and Liberal Governance during the 1847 Typhus Outbreak in Montreal'. *Journal of the Canadian Historical Association/Revue de la Société historique de Canada* 23 (2012): 65–100.

Horner, Dan. 'If the evil now growing around us be not staid': Montreal and Liverpool Confront the Irish Famine Migration as a Transnational Crisis in Urban Governance'. *Histoire sociale/Social History* 46 (2013): 349–66.

Joyce, Patrick. *Democratic Subjects: The Self and the Social in Nineteenth-Century England* (Cambridge: Cambridge University Press, 1994).

Joyce, Patrick. *Liberalism and the Modern City.* (London and New York: Verso, 2003).

Keller, Lisa. *Triumph of Order: Democracy and Public Space in New York and London* (New York: Columbia University Press, 2013).

Kinealy, Christine. *The Great Irish Famine: Impact, Ideology and Rebellion* (London: Palgrave Macmillan, 2002).

Levine, Philippa. ed., *Gender and Empire* (Oxford: Oxford University Press, 2007).

Mangan, James. ed. *Robert Whyte's 1847 Famine Ship Diary: The Journey of an Irish Coffin Ship* (Dublin: Mercier Press, 1994).

McCrady, David. *Living With Strangers: The Nineteenth-Century Sioux and the Canadian-American Borderlands* (Toronto: University of Toronto Press, 2009).

McKay, Ian 'The Liberal Order Framework: A Prospectus for a Reconnaissance of Canadian History', *Canadian Historical Review* 81 (2000): 617–45.

McLean, Stuart John. *The Event and its Terrors: Ireland, Famine, Modernity* (Redwood City: Stanford University Press, 2003).

McNairn, Jeffrey. *The Capacity to Judge: Public Opinion and Deliberative Democracy in Upper Canada, 1791–1854* (Toronto: University of Toronto Press, 2000).

Miller, Kerby. *Emigrants and Exiles: Ireland and the Irish Exodus to North America* (Oxford: Oxford University Press, 1998).

Mills, Sean. *The Empire Within: Postcolonial Thought and Political Activism in Sixties Montreal* (Montreal: McGill-Queen's University Press, 2010).

Mills, Sean. 'Quebec, Haiti and the Deportation Crisis of 1974'. *Canadian Historical Review* 94 (2013): 405–35.

Monet, Jacques. *The Last Cannon Shot: A Study in French-Canadian Nationalism, 1837–1850* (Toronto: University of Toronto Press, 1969).

Morgan, Cecilia. *Public Men and Virtuous Women: The Gendered Languages of Religion and Politics in Upper Canada, 1791–1850* (Toronto: University of Toronto Press, 1996).

Morris, Robert J. and Trainor, Richard H. eds. *Urban Governance: Britain and Beyond since 1750* (Aldershot: Ashgate, 2000).

Muir, Ramsay and Platt, Edith May. *A History of Municipal Government in Liverpool* (Liverpool: University of Liverpool Press, 1907).

Mulrooney, Margaret. ed. *Fleeing the Famine: North America and the Irish Refugees, 1845–1851* (Westport: Greenwood, 2005).

Neal, Frank. *Sectarian Violence: The Liverpool Experience, 1819–1914* (Manchester: Manchester University Press, 1988).

Noel, Jan. *Canada Dry: Temperance Crusades before Confederation* (Toronto: University of Toronto Press, 1992).

Palmer, Bryan. *The Working Class Experience: Rethinking the History of Canadian Labour* (Toronto: McClelland and Stewart, 1992).

Perry, Adele. *On the Edge of Empire: Gender, Race and the Making of British Columbia, 1849–1871* (Toronto: University of Toronto Press, 2001).

Podruchny, Carolyn. 'Unfair Masters and Rascally Servants? Labour Relations between Bourgeois, Clerks and Voyageurs in the Montreal Fur Trade, 1780–1821'. *Labour/Le Travail* 43 (1999): 43–70.

Poovey, Mary. *Making a Social Body: British Cultural Formation, 1830–1864* (Chicago: University of Chicago Press, 1995).

Potters, Simon. *Newspapers and Empire in Ireland and Britain: Reporting the British Empire c. 1857–1921* (London: Four Courts, 2004).

Richardson, David, Schwartz, Suzanne and Tibbles, Anthony. eds. *Liverpool and Transatlantic Slavery* (Liverpool: Liverpool University Press, 2007).

Rosenzweig, Roy and Blackmar, Elizabeth. *The Park and the People: A History of Central Park* (Ithaca: Cornell University Press, 1992).

Rowbotham Judith and Stevenson, Kim. eds. *Criminal Conversations: Victorian Crimes, Social Panic and Moral Outrage* (Columbus: Ohio State University Press, 2005).

Ryan, Mary. *Civic Wars: Democracy and Public Life in the American City in the Nineteenth Century* (Berkeley: University of California Press, 1997).

Sanderson, Michael. *Education, Economic Change and Society in England, 1780–1870* (Cambridge: Cambridge University Press, 1995).

Steedman, Carolyn. *An Everyday Life of the English Working Class: Work, Self and Sociability in the Early Nineteenth Century* (Cambridge: Cambridge University Press, 2013).

Taylor, David. *The New Police in Nineteenth-Century England: Crime, Conflict and Control* (Manchester: Manchester University Press, 1997).

Tosh, John. *A Man's Place: Masculinity and the Middle-Class Home in Victorian England* (New Haven: Yale University Press, 1999).

Vernon, James. *Politics and the People: A Study in English Political Culture, c. 1815–1837* (Cambridge: Cambridge University Press, 1993).

Waller, Philip. *Democracy and Sectarianism: A Political and Social History of Liverpool, 1868–1939* (Liverpool: Liverpool University Press, 1981).

White, Richard. *The Middle Ground: Indians, Empires and Republics in the Great Lakes Region, 1650–1815* (Cambridge: Cambridge University Press, 1991).

Winter, James *London's Teeming Streets, 1830–1914* (London: Routledge, 1993).

Chapter 4

Brubaker, Rogers. *Ethnicity without Groups* (Cambridge, MA: Harvard University Press, 2006).

Conzen, Kathleen Neils, Gerber, David A., Morawska, Ewa, Pozzetta, George E. and Vecoli, Rudolph J. 'The Invention of Ethnicity: A Perspective from the USA'. *Journal of American Ethnic History* 12 (1992): 3–41.

Deutsch, Sarah. *Women and the City: Gender, Space, and Power in Boston, 1870–1940* (New York: Oxford University Press, 2002).

Giddens, Anthony. *The Constitution of Society: Outline of the Theory of Structuration* (Berkeley: University of California Press, 1984).

Gordon, Colin. 'Lost in Space, or Confessions of an Accidental Geographer', *Journal of Humanities & Arts Computing: A Journal of Digital Humanities* 5 (2011): 1–22.

Gregory, Derek. *Geographic Imaginations* (Cambridge, MA: Blackwell, 1994).

Hagerstrand, Torsten. 'What about People in Regional Science?', *Regional Science Association Papers* 24 (1970): 7–21.

Katz, Michael. *Why Don't American Cities Burn?* (Philadelphia: University of Pennsylvania Press).

Knowles, Anne Kelly and Hillier, Amy. eds. *Placing History: How Maps, Spatial Data, and GIS are Changing Historical Scholarship*, (Redlands, CA: ESRI Press, 2008).

Nightingale, Carl H. *Segregation: A Global History of Divided Cities*, Historical Studies of Urban America (Chicago; London: The University of Chicago Press, 2012).

Pavlovskaya, Marianna. 'Theorizing with GIS: A Tool for Critical Geographies?', *Environment and Planning A* 38, (2006): 2003–20.

Pred, Allan. 'The Choreography of Existence: Comments on Hagerstrand's Time-Geography and its Usefulness', *Economic Geography* 53 (1977): 207–21.

Scherzer, Kenneth A. *The Unbounded Community: Neighborhood Life and Social Structure in New York City, 1830–1875* (Durham: Duke University Press, 1992).

Stanger-Ross, Jordan. *Staying Italian: Urban Change and Ethnic Life in Postwar Toronto and Philadelphia* (Chicago: The University of Chicago Press, 2009).

Stansell, Christine. *City of Women: Sex and Class in New York 1789–1869* (Champaign, IL: University of Illinois Press, 1987).

Vann Woodward, Comer. ed. *The Comparative Approach to American History*, rev. ed. (New York: Oxford University Press, 1997).

von Lünen, Alexander and Travis, Charles. eds. *History and GIS Epistemologies, Considerations and Reflections* (Dordrecht: Springer, 2013).

Wingo, Lowdon Jr ed. *Cities and Space: The Future Use of Urban Land*, (Baltimore: Johns Hopkins University Press, 1963).

Zelinsky, Wilbur. *The Enigma of Ethnicity: Another American Dilemma* (Iowa City: University of Iowa City Press, 2001).

Zelinsky Wilbur and Lee, Barrett A. 'Heterolocalism, An Alternative Model of the Sociospatial Behavior of Immigrant Ethnic Communities', *International Journal of Population Geography* 4 (1998): 281–98.

Zucchi, John. *Italians in Toronto: Development of a National Identity* (Montreal: McGill-Queens University Press, 1981).

Chapter 5

Adams, David. 'Everyday Experiences of the Modern City: Remembering the Post-War Reconstruction of Birmingham', *Planning Perspectives* 26 (2011): 237–60.

Arnold, Jörg. *The Allied Air War and Urban Memory. The Legacy of Strategic Bombing in Germany* (Cambridge: Cambridge University Press, 2011).

Barjot, Dominique, Baudouï, Rémi and Voldman, Danièle. eds. *Les Reconstructions en Europe (1945–1949)* (Brussels: Éditions Complexe, 1997).

Buchanan, Colin. *Traffic in Towns* (Harmondsworth: Penguin Books, 1963).

Clout, Hugh. 'Place Annihilation and Urban Reconstruction: The Experience of Four Towns in Brittany, 1940 to 1960', *Geografiska Annaler* 82 (2000): 165–80.

Cresti Carlo. et al. *Firenze 1945–1947. I Progetti della 'Ricostruzione'* (Florence: Alinea, 1995).

Deckker, Thomas. ed. *The Modern City Revisited* (New York: Spon Press, 2000).

Diefendorf, Jeffry. ed. *Rebuilding Europe's Bombed Cities* (Houndmills and London, Macmillan, 1990).

Diefendorf, Jeffry. *In the Wake of War. The Reconstruction of German Cities after World War II* (Oxford and New York: Oxford University Press, 1993).

Diefendorf, Jeffry. 'Reconstructing Devastated Cities: Europe after World War II and New Orleans after Katrina', *Journal of Urban Design* 14 (2009): 377–97.

Diefendorf, Jeffry. 'Urban Transportation Planning Influences and Legacies: Kurt Leibbrand, Germany's Acclaimed Postwar Traffic Planner', *The Journal of Transport History* 35 (2014): 225–35.

Diefendorf, Jeffry, M. *The Boston Contest* (London: Routledge, 2015).

Domhardt, Konstanze Sylva. 'The Garden City Idea in the CIAM Discourse on Urbanism: A Path to Comprehensive Planning', *Planning Perspectives* 27 (2012): 173–97.

Durth, Werner. *Deutsche Architekten. Biographische Verflecthugnen 1900–1970* (Braunschweig and Wiesbaden: Friedrick Vieweg & Sohn, 1986).

Durth, Werner, Düwel, Jorn and Gutschow, Neils. *Architektur und Städtebau der DDR*, vol. 2 *Aufbau. Städte, Themen, Dokumente* 2nd ed. (Frankfurt and New York, Campus Verlag, 1999).

Durth, Werner and Gutschow, Neils. *Träume in Trümmern. Planungen zum Wiederaufbau zerstörter Städte im Westen Deutschlands 1940–1950*, 2 vols (Braunschweig and Wiesbaden: Friedrick Vieweg & Sohn, 1988).

Düwel, Jörn and Gutschow, Niels. eds. *A Blessing in Disguise. War and Town Planning in Europe, 1940–1945* (Berlin: Dom Publishers, 2013).

Düwel, Jorn. *Baukunst voran! Archteiktur und Städtebau in der SBZ/DDR* (Berlin, Schelzky & Jeep, 1995).

Essex, Stephen and Brayshay, Mark. 'Vision, Vested Interest and Pragmatism: Who Re-made Britain's Blitzed Cities?' *Planning Perspectives* 22 (2007): 417–41.

Faludi, Eugenio Giacomo. 'Reconstruction: Italy', *Task*, nos 7–8 (1948): 37–8.

Flinn, Ceci. '"Exeter Phoenix": Politics and the Rebuilding of the Blitzed City', *Southern History* 30 (2008): 104–27.

Grebler, Leo. *Europe's Reborn Cities* (Washington, DC: Urban Land Institute, 1956).

Grebler, Leo. 'Continuity in the Rebuilding of Bombed Cities in Western Europe', *The American Journal of Sociology* 60 (1956): 463–9.

Gunn, Simon, 'The Buchanan Report, Environment and the Problem of Traffic in 1960s Britain', *Twentieth Century British History* 22 (2011): 521–42.

Hamm, Michael F. ed. *The City in Russian History* (Lexington, Kentucky: University Press of Kentucky, 1976).

Hein, Carola, Diefendorf, Jeffry M. and Yorifusa, Ishida. eds. *Rebuilding Urban Japan after 1945* (Houndmills, Basingstoke, Palgrave Macmillan, 2003).

Hein, Carola and Yorifusa, Ishida. 'Japanische Stadtplanung und ihre deutschen Wurzeln', *Die alte Stadt* 3 (1998): 189–211.

Hoppe, Bert. *Auf den Trümmern von Königsberg. Kaliningrad 1946–1970* (Schriftenreihe der Vierteljahrsheft für Zeitgeschichte, 80, Munich, Oldenbourg Verlag, 2000).

Hubbard, Phil, Faire, Lucy and Lilley, Keith D. 'Remembering Post-war Reconstruction: Modernism and City Planning in Coventry 1940–1962', *Planning History* 24 (2002): 7–20.

Jozefacka, Anna. 'Rebuilding Warsaw: Conflicting Visions of a Capital City, 1916–1956' (PhD diss., New York University, 2011).

Kallis, Aristotle. 'The "Third Rome" of Fascism: Demolitions and the Search for a New Urban Syntax', *The Journal of Modern History* 84 (2012): 40–79.

Kirschenbaum, Lisa A. *The Legacy of the Siege of Leningrad, 1941–1995: Myth, Memories, and Monuments* (Cambridge, Cambridge University Press, 2006).

Larkham, Peter J. 'Replanning Birmingham: Process and Product in Post-War Reconstruction', Faculty Working Paper series no. 2, Faculty of Law, Humanities, Development and Society, University of Central England, Birmingham (2007).

Larkham, Peter J and Yasuda, Takashi. eds. 'Reconstruction, Replanning and the Future of Cities in Japan and the UK' (Working Paper series no. 1, Faculty of Law, Humanities, University of Central England, Birmingham Institute of Art and Design, 2005).

Leibbrand, Kurt. *Verkehrsingenieurwesen* (Basel: Birkhäuser, 1957).

Leibbrand, Kurt. *Transportation and Town Planning*, Nigel Seymer, trans. (Cambridge, MA. and London: MIT Press, 1970).

Lincoln, Toby. 'The Rural and Urban at War: Invasion and Reconstruction in China during the Anti-Japanese War of Resistance', *The Journal of Urban History* 38 (2012): 114–32.

Mazower, Mark, Reinisch, Jessica and Feldman, David. eds. 'Post-War Reconstruction in Europe. International Perspectives, 1945–1949', *Past and Present* 210 (2011): 9–367.

Meng, Michael. *Shattered Spaces: Encountering Jewish Ruins in Postwar Germany and Poland* (Cambridge: Harvard University Press, 2011).

Ministry of Transport. *Traffic in Towns. A Study of the Long Term Problems of Traffic in Urban Areas. Reports of the Steering Group and Working Group appointed by the Minister of Transport* (London: Her Majesty's Stationery Office, 1963).

Netzwerk Autobahn, Special edition, *Werkstatt Geschichte*, 21 (December 1998).

Niemeier, Reinhold. *Städtebau und Nahverkehr* (Berichte zur Raumforschung und Raumordnung. Bd 8, 1941).

Pendlebury, John. 'Thomas Sharp and the Modern Townscape', *Planning Perspectives* 24 (2009): 1–2.

Pendlebury, John, Erten, Erdem and Larkham, Peter J. eds. *Alternative Visions of Post-War Reconstruction* (London: Routledge, 2015).

Qualls, Karl. *From Ruins to Reconstruction. Urban Identity in Soviet Sevastopol after World War II* (Ithaca and London, Cornell University Press, 2009).

Ruble, Blair A. *Leningrad: Shaping a Soviet City* (Berkeley: University of California Press, 1990).

Schmucki, Barbara. *Der Traum vom Verkehrsfluss. Städtische Verkehrsplanung seit 1945 im deutsch-deutschen Vergleich.* Deutsches Museum, Beiträge zur Historischen Verkehrsforschung, vol. 4 (Frankfurt and New York: Campus Verlag, 2001).

Shaw, Denis J.B. 'Planning Leningrad', *Geographical Review* 68 (1979): 183–200.

Sorensen, André. *The Making of Urban Japan. Cities and Planning from Edo to the Twenty-First Century* (London and New York: Routledge, 2002).

Tiratsoo, Nick, Hasegawa, Junichi, Mason, Tony and Matsumura, Takao. eds. *Urban Reconstruction in Britain and Japan, 1945–1955: Dreams, Plans and Realities* (Luton: University of Luton Press, 2002).

Vale, Lawrence J. and Campanella, Thomas J. eds. *The Resilient City: How Modern Cities Recover from Disaster* (Oxford and New York: Oxford University Press, 2005).

Voldman, Danièle. *La reconstruction des villes françaises de 1940 à 1954: histoire d'une politique* (Paris: L'Harmattan, 1997).

Volker, Langbehn and Mohammad, Salama. eds. *German Colonialism. Race, the Holocaust, and Postwar Germany* (New York: Columbia University Press, 2011).

von Petz, Ursula. 'tädtebau-Ausstellungen in Deutschland, 1910–2010', *disP – The Planning Review*, 174 (2008): 24–50.

Ward, Stephen V. 'A Pioneer "Global Intelligence Corps"? The Internationalisation of Planning Practice, 1890–1939' *The Town Planning Review* 76 (2005): 119–41.

Ward, Stephen V, Freestone, Robert and Silver, Christopher. 'Centenary paper: The "new" Planning History. Reflections, Issues and Directions', *Town Planning Review* 82 (2011): 231–62.

Wedepohl, Edgar, ed. *Deutscher Städtebau nach 1945* (Essen: Richard Bacht, 1961).

Chapter 6

Andreski, Stanislav. *Syphilis, Puritanism and Witch Hunts* (New York: St Martin's Press, 1989).

Andrew, Donna T. *Philanthropy and Police, London Charity in the Eighteenth Century* (Princeton: Princeton University Press, 1989).

Badinter, Robert. (dir) *Une autre justice : contributions à l'histoire de la justice sous la Révolution* (Paris: Fayard, 1989).

Batchelor, Jenny. 'Industry in Distress: Reconfiguring Femininity and Labor in the Magdalen House', *Eighteenth-Century Life* 28 (2004): 1–20.

Berger, Emmanuel. *La justice pénale sous la Révolution: les enjeux d'un modèle judiciaire libéral* (Rennes: Presses Universitaires de Rennes, 2008).

Binion, Robert. 'Marianne au foyer. Révolution politique et transition démographique en France et aux États-Unis', *Population* 55 (2000): 81–104.

Bristow, Edward. *Vice and Vigilance, Purity Movements in Britain since 1700* (Dublin: Gill and Macmillan, 1977).

British and Foreign Medical Review, 5 (1838).

Conner, Susan. 'Politics, Prostitution, and the Pox in Revolutionary Paris, 1789–1799', *Journal of Social History* (1989): 713–34.

Cranidge, John. *A Mirror for the Burgesses and the Commonality of the City of Bristol* (Bristol, 1818).

Danet, Vincent. 'Les commissaires de police de la ville de Nantes au XVIIIe siècle (1720–1792)', *Annales de Bretagne et des Pays de l'Ouest* 116 (2009): 39–72.

Denk, Thomas. 'Comparative Multilevel Analysis: Proposal for a Methodology', *International Journal of Social Research Methodology* 13 (2010): 29–39.

Denter, Bas and Mossberger, Karen. 'Building Blocks for a Methodology for Comparative Urban Political Research', *Urban Affairs Review* 41 (2006): 550–571.

Dresser Madge and Ollerenshaw, Philip. eds. *The Making of Modern Bristol* (Tiverton: Redcliffe Press, 1996), 1–24.

Emsley, Clive. *Crime and Society in England, 1750–1900* (London: Longman, 1996).

Emsley, Clive, Johnson, Eric and Spierenburg, Pieter. *Social Control in Europe v2: 1800–2000* (Ohio State University Press, 2004), 1–21.

Farge, Arlette. *La Vie Fragile: Violence, Pouvoirs et Solidarités à Paris au XVIIIe siècle* (Paris: Seuil, 1986).

Fielding, John. *A Plan for a Preservatory and Reformatory for the Benefit of Deserted Girls and Penitent Prostitutes* (London, 1758).

Fissel, Mary. *Patients, Power and the Poor* (Cambridge: Cambridge University Press, 2002).

Godfrey, Barry, Emsley Clive and Dunstall Graeme. eds. *Comparative Histories of Crime* (Cullompton: Willan Publishing, 2003).

Goubert, Jean-Pierre. 'Le phénomène épidémique en Bretagne à la fin du XVIIIe siècle', *Annales. Économies, Sociétés, Civilisations* 24 (1969): 1562–88.

Harvey, Alfred. *Bristol, a Historical and Topographical Account of the City* (London: Methuen and Co., 1906).

Henderson, Tony. *Disorderly Women in Eighteenth-Century London* (London: Longman, 1999).

Jones, Philip. 'The Bristol Bridge Riot and its Antecedents: Eighteenth-Century Perceptions of the Crowd', *Journal of British Studies* 19 (1980): 74–92.

Lafon, Jacqueline. *La Révolution française face au système judiciaire d'Ancien Régime* (Genève: Droz, 2001).

Lemmings, David. *Moral Panics, the Media and the Law in Early Modern England* (Basingstoke: Palgrave, 2009).

Meriens, Linda E. *The Secret Malady, Venereal Disease in Eighteenth-Century Britain and France* (University Press of Kentucky, 1997).

Milliot, Vincent. (dir.) *Les mémoires policiers, 1750–1850. Écritures et pratiques policières du Siècle des Lumières au Second Empire* (Rennes: Presses Universitaires de Rennes, 2006).

Mort, Frank. *Dangerous Sexuality: Medicomoral Politics in England since 1830* (London: Routledge, 2000).

Muchembled, Robert. *Une histoire de la violence* (Paris: Seuil, 2008).

Nye, Robert. *A Mad, Mad World, Crime, Madness and Politics in Modern France: The Medical Concept of National Decline* (Princeton: Princeton University Press, 1984).

Pedersen, Susan. 'Hannah More Meets Simple Simon: Tracts, Chapbooks, and Popular Culture in Late Eighteenth-Century England', *Journal of British Studies* 25 (1986): 84–113.

Perry, Mary E. *Crime and Society in Early Modern Seville* (University Press of New England, 1980).

Pluskota, Marion. *Prostitution and Social Control in Eighteenth-Century Ports* (Abingdon: Routledge, 2015).

Poole, Steve. 'Popular Politics in Bristol, Somerset and Wiltshire, 1791–1805' (PhD diss., University of Bristol, 1992).

Reynolds, Elaine. 'Sir John Fielding, Sir Charles Whitworth, and the Westminster Night Watch Act, 1770–1775', *Criminal Justice History, Policing and War in Europe* 16 (2002): 1–20.

Saupin, Guy. *Nantes au XVIIe siècle, vie politique et société urbaine* (Rennes: Presses Universitaires de Rennes, 1996).

Schutt, Russell K. *Investigating the Social World* (University of Massachusetts: Sage, 2012).

Sharpe, Pamela. ed. *Women, Gender, and Labour Migration: Historical and Global Perspectives : Routledge Research in Gender and History* (London: Routledge, 2001).

Smith, David A. 'Method and Theory in Comparative Urban Studies', *International Journal of Comparative Sociology* 32 (1991): 39–58.

van de Pol, Lotte. *The Burgher and the Whore* (Oxford: Oxford University Press, 2011).

Vincineau, Michel. *Proxénétisme, débauche ou prostitution depuis 1810* (Bruxelles: Bruylant, 2006).

Williams, Alan. *The Police of Paris 1718–1789* (Baton-Rouge: University of Louisiana Press, 1979).

Wilson, Ben. *Decency and Disorder* (London: Faber, 2007).

Chapter 7

Adridge, Henry. 'Report of the Society for National Housing Reform Council for England and Wales', *Actes du VIIme Congrès international des habitations à bon marché tenu à Liège, du 7 au 10 août 1905* (Liège: Imprimerie industrielle et commerciale, M. Thone, 1906).

Bertrand, Louis. *Commune de Schaerbeek, Construction d'habitations à bon marché par la commune* (Brussels: Becquart-Arien, 1898).

Bloch, Marc. 'Pour une histoire comparée des sociétés européennes', *Melanges historiques* (1928) 1 (Paris, EHESS, 1983).

Booth, Charles. *Improved Means of Locomotion as a First Step towards the Cure of the Housing Difficulties of London* (London: Macmillan, 1901).

Booth, Charles. *Life and Labour of the People in London* (London: Macmillan, 1902–03).

Booth, Mary Catherine. *Charles Booth: A Memoir* (London: Macmillan and Co., Ltd, 1918).

Buls, Charles. *Esthétiques des villes* (1894) (Brussels: Sint-Lukasdossier, 1981).

Chapman, Stanley D. *The History of Working Class Housing* (Newton Abbot: David and Charles, 1971).

Commission of the European Communities, White Paper. *European Transport Policy for 2010: Time to decide* (Brussels, 12.9.2001): http://ec.europa.eu/transport/themes/strategies/doc/2001_white_paper/lb_com_2001_0370_en.pdf.

Commission of the European Communities Brussels, Green Paper. *Towards a New Culture for Urban Mobility* (Brussels, 25.9.2007), http://eur-lex.europa.eu/legal-content/EN/TXT/PDF/?uri=CELEX:52007DC0551&from=EN.

Commission of the European Communities, White paper. *Roadmap to a Single European Transport Area. Towards a Competitive and Resource Efficient Transport System* (Brussels, 28.3.2011): http://eur-lex.europa.eu/legal-content/EN/TXT/PDF/?uri=CELEX:52011DC0144&from=EN.

Communication from the Commission to the European Parliament, the Council, the European Economic and Social Committee and the Committee of the Regions, *Together Towards Competitive and Resource-Efficient Urban Mobility* (Brussels, 17.12.2013): http://ec.europa.eu/transport/themes/urban/doc/ump/com(2013)913_en.pdf.

Dauby, J. *La question ouvrière en Belgique. Causes de nos crises ouvrières; remèdes possibles* (Brussels: Librairie de A.-N. Lebègue et Cie., 1871).

de Lettenhove, M. Kervyn. *Annales parlementaires. Chambre des représentants* 1868–69 (21 April 1869).

De Quéker, Charles. *Rapport sur les logements à bon marché à l'étranger* (Brussels: Wormhout, 1906).

De T'Serclaes de Wommerson, A. *La condition du logement de l'ouvrier dans la ville de Gand* (Ghent-Paris: H. Engelcke, 1889).

Dewsnup, Ernest. *The Housing Problem in London* (Manchester: Manchester University Press, 1907).

Didier, Charles. 'Notre programme', *Le Cottage* (June 1903).

Doré Gustave and Jerrold, Blanchard. *London. A Pilgrimage* (London: Grant & Co., 1872).

du Castillon, Léonce and Bansart, Fernand, *La question des habitations et des logements à bon marché en Belgique et à l'étranger* (Brussels: Etablissmeents Généraux d'imprimérie, 1914).

Dyos, Harold James. 'Railways and Housing in Victorian London', *Journal of Transport History* 2 (1955): 11–21; 90–100.

Dyos, Harold James. 'The Slums of Victorian London', *Victorian Studies* 9 (1967): 5–40.

Febvre, Lucien. 'Une esquisse d'histoire comparée', *Revue de Synthèse historique* 37 (1924): 151–2.

Garnier, H. *La législation et la réglementation anglaise en matière de salubrité de l'habitation* (Paris: Giard et Brière, 1902).

Green, Nancy. 'L'histoire comparative et le champ des études migratoires, *Annales Economies, Sociétés', Civilisations* 45 (1990): 1335–50.

Grew, Raymond. 'The Case for Comparing Histories', *The American Historical Review* 85 (1980): 763–78.

Hellemans, Emile. *Enquete sur les habitations ouvrières en 1903, 1904, 1905* (Brussels: Imprimerie des institutions de prévoyance, 1905).

Hole, James. *National Railways, An Argument for State Purchase* (London: Caswell & Co. 1893).

Jamar, M. *Annales parlementaires. Chambre des représentants 1868–69* (22 April 1869).

Johnson, James, H and Pooley, Colin G. eds. *The Structure of Nineteenth-century Cities* (London: Croom Helm).

Langerock, H. *De arbeiderswoningen in Belgie* (Ghent: Boekhandel J. Vuylsteke, 1894).

London County Council. *Housing of the Working Classes in London* (London: Oldhams Ltd, 1913).

London County Council. *Workmen's Trains and Trams, with Particular of the Council's Dwellings for Workmen* (2 February 1914).

Mahaim, Ernest. La législation sociale en Belgique, 1869–1919 (s.n., s.d.).

Mahaim, Ernest. *Les abonnements d'ouvriers sur les lignes de chemins de fer belges et leurs effets sociaux* (Brussels: Misch & Thron, 1910).

Mahaim, Ernest. *The Belgian Experience of State Railways* (London, 1912).

Max, Adolphe. Conseil Communal, *Moniteur des Comités de Patronage* (25 April 1911).

Mearns, Andrew. *The Bitter Cry of Outcast London. An Inquiry into the Condition of the Abject Poor* (London: James Clarke & Co., 1883).

Moniteur des Comités de patronage et des sociétés d'habitations ouvrières (25 October 1900).

Pauly, Joseph. *Le chemin de fer et le parlement 1835–1860* (Brussels: H. Wauthoz-Legrand, 1935).

Pedersen, Susan. *Family Dependence, and the Origins of the Welfare State* (Cambridge: Harvard University Press, 1993).

Pirenne, Henri. 'De la méthode comparative en histoire', in G. Des Marez and F.L. Ganshof, eds. *Ve Congrès international des sciences historiques* (Brussels: Weissenbruch, 1923).

Puissant, Jean. 'Le bon ouvrier, mythe ou réalité au XIXe siècle. De l'utilité d'une biographie. J.F.J. Dauby (1824–1899)', *Revue belge de philologie et d'histoire* 56 (1978): 879–929.

Raffalovich, Arthur. *Le logement de l'ouvrier et du pauvre, Etats Unis, Grande Bretagne, France, Allemagne, Belgique* (Paris, Librairie Guillaumin et Cie., 1887).

Rochette, M. 27 March 1899, *Bulletin communal de Bruxelles*, (1899).

Rowntree, Benjamin Seebohm. *Land & Labour. Lessons from Belgium* (London: Macmillan, 1911).

Rutten, Adolph. *Het Samenwonen in Steden. Een maatschappelijk Vraagstuk* (Ghent: A. Siffer, 1902).

Simey, Thomas Spensley and Simey, Margaret, B. *Charles Booth. Social Scientist* (London: Oxford University Press, 1960).

Smets, Marcel. *Charles Buls. Les principes de l'art urbain* (Brussels: Pierre Mardaga, 1995).

Sutcliffe, Anthony. ed. *Multi-Storey Living: the British Working-Class Housing* (London: Croom Helm, 1974).

The Housing Journal 1 (August 1900).

Unwin, Raymond. *Actes du VIIme Congrès International des Habitations à bon Marché tenu à Liège, du 7 au 10 Août 1905* (Liège: Imprimerie industrielle et commerciale, M. Thone, 1906).

Van der Linden, Edouard. *Etude sur l'amélioration des habitations ouvrières et sur l'organisation du domicile de secours* (Brussels: Librairie Polytechnique Decq & Duhent, 1875).

Vandervelde, Emile. *L'exode rural et le retour aux champs* (Brussels: A. Vromant & Co., 1901)

Waller, Phillip, J. *Town, City and Nation. England 1850–1914* (Oxford: Oxford University Press, 1983).

Williams, Robert. *London Rookeries and Collier's Slums: A Plea for More Breathing Room* (London: W. Reeves, 1893).

Young Ken and Garside, Patricia. *Metropolitan London* (London: Edward Arnold, 1982).

Chapter 8

Bayly, Christopher. *The Birth of the Modern World* (Hoboken: Wiley-Blackwell, 2003).

Bombay Chronicle, August 10–13, 1925.

Bose, Sugata. *A Hundred Horizons: The Indian Ocean in the Age of Global Empire* (Cambridge: Harvard University Press, 2009).

Bose, Sugata and Manjapra, Kris. *Cosmopolitan Thought Zones: South Asia and the Global Circulation of Ideas* (Basingstoke: Palgrave, 2010).

Chattopadhyay, Swati. *Representing Calcutta: Modernity, Nationalism and the Colonial Uncanny* (London: Routledge, 2006).

Chopra, Preeti. *A Joint Enterprise: Indian Elites and the Making of British Bombay* (Minneapolis: University of Minnesota Press, 2011).

Dossal, Mariam. *Theatre of Conflict, City of Hope: Bombay/Mumbai 1660 to Present Times* (New Delhi: Oxford University Press, 2010).

Glover, William. *Making Lahore Modern: Constructing and Imagining the Colonial City* (Minneapolis: University of Minnesota Press, 2007).

Hardy, Dennis. *From Garden Cities to New Towns: Campaigning for Town and Country Planning*, (London: E & FN Spon, 1991).

Haynes, Douglas E. and Rao, Nikhil. 'Beyond the Colonial City: Re-evaluating the Urban History of India, ca. 1920–1970', Introduction to Special Issue of *South Asia* co-edited by Haynes and Rao, *South Asia* 36 (2013): 317–33.

Hazareesingh, Sandip. *The Colonial City and the Challenge of Modernity: Urban Hegemonies and Civic Contestations in Bombay City 1900–1925* (Bombay: Orient Longman, 2008).

Home, Robert. *Of Planting and Planning: The Making of British Colonial Cities* (London: Routledge, 2011).

Hosagrahar, Jyoti. *Indigenous Modernities: Negotiating Architecture and Urbanism* (London: Routledge, 2005).

Kidambi, Prashant. *The Making of an Indian Metropolis: Colonial Governance and Public Culture in Bombay, 1890–1920* (Aldershot: Ashgate, 2007).

Kissan, B.W. *Report on Town Planning Enactments in Germany* (Bombay: Government Printing, 1913).

Ladd, Brian. *Urban Planning and Civic Order in Germany, 1860–1914* (Cambridge: Harvard University Press, 1990).

Manjapra, Kris. *Age of Entanglement: German and Indian Intellectuals Across Empire* (Cambridge: Harvard University Press, 2014).

Manjapra, Kris. 'Transnational Approaches to Global History: A View from the Study of German–Indian Entanglement', *German History* 32 (2014): 274–93.

Mead, P.J. *Report on the Possibilities of Development of Salsette as a Residential Area* (Bombay: Government Printing Press, 1909).

Mirams, A.E. 'Town Planning in Bombay Under the Bombay Town Planning Act, 1915', *British Town Planning Institute, Papers and Discussions* 6 (1919–20): 43–63.

Moyn, Samuel and Sartori, Andrew. eds. *Global Intellectual History* (New York: Columbia University Press, 2013).

Prakash, Gyan. *Mumbai Fables* (Princeton: Princeton University Press, 2010).

Proceedings of the Bombay Improvement Trust (15 March 1910).

Rajagopan, C. *The Greater Bombay: A Study in Suburban Ecology* (Bombay: Popular Book Depot, 1962).

Rao, Nikhil. 'Towards Greater Bombay. Town Planning and the Politics of Urban Growth, 1915–1964', manuscript article.

Rao, Nikhil. 'Community, Urban Citizenship and Housing in Bombay, ca. 1919–1980', *South Asia* 36 (2013): 415–33.

Rao, Nikhil. *House, but No Garden. Apartment Living in Bombay's Suburbs* (Minneapolis: University of Minnesota Press, 2013).

Report of the Committee Appointed to Consider the Reorganization of Local Self-Government in Salsette (Bombay: Government Printing, 1925).

Vasudevan Ravi. et al. eds. *The Cities of Everyday Life* (Delhi: Centre for the Study of Developing Societies, 2002).

Chapter 9

Bellamy, Christine. *Administering Central-Local Relations 1871–1919: The Local Government Board in its Fiscal and Cultural Context* (Manchester: Manchester University Press, 1988).

Bevir, Mark. 'Public Administration as Storytelling', *Public Administration* 89 (2011): 183–95.

Bevir, Mark and Richards, David. 'Decentring Policy Networks: Lessons and Prospects', *Public Administration* 87 (2009): 132–41.

Borrie, Gilles W.B. Florentinus M. Wibaut, *Socialisme: ('Fabian essays in socialism')* (Amsterdam: Van Looy Gerlings, 1891).

Borrie, Gilles W.B. *F.M. Wibaut, mens en magistraat: ontstaan en ontwikkeling der socialistische gemeentepolitiek* (The Hague: Staatsuitgeverij, 1987).

Borrie, Gilles W.B. *Pieter Lodewijk Tak (1848–1907): journalist en politicus, een gentleman in een rode broek* (Amsterdam: Aksant, 2006).

Bulkeley, Harriett. 'econfiguring Environmental Governance: Towards a Politics of Scales and Networks', *Political Geography* 24 (2005): 875–902.

Chandler, John A. *Explaining Local Government: Local Government in Britain since 1800* (Manchester: Manchester University Press, 2007).

Couperus, Stefan. et al. *In Control of the City: Local Elites and the Dynamics of Urban Politics, 1800–1960* (Leuven, Paris and Dudley, MA: Peeters, 2007).

Dale, Harold, E. *The Higher Civil Service of Great Britain* (Oxford: Oxford University Press, 1941).

de Liagre Böhl, Herman. *Wibaut de machtige. Een biografie* (Amsterdam: Bert Bakker, 2013).

Dogliani, Patrizia. 'European Municipalism in the First Half of the Twentieth Century: The Socialist Network', *Contemporary European History* 11 (2002): 573–96.

Doyle, Natalie J. and Sebesta, Lorenza. *Regional Integration and Modernity: Cross-Atlantic Perspectives* (London: Lexington Books, 2014).

Ewen, Shane. 'Le long XXeme siècle, ou les villes à l'âge des réseaux municipaux transnationaux', *Revue Urbanisme: Villes, Sociétés, Cultures* 383 (2012): 46–9.

Ewen, Shane and Hebbert, Michael. 'European Cities in a Networked World during the Long 20th Century', *Environment and Planning C: Government and Policy* 25 (2007): 327–40.

Fleddérus, Mary. eds. *World Social Economic Planning: the Necessity for Planned Adjustment of Productive Capacity and Standards of Living: Material Contributed to the World Social Economic Congress, Amsterdam, August 1931* (The Hague and New York: International Industrial Relations Institute, 1932).

Frioux, Stéphane. 'Henri Sellier, Un maire au service de la circulation des savoirs sur et pour la ville, 1919-1939', *Histoire urbaine* 37 (2013): 107–23.

Fry, Geoffrey K. 'More Than 'Counting Manhole Covers': The Evolution of the British Tradition of Public Administration', *Public Administration* 77 (1999): 527–40.

Geertz, Clifford. *The Interpretation of Cultures* (New York: Basic Books, 1973).

Griffiths, John. 'Were There Municipal Networks in the British World c.1890-1939?', *Journal of Imperial and Commonwealth History* 37 (2009): 575–97.

Harris, George M. *The Garden City Movement* (London: Garden City Association, 1906).

Harris, George M. *Problems of Local Government* (London: P.S. King & Son, 1910).

Harris, George M. *Local Government in Many Lands: A Comparative Study* (London: P.S. King & Son, 1925).

Harris, George M. *Local Government in Many Lands: A Comparative Study*, 2nd edition (London: P.S. King & Son, 1934).

Harris, George M. *Westward to the East: The Record of a World Tour in Search of Local Government* (Brussels and London: International Union of Local Authorities, 1935).

Harris, George M. *Municipal Self-Government in Britain: A Study of the Practice of Local Government in Ten of the Larger British Cities* (London: P.S. King & Son, 1939).

Harris, George M. *Comparative Local Government* (London: Hutchinson's University Library, 1948).

Harris, George M. and Wakelam, H.T. *The First International Road Congress, Paris, 1908* (London: Wyman & Sons, 1908).

Iriye, Akira and Saunier, Pierre-Yves. eds. *The Palgrave Dictionary of Transnational History: From the Mid-19th Century to the Present Day* (New York: Palgrave Macmillan, 2009).

Journal of the Town Planning Institute 13 (July 1927).

Kaiser, Wolfram. 'Bringing History Back in to the Study of Transnational Networks in European Integration', *Journal of Public Policy* 29 (2009): 235–6.

Laqua, Daniel. ed. *Internationalism Reconfigured: Transnational Ideas and Movements Between the World Wars* (London: I.B. Taurus, 2011).

Local Government Administration 2 (1936).

Meller, Helen, ed. *Ghent Planning Congress 1913. Premier Congrès International et Exposition Comparée des Villes* (London: Routledge, 2014).

Rhodes, Roderick Arthur William. 'Putting People Back into Networks', *Australian Journal of Political Science* 37 (2002): 399–416.

Rhodes, Roderick Arthur William. 'Everyday Life in a Ministry: Public Administration as Anthropology', *The American Review of Public Administration* 35 (2005): 3–25.

Rhodes, Roderick Arthur William. *Everyday Life in British Government* (Oxford: Oxford University Press, 2011).

Saunier, Pierre-Yves. 'Sketches from the Urban Internationale, 1910–50: Voluntary Associations, International Institutions and US Philanthropic Foundations', *International Journal of Urban and Regional Research* 25 (2001): 380–403.

Saunier, Pierre-Yves and Ewen, Shane. eds. *Another Global City: Historical Explorations into the Transnational Municipal Moment, 1850–2000* (New York: Palgrave Macmillan, 2008).

Vall, Natasha. 'Social Engineering and Participation in Anglo-Swedish Housing 1945–1976: Ralph Erskine's Vernacular Plan', *Planning Perspectives* 28 (2013): 223–45.

Ward, Stephen V. 'What did the Germans ever do for us? A Century of British Learning About and Imagining Modern Planning', *Planning Perspectives* 25 (2010): 117–40.

Wibaut, Florentinus M. *Xme Congrès international des habitations à bon marché, La Haye-Schéveningue, septembre 1913, rapports. Pt. 3* (Rotterdam: Nijgh en Van Ditmar, 1913).

Wibaut, Florentinus M. *Gemeentebeheer: (Financieel beheer. Bedrijfsbeheer)* (Amsterdam: Ontwikkeling, 1926).

Wibaut, Florentinus M. 'Organization for securing efficiency in the municipal service of Amsterdam', *3rd International Congress of Scientific Management Rome* (1927).

Wibaut, Florentinus M. 'Internationale gemeentepolitiek', *Haagsch Maandblad* 11 (1929): 484–95.

Wibaut, Florentinus M. *Private und gemeinnützige Wohnbautätigkeit: die sozialpolitische Bedeutung der Wohnungswirtschaft in Gegenwart u. Zukunft* (Frankfurt am Main: Verlag des Intern.Verbandes für Wohnungswesen, 1931).

Wibaut, Florentinus M. *Ordening der Wereldproductie* (Haarlem: Tjeenk Willink & Zoon, 1934).

Wibaut, Florentinus M. *A World Production Order* (London: George Allen & Unwin, 1935).

Wibaut, Florentinus M. *Levensbouw: memoires* (Amsterdam: Em. Querido's uitgevers-maatschappij, 1936).

Chapter 10

Agamben, Giorgio. *Homo Sacer: Sovereign Power and Bare Life*, trans. Daniel Heller-Roazen (Stanford: Stanford University Press, 1998).

Aly, Götz and Heim, Susanne. *Vorkenker der Vernichtung: Auschwitz und die deutschen Pläne für eine neue europäische Ordnung* (Hamburg, 1991).

Barnes, Trevor J. and Minca, Claudia. 'Nazi Spatial Theory: The Dark Geographies of Carl Schmitt and Walter Christaller', *Annals of the Association of American Geographers* 103 (2013): 669–87.

Blackbourn, David. *The Conquest of Nature: Water, Landscape and the Making of Modern Germany* (London: Random House, 2006).

Bridge, Gary and Watson, Sophie. eds. *The Blackwell City Reader*, 2nd ed. (Malden, MA and Oxford, UK: Blackwell, 2010).

Christaller, Walter. 'Die zentralen Orte in den Ostgebieten und ihre Kultur- und Marktbereiche'. Part 1 of a series entitled *Struktur und Gestaltung der zentralen Orte des deutschen Ostens*, for the Reichsarbeitsgemeinschaft für Raumforschung (Leipzig: K.F. Koehler Verlag, 1941).

Chu, Winson, Kaufman, Jesse and Meng, Michael. 'A Sonderweg through Eastern Europe? The Varieties of German Rule in Poland during the Two World Wars', *German History* 31 (2013): 318–44.

Closmann, Charles E. ed. *War and the Environment: Military Destruction in the Modern Age* (College Station, TX: Texas A&M University Press, 2009).

Cohen, Robin. *Global Diasporas: An Introduction* (New York: Routledge, 1997, 2nd ed. 2008).

Cole, Tim. *Holocaust City: The Making of the Jewish Ghetto* (New York: Routledge, 2002).

Davidovich, Joshua. 'How a Nazi Planner Shaped Early Israel', *The Times of Israel* (11 October 2013).

Diefendorf, Jeffry M and Ward, Janet. eds. *Transnationalism and the German City* (New York and Basingstoke, UK: Palgrave Macmillan, 2014).

Dörr, Heinrich. Bomben brechen die 'Haufen' Stadt: Stadtplanerische Betrachtung des Luftkrieges, *Raumforschung und Raumordnung* (1941).

Durth, Werner and Behnisch, Günter, eds. *Berlin Pariser Platz. Neubau der Akademie der Künste* (Berlin: jovis Verlag, 2005).

Düwel, Jörn, Durth, Werner, Gutschow, Niels and Jochen Schneider, eds. *1945. Krieg – Zerstörung – Aufbau. Architektur und Stadtplanung 1940–1960* (Berlin: Henschel Verlag, 1995).

Dwork, Debórah and Van Pelt, Robert Jan. *Auschwitz. 1270 to the Present* (New York: W.W. Norton, 1996).

Ely, Geoff. *Nazism as Fascism: Violence, Ideology, and the Ground of Consent in Germany 1930–1945* (New York: Routledge, 2013).

Golan, Arnon. 'Israeli Historical Geography and the Holocaust: Reconsidering the Research Agenda', *Journal of Historical Geography* 28 (2002): 554–65.

Gutschow, Niels. *Ordnungswahn: Architekten Planen Im 'Eingedeutschten Osten' 1939–1945* (Gütersloh: Bertelsmann Fachzeitschriften, 2001).

Gutschow, Niels and Klain, Barbara. *Vernichtung und Utopie. Stadtplanung Warschau 1939–1945* (Hamburg: Junius Verlag, 1994): 119–20.

Harvey, David. *The Condition of Postmodernity: An Enquiry into the Origins of Cultural Change* (Cambridge, MA: Blackwell, 1989).

Heidegger, Martin. *Poetry, Language, Thought*, trans. Albert Hofstadter (New York: Harper Colophon Books, 1971).

Hewitt, Kenneth. 'Place Annihilation: Area Bombing and the Fate of Urban Places', *Annals of the Association of American Geographers* 73 (1983): 257–84.

Jaskot, Paul B. *Architecture of Oppression: The SS, Forced Labor and the Nazi Monumental Building Economy* (New York and London, UK: Routledge, 2000).

Jenkins, Jennifer. Transnationalism and German History, H-Net (23 January 2006): http://geschichte-transnational.clio-online.net/transnat.asp?type=diskussionen&id=875&view=pdf&pn=forum.

Kiernan, Ben. *Blood and Soil: A World History of Genocide and Extermination from Sparta to Darfur* (New Haven, CT: Yale University Press, 2007).

Kunstplan, *Gravuren des Krieges. Scars of War. Dresden 1945: Stadtführer. City Guide* (Altenburg: DZA, 2006).

Leach, Neil. ed., *Architecture and Revolution: Contemporary Perspectives on Central and Eastern Europe* (New York: Routledge, 1999).

Leendertz, Ariane. *Ordnung schaffen. Deutsche Raumplanung im 20. Jahrhundert* (Göttingen: Wallstein Verlag, 2008).

Levi, Primo. *The Drowned and the Saved*, trans. Raymond Rosenthal (New York: Vintage International, 1989).

Levi, Primo. *Survival in Auschwitz* (New York: Collier, 1993).

Ley, David. 'Transnational Spaces and Everyday Lives', *Transactions of the Institute of British Geographers* 29 (2004): 151–64.

Lyotard, Jean-François. *The Inhuman*, trans. Geoffrey Bennington and Rachel Bowlby (Cambridge, UK: Polity Press, 1991).

Mai, Uwe. *'Rasse und Raum': Agrarpolitik, Sozial- und Raumplanung im NS-Staat* (Paderborn: Ferdinand Schoeningh, 2002).

Mandel, Ruth. *Cosmopolitan Anxieties: Turkish Challenges to Citizenship and Belonging in Germany* (Durham, NC: Duke University Press, 2008).

Meng, Michael. *Shattered Spaces: Encountering Jewish Ruins in Postwar Germany and Poland* (Cambridge, MA: Harvard University Press, 2011).

Neutzner, Reinhard, Matthias and Hesse, Wolfgang. eds. *Das rote Leuchten. Dresden und der Bombenkrieg* (Dresden: edition Sächsische Zeitung, 2007).

Sassen, Saskia. 'The Repositioning of Citizenship: Emergent Subjects and Spaces for Politics', *Berkeley Journal of Sociology* 36 (2002): 4–25.

Sebald, Winfried Georg. *On the Natural History of Destruction*, trans. Anthea Bell (New York: The Modern Library, 2004).

Seydewitz, Max. *Die unbesiegbare Stadt. Zerstörung und Wiederaufbau von Dresden* (Berlin: Kongress-Verlag, 1956).

Stockholm Peace Research Institute (SIPRI), *Incendiary Weapons* (Cambridge, MA: MIT Press, 1975).

Szejnmann, Claus-Christian W. and Umbach, Maiken. eds. *Heimat, Region, and Empire: Spatial Identities under National Socialism* (New York and Basingstoke, UK: Palgrave 2012).

Taut, Bruno. *Die Auflösung der Städte* (Hagen: Volkwang-Verlag, 1920).

Vonnegut, Kurt. *Slaughterhouse 5* (New York: Delacorte, 1969).

Weiß, A. Der bauliche Luftschutz im Nationalistischen Bund Deutscher Technik, *Baulicher Luftschutz* 1 (1942).

Wetzel, Erhard Dr 'Stellungnahme und Gedanken zum Generalplan Ost des Reichsführers SS' (Berlin, 27 April 1942), repr. *Vierteljahrshefte für Zeitgeschichte* 6 (1958).

Chapter 11

Atkinson, Rowland and Flint, John. 'Fortress UK? Gated Communities, the Spatial Revolt of the Elites and Time-Space Trajectories of Segregation', *Housing Studies* 19 (2004): 875–92.

Avila, Eric. *Popular Culture in the Age of White Flight* (Berkeley: University of California Press, 2004).

Banham, Reyner. *Los Angeles: The Architecture of Four Ecologies* (Berkeley: University of California Press, 2001 [1971]).

Bannister, Jon and Fyfe, Nick. 'Introduction: Fear and the City', *Urban Studies* 38 (2001): 807–13.

Blakely, Edward James and Snyder, Mary Gail. *Fortress America* (Washington, DC: Brookings Institution Press, 1997).

Blandy, Sarah. 'Gated Communities in England: Historical Perspectives and Current Developments', *GeoJournal* 66 (2006): 15–26.

Bobo, Lawrence. et al., eds. *Prismatic Metropolis* (New York: Russell Sage Foundation, 2000).

Castells, Manuel. *End of Millennium* (Malden, MA: Blackwell Publishers, 1998).

Chang, Edward T. and Leong, Russell. eds. *Los Angeles – Struggles toward Multiethnic Community* (Seattle: University of Washington Press, 1994).

Chang, Edward T. and Diaz-Veizades, Jeannette. *Ethnic Peace in the American City* (New York: New York University Press, 1999).

Clark, W.A.V. *The California Cauldron* (New York: Guilford Press, 1998).

Clark, W.A.V. *Immigrants and the American Dream* (New York: Guilford Press, 2003).

Cross, Brian. *It's Not About a Salary: Rap, Race, and Resistance in Los Angeles* (London and New York: Verso, 1993).

Davis, Mike. *The City of Quartz* (New York: Vintage, 1990).

Davis, Mike. *Magical Urbanism* (New York: Verso, 2000).

Davis, Mike and Bertrand Monk, Daniel. eds. *Evil Paradises* (New York: New Press: Distributed by W.W. Norton, 2007).

Evans, Peter B. *Dependent Development* (Princeton, N.J.: Princeton University Press, 1979).

Findlay, John M. *Magiclands* (Berkeley: University of California Press, 1992).

Fishman, Robert. *Urban Utopias in the Twentieth Century* (New York: Basic, 1977).

Fogleson, Robert M. *The Fragmented Metropolis* (Cambridge: Harvard University Press, 1967).

Foner, Nancy and Fredrickson, George, M. eds. *Not Just Black and White* (New York: Russell Sage Foundation, 2004).

Forman, Murray. *The 'Hood' Comes First: Race, Space, and Place in Rap and Hip-Hop* (Middletown, CT: Wesleyan University Press, 2002).

Forman, Murray and Neal, Mark Anthony. eds. *That's the Joint!* (New York: Routledge, 2004).

Foster, John Bellamy, McChesney, Robert W and Jonna, R. Jamil. 'The Global Reserve Army of Labor and the New Imperialism', *Monthly Review* 63 (2011): 1–31.

Fulton, William B. *The Reluctant Metropolis* (Baltimore: Johns Hopkins University Press, 2001 [1997]).

Gandy, Matthew. 'Urban Visions', *Journal of Urban History* 26 (2000): 368–79.

Gilbert, Alan, Hardoy, Jorge Enrique an Ramírez, Ronaldo. eds. *Urbanization in Contemporary Latin America* (Chichester, New York: J. Wiley, 1982).

Goldman, Stephen, L. 'Images of Technology in Popular Films: Discussion and Filmography', *Science, Technology, and Human Values* 14 (1989): 275–301.

Graziano da Silva, Jose F. 'Capitalist "Modernization" and Employment in Brazilian Agriculture, 1960–1975: The Case of the State of São Paulo', *Latin American Perspectives* 11 (1984): 117–36.

Guillermoprieto, Alma. 'In the New Gangland of El Salvador', *New York Review of Books* (10 November 2011): 45–8.

Hermes, Will. *Love Goes to Buildings on Fire* (New York: Farber and Farber, 2011).

Hill Maher, Kristen. 'Borders and Social Distinction in the Global Suburb', *American Quarterly* 56 (2004): 781–806.

Hise, Greg. *Magnetic Los Angeles* (Baltimore and London: Johns Hopkins University Press, 1997).

Hise, Greg. 'Border City: Race and Social Distance in Los Angeles', *American Quarterly* 56 (2004): 545–58.

Hollen Lees, Lynn. 'Urban Public Space and Imagined Communities in the 1980s and 1990s', *Journal of Urban History* 20 (1994): 443–65.

Horne, Gerald. *Fire This Time* (Charlottesville: University Press of Virginia, 1995).

Human Rights Commission/USA, *Gangs in Guatemala*, 2013. Available from http://www.ghrcusa.org/wpcontent/uploads/2011/12/GangFactSheet.pdf (accessed 8 July 2013).

Jones, Colin. *Paris* (1st American ed.; New York: Viking, 2005).

Jutersonke, Oliver, Muggah, Robert and Rodgers, Dennis. 'Gangs, Urban Violence, and Security Interventions in Central America', *Security Dialogue* 40, nos 4–5 (2009): 373–97.

Kowarick, Lucio. ed. *Social Struggles and the City: The Case of Sao Paulo* (New York: Monthly Review Press, 1994).

Kruse, Kevin Michael and Sugrue, Thomas J. eds. *The New Suburban History* (Chicago: University of Chicago Press, 2006), 205–19.

Lamb, Charles M. *Housing Segregation in Suburban America since 1960* (New York: Cambridge University Press, 2005).

Levine, Robert M. *The History of Brazil* (Westport, CT: Greenwood Press, 1999).

Marques, Eduardo Cesar and Bichir, Renata Mirandola. 'Public Politics, Political Cleavages and Urban Space: State Infrastructure Policies in Sao Paulo, Brazil, 1975–2000', *International Journal of Urban and Regional Research* 27 (2003): 811–27.

McKenzie, Evan. *Privatopia* (New Haven: Yale University Press, 1994).

Mueller, Charles. 'Environmental Problems Inherent to a Development Style: Degradation and Poverty in Brazil', *Environment and Urbanization* 7 (1995): 67–84.

Neill, William J.V. 'Marketing the Urban Experience: Reflections on the Place of Fear in Promotional Strategies of Belfast, Detroit, and Berlin', *Urban Studies* 38 (2001): 815–28.

Nevin Willard, Michael. 'Nuestra Los Angeles', *American Quarterly* 56 (2004): 807–43.

Newman, Oscar. *Defensible Space* (New York, 1972).

Nugent, Walter T.K. *Into the West* (New York: A.A. Knopf, 1999).

O'Connor, Carol A. 'Sorting out the Suburbs: Patterns of Land Use, Class, and Culture', *American Quarterly* 37 (1985): 382–94.

Parkman Pardue, Derek. 'Blackness and Periphery: A Retelling of Marginality in Hip-Hop Culture of São Paulo, Brazil' (PhD diss., University of Illinois, 2004).

Pasternak, Suzana. 'Squatter Settlements as a Kind of Perverse Outcome: History of Popular Housing Policies in São Paulo', *Proceeding of the 13th*

Meeting of the International Planning History Society (Chicago: IPHS, 2008): 1182–201.

Paulo, Andres, Rodriguez-Pose, John and Tomaney, John. 'Industrial Crisis in the Centre of the Periphery: Stabilization, Economic Restructuring and Policy Responses in the São Paulo Metropolitan Region', *Urban Studies* 36 (1999): 479–98.

Pires do Rio Caldeira, Teresa. *City of Walls* (Berkeley: University of California Press, 2000).

Platt, Anthony M and Cooper, Lynn. eds. *Policing America* (Englewood Cliffs, NJ: Prentice Hall, 1974).

Pulido, Laura, Sidawi, Steve and Vos, Robert. O. 'An Archaeology of Environmental Racism in Los Angeles', *Urban Geography* 17 (1996): 419–39.

Pulido, Laura. 'Rethinking Environmental Racism: White Privilege and Urban Development in Southern California', *Annals of the Association of American Geographers* 90 (2000): 12–40.

Randall, Gregory C. *America's Original GI Town – Park Forest, Illinois* (Baltimore: Johns Hopkins University Press, 2000).

Read, Justin A. 'Obverse Colonization: São Paulo, Global Urbanization and the Poetics of the Latin American City', *Journal of Latin American Cultural Studies* 15 (2006): 281–300.

Robinson, William I. *Transnational Conflicts* (London and New York: Verso, 2003).

Robinson, William I. 'Globalization and the Sociology of Immanuel Wallerstein: A Critical Appraisal', *International Sociology* 26 (2011): 723–45.

Romero, Simon. 'At War with São Paulo's Establishment, Black Paint in Hand', *New York Times* (29 January 2012).

Romo, Ricardo. *East Los Angeles* (Austin: University of Texas Press, 1983).

Ross, Andrew and Rose, Tricia. eds. *Microphone Fiends* (London, New York: Verso, 1994).

Sá, Lúcia. *Life in the Megalopolis* (New York: Routledge, 2007).

Sanchez, Thomas W., Lang Robert E. and Dhavale, Dawn M. 'Security Versus Status?: A First Look at the Census's Gated Communities', *Journal of Planning Education and Research* 24 (2005): 281–91.

Sandercock, Leonie. *Cosmopolis II* (New York: Continuum, 2003).

Sides, Josh. 'Straight into Compton: American Dreams, Urban Nightmares, and the Metamorphosis of a Black Suburb', *American Quarterly* 56 (2004): 583–604.

Sites, William. 'Global City, American City: Theories of Globalization and Approaches to Urban History', *Journal of Urban History* 29 (2003): 222–46.

Soja, Edward W. *Thirdspace* (Cambridge, MA: Blackwell, 1996).

Soja, Edward W and Scott, Allen John. eds. *The City* (Berkeley: University of California Press, 1996).

Sonenshein, Raphael. *The City at Stake* (Princeton, NJ: Princeton University Press, 1993).

Sorkin, Michael. ed. *Variations on a Theme Park* (New York: Noonday, 1992).

Stolcke, Verena. *Coffee Planters, Workers, and Wives* (New York: St Martin's Press, 1988).

Takaki, Ronald T. *A Different Mirror* (Boston: Little, Brown & Co., 1993).

Toledo, Ricardo Silva. 'The Connectivity of Infrastructure Networks and the Urban Space of São Paulo in the 1990s', *International Journal of Urban and Regional Research* 24 (2000): 139–64.

Toop, David. *Rap Attack 2* (London and New York: Serpent's Tail, 1994).

United Nations Human Settlements Programme, *The Challenge of Slums 2003* (London and Sterling, VA: Earthscan Publications, 2003).

United Nations Human Settlements Programme, *Enhancing Urban Safety and Security* (London and Sterling, VA: Earthscan Publications, 2007).

Valdez Estrada, Gilbert. 'How the East Was Lost: Mexican Fragmentation, Displacement, and the East Lost Angeles Freeway System, 1947–1972' (Master's Thesis, California State University Long Beach, 2002).

Von Hoffman, Alexander. *House by House, Block by Block* (New York: Oxford University Press, 2003).

Wallerstein, Immanuel Maurice. *World-Systems Analysis* (Durham: Duke University Press, 2004).

Watson, Hilbourne A. 'Globalization as Capitalism in the Age of Electronics: Issues of Popular Power, Culture, Revolution, and Globalization from Below', *Latin American Perspectives* 29 (2002): 32–43.

Weinstein, Barbara. 'Presidential Address: Developing Inequality', *American Historical Review* 113 (2008): 1–18.

Whyte, William Hollingsworth. *The Organization Man* (New York: Simon and Schuster, 1956).

Williams, Richard J. ed. *Globalization, Violence, and the Visual Culture of Cities* (London and New York: Routledge, 2010).

Wyeld, Theodor G. and Allan, Andrew. 'The Virtual City: Perspectives on the Dystopic Cybercity', *Journal of Architecture* 11 (2006): 613–20.

Zilberg, Elana. 'Fools Banished from the Kingdom: Remapping Geographies of Gang Violence between the Americas (Los Angeles and San Salvador)', *American Quarterly* 56 (2004): 759–79.

Zilberg, Elana. *Space of Detention: The Making of a Transnational Gang Crisis between Los Angeles and San Salvador* (Durham and London: Duke University Press, 2011).

Chapter 12

Bairoch, Paul. *Cities and Economic Development* (Chicago: University of Chicago Press, 1988).

Bass Warner Jr, Sam. 'When Urban History is at the Center of the Curriculum', *Journal of Urban History*, 18 (1991): 3–9.

Braudel, Fernand. *Capitalism and Material Life 1400–1800* (London: Weidenfeld and Nicolson, 1973).

Cairncross, Alexander Kirkland. 'The Glasgow Building Industry 1870–1914', *Review of Economic Studies* 2 (1934): 1–17.

Castells, Manuel. *The City and the Grassroots: A Cross-Cultural Theory of Urban Social Movements* (Berkeley: University of California Press, 1988).

Dyos, Harold James. 'Editorial', *Urban History Yearbook* (1974).

Dyos, Harold James. 'Editorial', *Urban History Yearbook* (1975).

Fraser, Derek and Sutcliffe, Anthony. eds. *The Pursuit of Urban History* (London: Edward Arnold, 1983).

Harvey, David. *Social Justice and the City* (London: Edward Arnold, 1973).

Jansen, Harry S.J. 'Wrestling with the Angel: Problems of Definition in Urban Historiography', *Urban History* 23 (1996): 277–99.

Knox, Paul. ed. *Atlas of Cities* (Princeton: Princeton University, Press, 2014).

Koditschek, Theodore. *Class Formation and Urban Industrial Society: Bradford 1750–1850* (Cambridge: Cambridge University Press, 1990).

Lees, Andrew and Hollen Lees, Lynn. *Cities and the Making of Modern Europe 1750–1914* (Cambridge: Cambridge University Press, 2007).

Lepetit, Bernard. *The Pre-industrial Urban System: France 1740–1840* (Cambridge: Cambridge University Press, 1994).

Massard-Guilbaud, Geneviève and Rodger, Richard. eds. *Environmental and Social Justice in the City: Historical Perspectives* (Cambridge: The White Horse Press, 2011).

Mitchell, Wesley C. *Business Cycles and their Causes* (Berkeley: University of California Press, 1941).

Monkkonen, Eric H. *America Becomes Urban: the Development of U.S. Cities and Towns 1780–1980* (Berkeley: University of California Press, 1988).

Rodger, Richard. 'Historiens du dimanche', *Urban History* 23 (1996): 86–9.

Saunier, Pierre-Yves and Shane Ewen. eds. *Another Global City: Historical Explorations into the Transnational Municipal Moment 1850–2000* (New York: Palgrave Macmillan, 2008).

Topalov, Christian et al., *L'aventure des mots de la ville: à travers le temps, les langues, les societies* (Paris: Robert Laffont, 2010).

Index

For Product Safety Concerns and Information please contact our
EU representative GPSR@taylorandfrancis.com, Taylor & Francis
Verlag GmbH, Kaufingerstraße 24, 80331 München, Germany